e Right Har

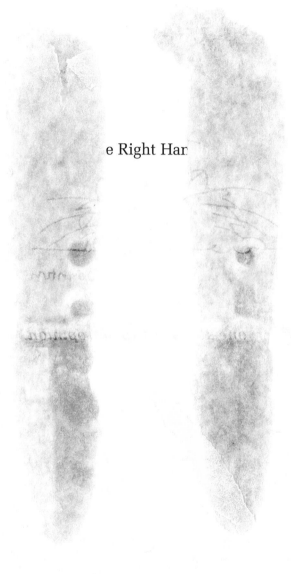

Everyone's entitled to our opinion.

THE Right

Second Edition

HANDBOOK

Grammar and Usage in Context

Pat Belanoff
State University of New York at Stony Brook

Betsy Rorschach
The City College of the City University of New York

Mia Oberlink
Mt. Sinai School of Medicine
of the City University of New York

BOYNTON/COOK PUBLISHERS
HEINEMANN
PORTSMOUTH, NH

Boynton/Cook Publishers
A Subsidiary of
Heinemann Educational Books, Inc.
361 Hanover Street, Portsmouth, NH 03801-3959
Offices and agents throughout the world

Library of Congress Cataloging-in-Publication Data

Belanoff, Pat.
   The right handbook : grammar and usage in context / Pat Belanoff, Betsy Rorschach, Mia Oberlink. – 2nd ed.
    p. cm.
   Rev. ed. of: The Right handbook / Pat Belanoff . . . et al. c1986.
   Includes index.
   ISBN 0-86709-316-1 (acid-free paper)
   1. English language—Rhetoric—Handbooks, manuals, etc.
   2. English language—Grammar—1950—Handbooks, manuals, etc.
   3. Report writing—Handbooks, manuals, etc. I. Rorschach, Betsy.
  II. Oberlink, Mia R. III. Title. IV. Title: Right handbook.
  PE1408.R567 1993
  808′.042–dc20   92-28851
                                              CIP

Cover design by Tom Allen, Pear Graphic Design
Printed in the United States of America
Printed on acid free paper
93 94 95 96 97   10 9 8 7 6 5 4 3 2 1

Contents

Preface

This is not a traditional handbook. That is, if you have a question about the punctuation of a particular sentence, or about word choice, you won't find the answer in here. Because every sentence you write is new, because it has never existed before in the context you have created for it, no handbook can tell you what to do with it. What that sentence offers you is the opportunity for choices. This book is meant to help you make those choices by presenting to you some ideas about English—some guidance to understanding what you already know about your language, some reasons for the ways people discuss it, some new ways to think about how you use it when you write, some awareness of the role of context. We hope that what you find here will not just ease some of your writing anxieties, but also spark an appreciation of how your language works and an understanding of its richness and diversity.

At the end of the book, we've included a short index. We debated among ourselves about having one at all since its very existence suggests you can look in one spot and find answers to specific questions—and you can't. But, we decided to provide one and ask you to use it sensibly—just as a way to send yourself to spots in the book to read related discussions—*after* you've already read the book; that is, the index can help you get back to a spot you remember reading, but can't find.

We would like to thank our colleagues and students at New York University and SUNY Stony Brook for their support and encouragement as we wrote and rewrote. We would especially like to thank Paula Johnson for asking us to write this book; Lil Brannon, Paul Connolly, Peter Elbow, and Peter Stillman, who gave extensive critical comments that helped us revise it; Sandra Boynton for giving us permission to use her delightful observations on us language animals; and Bob Boynton for all his suggestions, but mostly for thinking as we do about language handbooks.

Preface to the Second Edition

The biggest change we've made in this second edition is to add practices at the end of many sections. We made this change because so many of the teachers who used the first edition told us that they needed to give students samples to practice our suggestions on.

Frankly, we debated taking up this advice since we had decided against exercises for our first edition for reasons that still seem valid to us. In our early careers as teachers, we had assigned grammar exercises to our students. Most of them, with some instruction, did quite well on these exercises—but continued to make the mistakes covered by the exercises when they did their own writing. Our experience is supported by several research studies which conclude that teaching grammar apart from students' own writing is not helpful and may even be harmful if it takes away from the time students spend writing. Almost all exercises in grammar books and handbooks identify fairly narrowly what errors are being tested. Thus, students know what the possible answers are and what errors to look for. Such pre-identification of possible errors doesn't exist when students do their own writing. Some bell has to ring in a writer's head before she or he can even know there's a decision to be made. Knowing this led us to decide against exercises in the first edition of *The Right Handbook*.

Another reason we decided against exercises in the first edition was that they seemed to contradict so much of what we are saying. We spend a fair amount of time telling you that decisions on grammatical and usage issues are *always* contextual. It's often hard to tell whether something is an error without examining what comes before and after. Exercises decontextualize language and ask students to consider error apart from important rhetorical features of writing such as situation, audience, levels of formality, and so forth. We concluded that to insert exercises in our book would undermine our own advice!

The feedback we got from those who used the first edition of this book required us to relook at this decision. (After all, in this book we ask you to consider feedback; we can hardly ignore our own advice!) After talking over the issue at some length, we decided to include practices (not exercises) in this second edition. But you'll notice that most of the practices consist of fairly extensive pieces of student writing so that possible errors can be considered in the contexts in which they occur. And we've also placed the practices in such a way that the range of types of errors possible in each practice is fairly broad. By setting the practices up this way, we hope we're not pre-identifying possible errors as narrowly as most exercises in most grammar books do.

We've made some other changes too—mostly additions. We've added a chapter on global revision because we wanted to demonstrate concretely that writers have to get straight what they want to say before they begin doing any editing and proofreading. Two new chapters have been added to make our book more useful to both teachers and students. The first of these new chapters, "If English Is Not Your First Language," addresses the needs of the increasing number of students whose native language is *not* English. We believe that these students benefit from the same kind of instruction native-speaking students benefit from, but we recognize that they have some special needs too.

And we also recognize that not all writers are in a writing class— many are not in school at all. We wanted to provide advice for both of these groups. We hope that the second new chapter, "Writing Outside The English Class," will make students currently in writing classes aware of the large world outside those classes where people write many different things in many different ways for many different purposes. As our colleague Peter Elbow once said, "School is short; life is long."

Our final addition is an Appendix in which we look at how two students used this new edition of *The Right Handbook* in the process of writing, revising, and copyediting their papers.

We want to give special thanks to all those who provided us with the feedback that led to this second edition. Many of them are anonymous to us now because we forgot to record who told us what in casual encounters at conferences and in hallways. But we can thank several by name: Vara Neverow-Turk whose class at New York University's Continuing Education Division sent us extensive comments and suggestions; Glenn Klopfenstein and his students at Stony Brook who sent us chapter-by-chapter responses; Melinda Knight of New York University's Stern School of Business and Gene Doty of the University of Missouri-Rolla, both of whom responded extensively to a questionnaire we distributed before undertaking this revision. We also want to extend a special thanks to Alberta Grossman whose enthusiasm for the book has enabled her to give us excellent advice about how to make it better. And, once again and finally, we'd like to thank Bob Boynton for his confidence in us and this book.

Introduction

We're teachers of writing. We're not grammar teachers; we're not even English teachers in the usual sense; we're writing teachers. We believe it's important for people to write effectively because communication nurtures individual fulfillment and societal health. We know also that this is a belief each writer discovers for herself; it can't be imposed by a teacher.

What does it mean to write "effectively"? Most of us recognize an effective piece of writing—we recognize it by the "effect" it has on us. Such a statement presupposes that not all of us would agree on what's effective—that's true, we don't—all we're saying is that each of us can make the judgment.

How do we, as teachers of writing, help students become "effective" writers? Because of how we define "effective," we believe that the best way to help student writers is to create a classroom situation in which they can judge for themselves the effect of their writing on others—not just on teachers, but on classmates. All writing involves saying something to someone (including oneself) for some reason; that is, all writing is created within a context and has its effect within that context. If you were in our classroom, we'd ask you to discuss with your peer-readers which parts of your writing they find effective and which parts don't work well for them. We hope you would care enough to let that discussion guide your revisions. Notice we said "guide"; your writing belongs to you as well as to your audience. Consequently, your idea of what's effective is important also.

In some sense, all of us can improve on everything we write. W. B. Yeats revised almost everything he had written when it was reprinted. (He hoped that the thirteenth reprinting, in 1895, of his continually revised poems would be "the final text of the poems of my youth; and yet it may not be.") At some point, however, a writer must, for whatever reasons, cease work on a particular piece, at least for the moment. In the classroom, you usually stop at some point because your teachers need to fulfill their obligations by giving you grades. In our classes, just before students submit papers for a grade, we ask them to do careful proofreading and copyediting. At its most basic level, proofreading locates and corrects typographical errors. (Writing can't be very effective if your reader has to supply missing

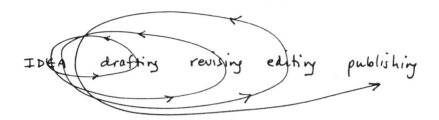

words or substitute one letter for another.) At a level slightly above this, copyediting locates and corrects usage errors.

It's important to emphasize here the appropriate time to proofread. We said that we ask our students to proofread *just before they submit their papers for evaluation.* That is, when they are generating and developing their ideas—getting started and then figuring out what they want to say—we don't ask for or expect perfect texts. Writing is a recursive rather than linear process; that is, writers don't go straight from drafting to revising to editing without backtracking or repeating any steps. We imagine the process as something like the diagram above. The writer starts with the core of the idea, moving outward and then back, passing through revision and drafting and editing repeatedly, but with drafting and then revising receiving less attention as editing becomes the focus. But at the early stage, when writers are concentrating on ideas, they don't have time to worry about punctuation and verb tenses.

After writers are satisfied that they've said all they had to say, and that they've made it as clear and as complete as possible, then is the time to look carefully at the language and mechanics to see if they conform to the conventions appropriate to the subject and audience. These conventions include both grammar and usage, and this book deals specifically with usage. (In Chapter 1 we discuss the differences between grammar and usage.)

Usage depends highly on context—on subject and audience, on purpose, even on the writer herself. When you write a letter to a friend, your language and tone may depend on your own mood as well as on what you have to say; and the language of any letter you write to a friend will probably differ greatly from that of an essay you write for a professor. Your friend may not be bothered by words like "ain't" or by an overabundance of "I," but your professor may feel strongly that such usages are unacceptable in an essay written for his course. Experienced writers take the time before writing to define explicitly their purpose and their audience, and to redefine these as necessary throughout the process of writing their text. Every time you write something, you're working within a context that is defined by you, by your subject, by your purpose for writing, and by your audience. Our aim in this book is to help you learn which usage is appropriate in which context.

Providing you want to, how can you learn usage? First, you need to be sensitive to the demands of your audience. You become sensitive through feedback—if for example, your history teacher fails you because you use contractions and too few commas. If you leave a note for your roommate written in the same language you use for your history paper, your roommate may look at you peculiarly the next time the two of you meet. This too is feedback. Second, exposure to language, spoken or written, contributes a great deal to your developing intuitions about usage. The more you read, write, listen, and speak, the more you're likely to feel comfortable about usage. For example, reading essays on historical issues and listening to your professor lecture, and engaging in discussion about the subject both in and out of class should make you more aware of the usage acceptable in this field, just as reading the sports page tunes you in to acceptable usage in sports writing. Third, consulting an expert, text or person, as one would consult a dictionary for spelling, is another way to strengthen intuitions. As you get more answers to more questions, you begin to internalize a sense of what the appropriate answers are.

Finally, becoming familiar with the basics of usage by reading a book like this one also strengthens your intuitions. This is why we suggest that you read this whole book now, to get a sense of what it's about and also to get a sense of your own abilities to make appropriate choices. Maybe the best reason for reading the whole book first is to get a sense of the right attitude toward language use.

If you're a native speaker of English, you probably make appropriate choices most of the time when you speak. After all, you've had lots of practice. You understand the different contexts of speaking to a friend, parent, teacher, stranger, potential lover, etc. And you can switch roles—"voices"—in a matter of moments to meet the demands of each context. Reading this book will help you understand how to make appropriate choices for the different contexts of writing. If you're not a native speaker of English, you have to actively seek out situations where language is integral to the activity, where you *have* to interact with others in English, so that you can start to develop a feeling for what is correct. The amount of language you hear and read will influence the speed with which you acquire fluency; so will the amount you speak and write. Reading this book will give you ideas about how to evaluate your writing, as well as ideas about how context influences choices you make as a writer.

Our goal, then, for all our readers, is to help you develop an awareness of what you do intuitively. Our discussions of the various aspects of usage should make you notice how you and others use language; after reading this book you should be able to explain the reasons behind the choices you make when writing. Instead of saying, "I don't know why I wrote that, it just sort of came to me," you'll be able to say, "Within the context of this idea, my choice makes sense because I was trying to . . ." The practices at the end of each chapter will give you more opportunities to discuss context and choice with others in your class.

When you have questions about your writing, we hope you come back to this book to help you make your decision. We've organized the book to make it easier for you to find help with your writing and usage problems. Each of the sections is designed as a unit. If you have a problem to solve, see if you can categorize it—as a problem in verb tense, in paragraphing, in pronouns, or whatever. Having done this, you should reread the entire section on that topic. We suggest, for example, that if you have a decision to make about a comma, you reread the punctuation section and then make a decision. Commas are part of a system; knowing that system is more helpful in making decisions than memorizing a list of rules about commas, almost all of which have exceptions.

If you can't categorize your problem, reread the following paragraphs which will help you decide what kind of problem you're dealing with and where to look for suggestions to solve it.

Chapter 2 ("Global Revision") covers the all-inclusive sort of revision of ideas, scope, emphasis, focus, and structure necessary before tackling editing and proofreading.

Chapter 3 ("Paragraphs") doesn't need much explanation; in it, we talk about grouping sentences into paragraphs.

Chapter 4 ("Sentences") covers sentence division (run-ons and fragments), sentence structure (syntax, active vs. passive voice, subordination, parallelism, comparisons, variety, "awkwardness"), word order (dangling participles, misplaced modifiers), punctuation, and so forth. If one of your sentences doesn't seem right to you (or to your teacher, another student, or a friend), we suggest that you look in this chapter for possible strategies for revision.

Chapter 5 ("Phrases") covers problems which don't require a reworking of a whole sentence, but do require more than the alteration of one word. These problems include subject-verb agreement, double negatives, double comparisons, split infinitives, and pronouns.

Chapter 6 ("Words") is divided into two parts. The first covers the form (usually endings) of nouns, verbs, adverbs, and adjectives; the second covers the choice of words (slang, colloquialisms, repetition) and includes a list of common errors and words often confused.

Chapter 7 ("Mechanics") covers the mostly conventional rules about typing, printing, and documentation.

Within each of these chapters, you'll discover that we refer you to one of the other chapters (sometimes even to all of them!). We hope this doesn't confuse you, but the truth of this book's philosophy makes this cross-referencing inevitable; choices made while writing depend upon context: immediate context (words before and after), and context within the sentence, within the paragraph, within the entire piece. And because a text is a unit, changing a part may affect the whole.

Once you've categorized your problem, what happens next? If you've done a lot of searching through grammar books in the past, looking for the answer to your particular question, you've probably noticed that none of the examples match your problem sentence exactly. The search for an answer is always frustrating, because usage isn't like spelling. Most words have only one spelling, so once you've found the word in the dictionary, you've found the answer to your question. Usage, however, as we've said before, depends on context; as the context varies, so do the possible answers to your questions about which choices to make. No handbook can give all the answers to all the questions, because there simply isn't enough space for a handbook that big—and it would take a few thousand lifetimes to write it in the first place, even with the help of computers. There are just too many questions, each with too many answers.

This handbook can't provide absolute answers, and it isn't meant to. We've designed it to help you find ways to arrive at answers on your own, relying on your own intuitions about which choices are best and trusting that your intuitions are well founded. Which brings us back to what we said earlier: each time you use the language, receive feedback on the effectiveness of your choices, and think about that feedback, you'll strengthen your intuitions. As you do more writing and as you read more, you'll become more familiar with the different contexts for language and more secure about your own abilities to write effectively.

Chapter One

Debunking Myths
Or, the Truth About Language, Plus a Few Explanations

Maybe you never read "Dear Abby," or maybe recently people's concerns have shifted away from language etiquette, but several years ago there were letters to Ms. Van Buren asking whether, when answering the telephone, one should say "This is I" or "This is me." Now here's a person whose job is to advise people about the things that matter, and evidently enough people wrote about this telephone problem that she felt compelled to publish a representative letter and then give some advice. (She suggested you choose a third alternative, "This is [your name here].")

This is a long way of getting to an important point about language: people, for often unfathomable reasons, are insecure about their language. So insecure that many adults, when introduced to English teachers, suddenly become nervous about the way they talk. So insecure that some people make efforts to disguise their regional accents. So insecure, in fact, that the business of giving advice about how to "fix" your language will always support a few writers. This is part of the reason why we have popular, or "pop," grammarians—people like John Simon, Edwin Newman, William Safire—telling us about the mistakes we make when we use English without watching our grammar.

But there's one thing that these pop grammarians rarely mention: the "decline" of the language is no new phenomenon; popular writers have been complaining about the sorry state of the English language for several hundred years. Samuel Johnson wrote his *Dictionary of the English Language* in the 1750s. In the Preface he complained about how the language had been allowed to run out of control, "exposed to the corruptions of ignorance, and caprices of innovation"; and he wrote yearningly of his wish "that the instrument might be less apt to decay, and that signs might be permanent, like the things which they denote." Several decades earlier, Jonathan Swift had complained that the English language was being allowed to deteriorate through the forces of various bad influences. And Chaucer, in 1385, though not complaining, had obviously noticed that the language was changing:

> Ye knowe ek that in forme of speche is chaunge
> Withinne a thousand yer, and wordes tho
> That hadden prys now wonder nyce and straunge
> Us thenketh hem, and yet they spake hem so.
>   —Troylus and Criseyde, *II, 22-25*

Why so much continual concern and alarm? Has English always been on the verge of collapse because of outrageous misuse by the untutored masses? No, that's not the problem. The problem is with linguistic snobs, people who see the language changing and who don't like the changes they can see happening. Swift complained about the influence of pedants—i.e., scientists—on the language; Johnson deplored the new words introduced by translators, words that diluted the purity of English. This moralistic tone has resurfaced today: William Safire, in his column "On Language," once wrote that Brooke Shields "Is pure in construing the verb of her relative clause as plural" (*The New York Times,* May 12, 1985). The 1991 publication of *Random House Webster's College Dictionary* was accompanied by the familiar furor over the dictionary's sanctioning of new usages, and reviewers warned again of the results of these kinds of "attacks" on the language. (See our section on dictionaries in Chapter 10 for further discussion of this issue.) All these self-styled experts respond emotionally to changes in the language; they'd like to freeze it in a "perfect" state, one that has never existed except in their heads.

But language changes. Always. You can't stop it. People who write dictionaries or grammar handbooks can't stop it. Even people writing language columns for newspapers or journals can't stop it. The only time a language stops changing is when people stop using it. Latin, a dead language, stopped changing the moment people stopped using it in everyday give and take. Latin grammar books don't have to be revised, but handbooks for living languages do, in order to take into account the changes since the last editions of those books.

Languages and Dialects

Because languages change, or evolve, dialects develop. When people spend extended periods of time separated from others who speak the same language, they naturally develop their own ways to say things. (Darwin's theory of evolution, somewhat modified, applies to language as well as to species. Obvious examples of divergent evolution in the English language are British "lift" and American "elevator," British "in hospital" and American "in the hospital.") All major languages have a standard or "high" dialect, with various other nonstandard or "low" dialects: Demotic Greek, Low German, Cockney English, Black English—each an example of a dialect that is not accepted as standard. Any widespread language needs a standard dialect to ease communication. Without Mandarin, the Chinese could communicate only in writing; without official state languages, several African nations would comprise tribal groups who could never talk to each other.

But nonstandard dialects do have their own grammars, their own systems for structuring sentences. Native speakers of each dialect have an intuitive knowledge of the grammar, and when they speak they rarely make mistakes. These dialects are judged to be nonstandard, not because of any inherent lack of value—no language or dialect is any better or worse than any other language or dialect—but because those in power insist, consciously or unconsciously, that their dialect is the standard one.

We don't want this handbook to be a political diatribe about language and power. What we want you to get out of this discussion are two points, which few pop grammarians acknowledge: every dialect and language has a systematic structure, and every native speaker of each dialect and language speaks it fluently without any explicit knowledge of that system.

Problems arise when people are faced with new situations in which to use language or when they are asked to make their tacit knowledge explicit. A new situation may be something as basic as your first job interview; or it could be that you're trying to express new, complex ideas that you're not quite sure about; or you could be trying to learn how to use a new dialect; or your teacher has asked you to explain the difference between adjectives and adverbs. All of these situations, and others like them, could cause you difficulty, and in all of them you might make mistakes. But the mistakes aren't the result of any moral inadequacy or mental deficiency on your part—they just prove that you're operating in unfamiliar territory. So, the problems you may have with academic writing—for many people, an unfamiliar territory when they begin college—could simply result from your attempt to write in a wholly new context about ideas that may be new as well.

Grammar Books and Handbooks

As we mentioned earlier, a standard dialect develops to aid communication in a widespread language. Eventually, this dialect is codified in grammar and usage books, where discussion of the language is divided into sections for each term (nouns, verbs, clauses, fragments, etc.) and each problem (spelling, punctuation, etc.). Then these versions of the language are presented to students for them to memorize and master, the terms providing a convenient way to talk about the language. Somehow (probably because of the types of discussions in language classes), students get the impression that these categories and terms have always existed in the form the books present.

Nothing could be further from the truth. This belief is, in fact, one of the myths about language, and our purpose in this chapter is to debunk the myths that hobble language users. Grammar books have perpetuated many myths about language, myths that people accept unquestioningly. That is, after all, what myths require: faith, acceptance. The problem with myths, though, is that most people have the impression that they can't control or change myths. They believe that myths are self-generated, rather than human creations that have gained supernatural power. If you believe the world is flat, you won't try sailing around it; if you believe that certain groups of people are inferior, you'll enslave and refuse to educate them; if you believe that language is outside your control, you'll open yourself to being controlled by others through language. The linguistic myths that have been passed down all these years, myths about decline, superiority, and correctness, hinder people, making them feel insecure and thus at best making them prey to the often foolish cautions of pop grammarians. At worst, this makes them unable to write.

So, because we believe that knowing about language helps you get control over it, that is, helps make you a more effective language user, we've included a chapter that will explode some of the myths about language and give you some background that will help you recognize other myths. First, let's look at the myth that the "rules" presented in grammar books are immutable.

Historical studies help us use the past to understand the present, and the history of languages (etymology and historical linguistics) provides evidence that the grammars and lexicons of languages do change. On the surface, the myth of nonchange makes sense: Major grammatical structures and lexical forms change so slowly that differences aren't noticed immediately—you can't point to the specific dates when Chaucer's English changed into Shakespeare's English and then into the English we use now, just as you can't observe the changes in your physiognomy actually happening. Yet photos of you, separated by twenty years or so, will reveal quite marked changes. You can't deny that those changes occur.* And, in a sense, grammar and other books about language are like photos, stop-action records of an unending process. Because of this process, some books, especially dictionaries, are out of date even before they reach the bookstores. The *Oxford English Dictionary,* an immensely useful reference tool for anyone reading books written one hundred years ago or earlier, took fifty years to write—by the time the tenth volume had come out in 1928, the first volume was fifty years out of date. Supplements have since been published, to update the earlier volumes to 1986. Other dictionaries are usually revised every five to ten years, to incorporate newly coined words and phrases as well as new meanings for old words. But, especially with regard to slang expressions, it's safe to assume that if a saying has been around long enough to get itself into a dictionary, it's probably no longer in vogue, and new connotations for words develop almost daily. Dictionaries simply can't keep up with the changes.

It's a bit easier for books about grammar to keep up, but since most of them are prescriptive rather than descriptive—they tell you how you ought to speak and write, rather than how most people actually do speak and write—these books also lag behind actual language use. For many years into the 1950s and 1960s, grammar books were urging the shall/will distinction despite the fact that few people actually made that distinction when writing or speaking. (Many of you probably won't even know what the fuss was about.) And there's another problem with prescriptive grammar books: They tend to contradict each other, since grammar-book writers don't always agree on what correct usage is.

But if grammar books are supposed to guide your choices about usage and mechanics, what good are they if they don't agree and if they're not completely up to date? And if they're no good, why do

---

* Our physiognomy analogy makes us wonder if the writings of pop grammarians are like facelifts—the nip and tuck approach to language, in the hope of hiding the inevitable changes for a few more years.

teachers keep requiring students to buy them? It's sad to say, but some teachers don't look at the handbooks they ask their students to read, because they don't need to. They rarely have questions about their own usage (and to answer the few questions they do have, they usually ask a colleague, check a dictionary, or refer to their own rarely used, out-of-date handbooks). They don't realize that handbooks are helpful only for those who feel confident about their own language abilities and understand enough about language to be able to make informed decisions about the suggestions handbooks make. In the same way, popular grammarians are able to bully only the insecure language users, the ones who have always had doubts about the difference between *who* and *whom*, for instance. People who know about language read the columns to keep track of attitudes about usage issues, not only to change or adjust their own usage.

People who know about language also understand how to use the directions given by handbooks. Reading through these books and doing the exercises could give a person the impression that there is no connection between form and meaning. The exercises require simple correction and simplistically imply that editing texts is only a matter of replacing the wrong form with the right one. Another myth. For a handful of writers, the handbook exercises may be instructive, but in almost all writing, correcting "errors" actually affects meaning, and writers have to reread each correction within its context (sentence, paragraph, essay) to see if the new meaning still fits the old context. Editing isn't easy, and it requires paying attention to your initial purpose.

Another myth concerns "academic style." People, especially students who've done a lot of academic reading, get an image of acceptable academic prose that excludes concrete, subjective, personal writing. Every field has its cadre of incomprehensible writers that students must wade their way through in order to pass courses and graduate. Since the writers are recognized experts, the students assume theirs is the expert style. And since handbooks do nothing to correct this impression about academic prose, it's no wonder that students try, with disastrous effects, to imitate it by not breaking an imagined set of "rules."

Look at the following paragraphs. How many "rules" does the writer break?

> But let us go further. Consciousness is a much smaller part of our mental life than we are conscious of, because we cannot be conscious of what we are not conscious of. How simple that is to say; how difficult to appreciate! It is like asking a flashlight in a dark room to search around for something that does not have any light

shining upon it. The flashlight, since there is a light in whatever direction in turns, would have to conclude that there is light everywhere. And so consciousness can seem to pervade all mentality when actually it does not.

The timing of consciousness is also an interesting question. When we are awake, are we conscious all the time? We think so. In fact, we are sure so! I shut my eyes and even if I try to think, consciousness still streams on, a great river of contents in a succession of different conditions which I have been taught to call thoughts, images, memories, interior dialogues, regrets, wishes, resolves, all interweaving with the constantly changing pageant of exterior sensations of which I am selectively aware. Always the continuity. (*Julian Jaynes,* The Origin of Consciousness and the Breakdown of the Bicameral Mind)

We gave these paragraphs to a class of college freshman to read and analyze, and they came up with the following diagnosis: repetitious, too much "I," too personal, some fragments, a not very serious comparison (the flashlight), sentences starting with "but" or "and." The students' final judgement was that this selection represented poor academic prose. And what handbook has any discussion that would make the students doubt their analysis?

Handbooks give no hint that context guides a writer's decisions. Rather, they imply that one kind of writing is best for all contexts, and people who don't know about language are left once again with myths instead of truths. Worse still, if one of these people happens to be observant and asks why George Orwell's "Shooting an Elephant" is so admired when it obviously is not objective or impersonal, that person is told, "Yes, but Orwell is a professional writer and knows how to do these things." This, perhaps, is the most insidious myth of all, that professional writers can break rules that students can't. It's an amazing fact that English teachers will tolerate, even enjoy, broken "rules" in published texts but move to stamp out the same broken "rules" in students' writing. Teachers assume that writers break rules on purpose, but that students break rules because they don't know any better. Why the double standard? What have professional writers got that students haven't got? Experience, which comes from writing and reading, but not from handbooks.

Where, then, if not in handbooks, do people who don't know much about language, or who are insecure, get help? We can only suggest some analysis of the situation—ignorance leads to insecurity, *not* to bliss. First, within your own speech community, you needn't worry about making mistakes. Any listener will assume that the few mistakes you do make are slips of the tongue rather than errors caused by ignorance. In a different speech community, people will rarely notice your language until you do something wrong by their standards. You'll never hear anyone say, "I like the way you constructed that sentence correctly," but you will hear "*What* did you say?" if you do something wrong. But note here that the focus of the listener's question is on your ideas, not on the form they're in. Most people will ask you to rephrase something they haven't understood; only the pickiest listener will question your verb tenses or adverb forms. To keep up with what you're saying, your listeners have to pay attention to meaning alone.

Only when language is written down do people—readers—attend to form as well as to meaning. Perhaps students are surprised by the sudden focus on form as they begin academic writing. When writers expect a certain kind of response, the kind they've received while speaking, they're frustrated when they get something else. So part of adjusting to writing is getting used to the fact that people will look at the form as well as the ideas (if you're lucky; some readers, unfortunately, only look at form).

Second, because others only tell you what you do wrong, you have to find out for yourself what you do right. If you speak the standard, accepted dialect, you probably have very few problems. Examine the last paper that a teacher of yours corrected, and look at all you got right.

If you speak a nonstandard dialect or if English isn't your first language, there will probably be a greater number of corrections on your essays, but analysis of those corrections can tell you a lot: most of your errors will probably fall into just a few categories (punctuation, pronoun reference, verb form/tense). Don't be put off by the number of errors—look at what *kind* you make and categorize them. (We hope this book will help you do that.) Then you can work on learning how to correct those errors: by reading more, writing more, and becoming more aware of the way language is used in different contexts.

One thing you need to be aware of is the difference between grammar and usage. If you look at grammar handbooks, you'll notice that in certain areas they all agree. In fact, you could gather all the handbooks written since the late 1800s and, after comparing them, note that they agree with each other in a large number of areas—like subject-verb agreement, adjective and adverb formation, verb tense formation, word order, pronoun case. These areas of agreement are all rightly placed under the rubric of "grammar," and the grammars of many nonstandard dialects match the grammar of the standard dialect. Areas of disagreements among the handbooks all belong under "usage"—this is where arguments occur: *who* vs. *whom,* split infinitives, dangling participles. Usage causes the most difficulties in the written form of the language. Learning the idiosyncracies of the graphics (their/they're/there; comma vs. period) with all the complexities (*'s* in *Hermione's* shows possession, *'s* in *it's* shows contraction) makes just about everyone feel insecure for a while. In time, if your dialect is the standard one, you get the hang of it, and most of these problems disappear from your writing. If you speak a nonstandard dialect, you have to learn the standard one while you're also learning the graphics, which is a difficult process.

But, if no dialect is better than any other dialect, why should anyone bother to learn the standard dialect? That's a reasonable question to raise in the context of our earlier discussion. That question is only slightly different from "Why learn French/German/Chinese/etc.?" If you're never going to live, work, or travel in the countries where these languages are spoken (or never going to read texts written in these languages), there really isn't much point to learning them. But you won't get far hunting for a job in Paris if you don't know French. To become a part of the French-speaking community (which includes other European countries besides France, as well as about one-third of Africa), you have to know the language of that community. Some linguists think that every language throws a slightly different light on the concrete world and on the abstract world of concepts. The same may be true of dialects within a language. Those who accept these conclusions will argue that learning a new language or a new dialect expands one's perspectives on the world. We agree.

But back to being more pragmatic. If you want to become a part of the mainstream community in the U. S., you have to know the written language of that community as well. You've already begun to learn it: you're in school. Eventually you'll be applying for jobs. To succeed in either of those ventures, you have to know the standard written dialect, even if you choose to ignore the standard spoken dialect.

The Truth About Language

So far, we've debunked a few myths, but we haven't yet explained the truth about language. It's unsettling, and few people like to think about it, but the truth is that language is so tied up in the way we view the world, and our view of the world so controlled by our language, that when one changes, so does the other. As your proficiency in the standard dialect increases, you'll find yourself looking at the world in a new, slightly different way. Eliza Doolittle, in *My Fair Lady,* is a good example of this change; once she'd learned the language of the rich, which allowed her to experience the life of the rich, she found she couldn't return to her old life as a flower-seller. Richard Rodriguez, in *Hunger of Memory,* describes the even more poignant change that happened to him. As he learned English, he found himself moving further away from his Spanish-speaking parents; now he's a successful writer, but he recognizes that he has lost a close relationship with his family in the process.

As long as the world changes, so will language, and as long as language changes, so will the world. We quoted Dr. Johnson earlier, in his wish that language could be as unchanging as the things languages refers to. We think Dr. Johnson was also subconsciously wishing for an unchanging world. In fact, we suspect that all the people who berate the "illiterates" who take the language and "misuse" it are actually mourning the loss of something in the world— beliefs, innocence, whatever. It's possible that those who attack feminist language are wishing for the secure days of male dominance. At least then we each (men and women) had limited roles; now, far too much is expected of us. Perhaps those who complain about the increasing incidence of mechanistic, computer terminology in discussions about noncomputer-related subjects are actually bewailing the increasing prevalence of computers in our society. (Some of the most vitriolic prose has come out of people's shock at changes in their language. One letter writer in *The New York Review of Books* called people who argue for nonsexist language "extremist nuts.") Since language is so personal, it's easy to understand why people get upset when they see language changing: they feel personally attacked. Yet the world is unstable, and so is language.

How, then can you feel secure in a world where there's instability? We can only counter this question with our own epigram: ignorance is the worst form of oppression. Knowing about language can keep people from being oppressed by linguistic snobs; by understanding the power inherent in language, people can become better language users and more certain that they're in control of their lives.

By now, you should have the impression that language is actually too complex to encapsulate in a book. All our discussion so far has been in support of this assertion. This is why most handbooks are misleading; they give the impression that they've painted the whole picture, rather than just a part. Our book doesn't come any closer to painting the whole picture; that can't be done. What it does instead is draw an outline that you can work within, as well as provide the tools for you to work with. We discuss paragraphs and sentences that come from the work of students and professional writers. We explain the development of certain conventions and the disappearance of others. We show the complexity of language and admit the impossibility of saying it all.

We also have to admit, as a way of disarming linguistic snobs, that there'll be mistakes in this book, advertent as well as inadvertent. It'll be interesting for us, though, to watch the reactions from our critics, to see which mistakes they haul out of these pages for the world to look at as proof of our mistaken views. In fact, we like to date pop grammarians by their pet peeves, the linguistic equivalent of carbon 14.

But even the pop grammarians will admit, when pressed, that "perfect language" doesn't exist and never has. Their jobs compel them to maintain the myth about the linguistic Eden that our language has fallen from, about the purity that English has lost because of laxness, but once that myth is dispelled, then all the others become wonderfully easy to discard.

I am eruditer than you.

Boynton

Chapter Two

Global Revision

We're not going to be talking here about the almost daunting challenges facing map-makers (not to mention the countries themselves) during these early years of the 1990s. But the changes in the former U.S.S.R., Germany, and other countries may provide a useful analogy for how revision affects a text. Imagine a truck factory in Kazakhstan which in the past relied on an Armenian tire factory—more than a thousand miles away—for all its tire supply; with the dissolution of the Soviet Union, the truck factory may not be able to get the tires it needs. Life for the Kazakh factory workers will change drastically because of the complicated chain of events begun by Armenia's declaration of independence from the U.S.S.R.

Now imagine your text as you're revising it. You're rereading the first paragraph and you decide to rephrase a sentence. Then you notice that this rephrasing requires that you change something in the third paragraph—maybe you have to add some more information. But this new information contradicts a point you make on your fourth page, so you have to account for the contradiction there. Then you remember a great quote from a book that would fit perfectly back on page two as well as set up the later discussion of the contradiction, so you add it, in the process of which you decide you'd better check your conclusion. Sure enough, that needs revising, to include the new points raised by the contradiction. . . .

And so it goes. A seemingly minimal revision at any point may lead to revisions elsewhere—an effective writer is aware of this possibility. She will reread the revised paragraph, then the section, then the introduction and conclusion—all to make sure that her revised text continues to fit neatly together.

But don't let the prospect of all this complicated working and reworking scare you away from revising. Having to revise is not a sign of having done something wrong; your teacher asking you to revise shouldn't be considered a punishment. If you're writing about something that truly appeals to you, you'll probably want to take the time to consider how each change affects the whole text, and you'll follow up on these changes. If you're writing about something that doesn't appeal to you, large-scale revision may help you tailor the assignment to your interests; it may help you discover a related something that does appeal to you.

How do you know when you need to do a global revision? One clue, as we implied above, is when you're dissatisfied or bored with what you're writing about. Change your stance, your angle of view, on the topic; choose a smaller part of it, or combine it with something else to make it bigger. Adjust it so that it becomes something you want to write about while still meeting the requirements of the assignment. (And be sure to check any major change with your teacher; a strict teacher may want "approval rights," a less strict one may want to make helpful suggestions.)

Other signals to revise will come from your readers. Their comments will help you see what they liked, what confused them, and what made them want to hear more. Your readers' comments can help you find parts of your text that need revising, and can then help you see if your revisions are effective. Keep in mind, however, that your readers' comments are at most suggestions, not directives; you are the writer, and you get to make the final decisions about what to change and how to change it. (And keep in mind one of the many benefits of reading aloud to others: sometimes the presence of a *listener* can make you aware of gaps that you hadn't noticed while reading silently to yourself.)

The signal that you'll grow to rely on more and more as you become a more experienced writer is your own sense of how well what you wrote matches what you intended to write. This is why rereading your text—frequently—is a critical part of revising. The act of rereading helps remind you of what your original intentions were, helps you decide whether to change those intentions, and helps you keep track of what you haven't yet written. For a long paper, a written plan helps as well, but as you discover new ideas this too may end up being revised during the process of writing.

Throughout the process of revision, however, keep yourself focused on the ideas in your text—don't get bogged down in extensive editing until you're sure you won't be revising any more. If you notice a mistake that you can change effortlessly, there's no reason not to. But if you're wrestling with a tough section, trying to get all your ideas into a sensible order, don't stop to look up a word's spelling—save that for later, when you're ready to create the final draft.

Practice 1

Below is a draft of a text, the readers' comments, and then the revision. After reading the first draft, write your own comments for Sally, and compare your comments with what Sally's peers and teacher wrote. Then, before reading the revision, decide how you would use the comments to revise, and compare your decisions with Sally's. Discuss the comments and the revision with others in your class, and decide if you think Sally's choices were effective.

Sally's First Draft

According to the Webster's Dictionary, insanity is defined to be a deranged state of mind, usually occurring as a specific disorder; unsoundness of mind or lack of understanding as prevents one from having the mental capacity required by law to enter into a particular relationship, status or transaction or as removes one from criminal or civil responsibility; unreasonableness or something utterly foolish.

Insanity can be classified into two categories: namely, insanity in its technical sense, that is, the loss of reality and in its broad sense, mass insanity.

Certain activity or obsession can be viewed not as individual insanity but mass insanity in the accepted mode of society. From my point of view, people rushing to and from work, housewives "grabbing" goods during after-Christmas sales in department stores and fans waiting overnight to purchase tickets for football games or rock concerts are all acts of insanity. But in our society where the law determine the status of sanity in an individual, we cannot simply lock those people who committed the above acts in an asylum. As so, people would think that such acts or behavior are "normal" but crazy. However, the term "insane" is used casually by everyone to refer to behavior that society has not defined as insane.

(If someone who is sane, that is able to function properly in society hurts others physically for some psychological reasons, he can plead not guilty, as the law permits on grounds of insanity. Here again, the law system defines insanity.)

In New York City, there are reports about mental patients being released because the city cannot accomodate them or provide them with proper treatment. It is most likely that some of those bag ladies seen crouching on dirty sidewalks, subway stations and alleys, destitutes wandering aimlessly and scavenging for leftovers in garbage cans are former mental patients. They are turning our streets into open asylums. I always find them disturbing for the fact that they should be taken care of in appropriate institution or place. The majority of the American society tend to ignore these people for fear of being hurt or perhaps, for not able to do much to help improve the situation. Perhaps, it's due to my upbringing that my level of tolerance is lower than the majority of the American society. I was brought up in a completely sheltered environment where the mentally ill are placed in asylums and anyone who committed murder are sentenced to death or a life sentence without plea bargaining. Capital punishment may not be the best solution to deal with insane criminals, but it can ensure safety to the general public. Here, in the States, the law permits an alleged killer to plead innocent on grounds of insanity. I would say that the law system defines insanity.

I hardly see or witness "society's illnesses" till I came to the States. What I mean by society's illnesses are the problems arising as a result of the social unrest or behavior. In the past, movies constantly depicted the good life of the American families. The ugliness of the American society was so well-hidden that insanity becomes a dirty word.

Comments on the first draft

From John: I'd like to know more about your upbringing—about your country's attitude toward insane people. How well are they taken care of? The paper's organization is confusing to me, but I don't know what to suggest. By the way, where are you from?

From Andrew: Do you need to include the death penalty here? That seems like something else. Are you trying to define insanity? Everyone has a different definition of it. That seems too hard to me. Maybe you should just write about some examples of what *you* consider to be insane behavior.

From Milly: I really hate the way the poor, insane people are treated in this country. No one seems to care about them. I think you should write about that. It's really a crime that they have no place to go, no way to tell people they need help except by committing some kind of terrible crime. Is it really better in your country? I've heard that asylums in a lot of places are awful.

From Sally's teacher: Your partners' comments show some confusion about your main idea—you're writing about a lot of different things, all having to do with insanity, but not connected closely enough. If you decide to define insanity, try not to rely on the dictionary's words. What is *your* definition? However, I think I'd much rather hear your opinions about how insane people are treated in NYC and in your country.

Sally's Revision

In New York City, there are reports about mental patients being released because the city cannot accomodate them or provide them with proper treatment. It is most likely that some of those bag ladies seen crouching on dirty sidewalks, subway stations and alleys, destitutes wandering aimlessly and scavenging for leftovers in garbage cans are former mental patients. They are turning our streets into open asylums. I always find them disturbing for the fact that they should be taken care of in the appropriate institution or place. The majority of the American society, however, tend to ignore these people for fear of being hurt or perhaps, for not being able to do much to help improve the situation.

I was brought up Singapore, in a completely sheltered environment where the mentally ill are placed in asylums. I hardly see or witness "society's illnesses" till I came to the States. What I mean by society's illnesses are the problems arising as a result of the social unrest or behavior. In the past, movies constantly depicted the good life of the American families. The ugliness of the American society was well-hidden and insanity becomes a dirty word. Now, Americans don't want to discuss the problem of insane people living on the streets and so these people continue to roam, with no one to offer help to them.

In Singapore, insane people are sent to asylums, or they stay with their families. They aren't allowed to live on the street. If a family is too poor to pay for an asylum, the government pays. The asylums aren't pleasant places to live, but at least these people are cared for.

No one, in any country, enjoys talking about insanity. Only doctors seem interested in understanding the causes of insanity. In Singapore, doctors study the patients in asylums and learn more about their behavior and how to treat them. Family members come to visit them, bringing food and clothing. If a patient recovers, he is taken home by his family. But in New York City, with the insane people on the streets, they can't be treated and can't recover. People just turn their heads as they go by, and family members don't know where to find their homeless relatives in order to offer help. (Some may not even want to offer help.)

I think Americans don't care about these people. This society is very cold if it lets insane people remain outside, threatening themselves and others.

Chapter Three

Paragraphs

Before you begin the close reading of individual sentences and words which proofreading and copyediting demand, you should check your paragraphing. In the process, you may discover that you need to do some reorganizing of your ideas: rearranging, adding transitions, deleting the unnecessary. We think it makes sense to do all that before you begin checking smaller elements such as sentences and phrases.

We like to think of paragraphs as higher-order punctuation marks that extend the connections shown by commas, semi-colons, and periods. Just as these punctuation marks divide words into groups which help readers make sense out of what they're reading, so paragraph indentations and spacing divide sentences into groups which help readers judge the relative importance of particular ideas within an essay.

Paragraphs and Ideas

It could be that paragraphing "skills" are intuitive—that is, through reading and writing and talking about writing you get a sense of how paragraphing works. At any rate, a writer's decisions about when to begin a new paragraph are guided by the relationships he sees between his ideas. Because of this, writers rarely share paragraphing styles. Any text can be divided several ways, depending on what needs to be emphasized.

This chapter has four paragraphs so far (counting this one). We could have divided it just as easily into two or three paragraphs, or left it as one. But we saw a special purpose for the first paragraph as an introduction and a distinct division between the central idea in the second paragraph (paragraphing as a form of punctuation) and the third one (paragraphing "skills" as intuitive and idiosyncratic), and we wanted to make sure those ideas were given equal weight. And since this paragraph is a commentary on *all* the preceding paragraphs, it didn't seem right to attach it to the third one.

Let's see if we can make these ideas more concrete by looking at an example. One of our students wrote the following to introduce a paper on the relationship between television and politicians' successes and failures:

> By the summer of 1960 there was a close presidential race developing between Vice-President Richard Nixon and a lesser known Catholic John Kennedy. There were many who felt the entire election would be settled in a series of television debates, the first such debates ever held. When the first debate began Kennedy was sharply dressed, with his hair well groomed and his makeup just right. Nixon on the other hand looked nervous and sweaty, in a bland grey suit. J.F.K.'s composure and boyish good looks were a great visual contrast to the shifty-eyed, sweaty-browed Nixon. It was this visual effect which is generally accepted as having been the most important factor in the Kennedy debate victory which led to his subsequent election victory. The public worry as to Kennedy's relative youth and inexperience was calmed and Kennedy had a new image which he would continually fuel through the media as President. Strangely enough many who listened to the debate on radio were left with a far different impression as to the outcome of the debate. Nixon was later to admit that he put far too much emphasis on substance and not enough on creating an image.

As one paragraph, this introduction gives an overview of the Kennedy-Nixon debate, with some points (visual effects, response of the radio audience) almost getting lost in the midst of everything else. The contrast between the appearance of the two candidates seems almost as important as the contrast between the effects of television coverage and radio coverage. Divided into paragraphs, the introduction would emphasize various points, showing closer connections between some than between others.

If, for example, the writer had begun a new paragraph with "Strangely enough," the last two sentences might become more of an aside, a bit of information not critical to the paper, but added for the reader's benefit. The ideas of these sentences might no longer seem to be either a summary or conclusion to what goes before and/or a foreshadowing of what follows. With the last two sentences in a separate paragraph, the final sentence of the first paragraph would

be: "The public worry as to Kennedy's relative youth and inexperience was calmed and Kennedy had a new image which he would
continually fuel through the media as President." This sentence
might now serve as a summary or conclusion to what precedes and
a foreshadowing of the paper's focus. On the other hand, it's possible
that the new paragraph beginning "Strangely enough" might introduce the real subject of the paper. We wouldn't know that until we
read on. At any rate, here's what it would look like:

> By the summer of 1960 there was a close presidential race
> developing between Vice-President Richard Nixon and a lesser
> known Catholic John Kennedy. There were many who felt the entire
> election would be settled in a series of television debates, the first
> such debates ever held. When the first debate began Kennedy was
> sharply dressed, with his hair well groomed and his makeup just
> right. Nixon on the other hand looked nervous and sweaty, in a
> bland grey suit. J.F.K.'s composure and boyish good looks were a
> great visual contrast to the shifty-eyed, sweaty-browed Nixon. It
> was this visual effect which is generally accepted as having been
> the most important factor in the Kennedy debate victory which led
> to his subsequent election victory. The public worry as to Kennedy's
> relative youth and inexperience was calmed and Kennedy had a
> new image which he would continually fuel through the media as
> President.
> Strangely enough many who listened to the debate on radio were
> left with a far different impression as to the outcome of the debate.
> Nixon was later to admit that he put far too much emphasis on
> substance and not enough on creating an image.

If the student had divided this introductory section into three
paragraphs, at "When the first debate" and at "Strangely enough," we
would see closer connections between certain ideas and weaker
connections between others. Here's what it would look like:

> By the summer of 1960 there was a close presidential race
> developing between Vice-President Richard Nixon and a lesser
> known Catholic John Kennedy. There were many who felt the entire
> election would be settled in a series of television debates, the first
> such debates ever held.
> When the first debate began, Kennedy was sharply dressed, with
> his hair well groomed and his makeup just right. Nixon on the other
> hand looked nervous and sweaty, in a bland grey suit. J.F.K.'s
> composure and boyish good looks were a great visual contrast to the
> shifty-eyed, sweaty-browed Nixon. It was this visual effect which is
> generally accepted as having been the most important factor in the
> Kennedy debate victory which led to his subsequent election victory.
> The public worry as to Kennedy's relative youth and inexperience

was calmed and Kennedy had a new image which he would continually fuel through the media as President.

Strangely enough many who listened to the debate on radio were left with a far different impression as to the outcome of the debate. Nixon was later to admit that he put far too much emphasis on substance and not enough on creating an image.

Paragraphed in this way, the connection between what people had seen on television (visual effects) and the public response to the debate (worry was calmed) would be emphasized because these ideas would now be together in their own paragraph. The relationship between these two ideas and the impression made by the radio broadcast would change because of the intervening paragraph break. We think that the contrast between the effect on television and the effect on radio is made more significant by this division. If you're attentive to your reading as you read, you'll sense a difference too, even though you may explain it somewhat differently than we have. The significant point is that we all react to the paragraph break.

The student actually divided this section into four paragraphs:

By the summer of 1960 there was a close presidential race developing between Vice-President Richard Nixon and a lesser known Catholic John Kennedy. There were many who felt the entire election would be settled in a series of television debates, the first such debates ever held.

When the first debate began, Kennedy was sharply dressed, with his hair well groomed and his makeup just right. Nixon on the other hand looked nervous and sweaty, in a bland grey suit. J.F.K.'s composure and boyish good looks were a great visual contrast to the shifty-eyed, sweaty-browed Nixon. It was this visual effect which is generally accepted as having been the most important factor in the Kennedy debate victory which led to his subsequent election victory.

The public worry as to Kennedy's relative youth and inexperience were calmed and Kennedy had a new image which he would continually fuel through the media as President.

Strangely enough many who listened to the debate on radio were left with a far different impression as to the outcome of the debate. Nixon was later to admit that he put far too much emphasis on substance and not enough on creating an image.

Now we can see a developing focus on "image"—the new third paragraph brings this point to our attention, and with the next (the fifth) paragraph (not reprinted here) beginning: "Clearly the emphasis on image is an accepted part of the television media," we can see that the fourth paragraph is *not* incidental information. Instead, it acts as a link between the introductory paragraphs and the next section of the paper.

How can you use what we've been saying here? If you stayed with our explanation all the way through, you undoubtedly noticed that you had to read quite carefully and attend closely to the student's ideas. What we were saying was specifically directed to the particular essay we were looking at. None of it was general. That's how it is with paragraphs—it's very difficult to say anything about them in general since whether or not they seem right is almost solely a matter of their context—of the paragraphs before and after them. The only general statement about paragraphs we feel comfortable making is the one we've already made: paragraphs group related sentences into a unit. Psychologists tell us that we can remember things better and longer if we can group related ideas into clusters. Paragraphs help readers do this.

Paragraphs "Say" and "Do"

Think a bit about how you paragraph as you write. Do you tend to write first drafts which are one long paragraph? Or do you do the opposite: write a series of sentences each indented as though it were a paragraph? Probably you do neither, instead paragraphing where it seems "right" to do so and then making adjustments. So we're going to assume that the paper you're copyediting has at least two paragraphs—probably three or more. If you want to test out the validity of your paragraphing, we suggest that you forget general statements about what paragraphs are and do some close reading of the paragraphs in your paper. All paragraphs "say" something. In addition, all paragraphs "do" something: they introduce, provide proof, give illustrations, serve as transitions, restate something particularly important, conclude a particular development, and so forth. Since paragraphs "say" and "do" at the same time, it's artificial to talk about these matters separately. On the other hand it's impossible to talk about both at the same time.

We suggest that you read each paragraph in your essay closely. Once you've done that, write in the margin as briefly as possible what the paragraph says; this will be a summary of its content. Under the content statement, jot down what the paragraph "does" (see the list in our previous paragraph for suggestions). If you have trouble doing either of these, you've got more writing and thinking to do. If you can't give a brief summary of the content of a paragraph, perhaps the paragraph is trying to say too much. If you find more than one sentence in a paragraph which can serve as a statement of its central idea, you'll want to check and make certain that the ideas in the paragraph are developed, not just restated. If you can't figure out what a particular paragraph is "doing," either there's no reason for the paragraph to be there or—what's more likely—you need to re-trace your prior thinking and try to recapture what was in your mind when you first wrote the paragraph. Very few of us write something without a reason. What *is* possible is that after you revise your paper, some ideas you had originally no longer belong. All of us have had the experience of wanting to keep words we've become particularly attached to. Sometimes, though, we have to give them up—or store them away for use some other time.

Once you've written down what each paragraph "says" and "does," you'll have a clear picture of the structure of your essay. You can look at the overall development of your ideas from paragraph to paragraph and see if it's logical. The summary statements for each paragraph become a kind of outline. (We don't believe in writing outlines *before* writing papers because most writers don't know what they're going to say until they've said it.) If you notice that most of your paragraphs "do" the same thing, you can question yourself about the usefulness of that; if, for example, you discover that you have four paragraphs which explain and only one paragraph which gives concrete evidence or illustrations, you can make a decision about whether such a heavy dose of explanation serves your purpose. It may or it may not; its usefulness can only be assessed within the context of your essay.

Here's an essay written by one of our students. Using it, practice the process we've just described; that is, write down in the margin what you think each paragraph "says" and "does."

My life changed drastically when I reached the age of seventeen. I had to adjust to the newly gained responsibilities. At seventeen, many things were expected of me. People demanded much more from me. I was expected to do things without being told, to understand things that made no sense to me, and to set a good example for my younger brother and sister.

I have had responsibility before in my life, but I never had so much at one time before. My responsibilities ranged from taking care of the yard to more difficult tasks, like taking care of my younger brother and sister. At the age of seventeen I also noticed that it was not just an age filled with a lot of responsibilities. Along with the responsibility came privileges that I never had before. I was allowed to stay out later at night when I went to parties. The decisions that I made were not questioned as they were when I was younger. Since I was given these privileges I can say that turning seventeen has its advantages along with its disadvantages. These advantages and disadvantages that I was abruptly introduced to are what changed my life drastically. In school, the classes became more challenging and the competition was fierce. With so many new experiences occurring at the same time it was difficult for me to adjust to my life. Someone may say that every age group has responsibilities, competition and privileges, but somehow at seventeen all of these things seem to play a major role in a person's life. I feel this is where the transformation from child to adult takes place, because if you do not handle your responsibilities and if you do not live up to your expectations then you are looked upon as a failure.

When you turn seventeen you are really being prepared for the outside world. You are preparing to leave high school and go into a world that you have been sheltered from for seventeen years. Turning seventeen is like being in a protective bubble all of your life and each year you get bigger until finally you are too big for the bubble and you must face life without your protection. This analogy is really saying that life is unbalanced. Life starts out easy in the beginning and gets harder as you get older. Even though I am eighteen now and I have even more pressures than I had when I was seventeen, I could not say that eighteen was the turning point in my life, because at seventeen the pressures hit me without any warning and at eighteen I expect these pressures.

My attitude toward certain things had changed. My attitude toward things like the presidential election and the United States foreign policy had changed from one of indifference to one of interest. My values toward some issues like sex, marriage and friendship had changed. My expectations became very clear to me. I expected to get into a good university and to make it to medical school, so that I could become a doctor. The things that I enjoyed doing with my friends didn't seem enjoyable anymore. My friends and I went down to the park to play handball everyday. I became bored with the park. When I changed my attitude, some of my friends and I were not really communicating as we once had been. We seemed like strangers, so they went their way and I went mine.

If someone asked me if I like the changes that had taken place, I would have to say no, because no one really likes to change the way they have been doing things. Even though I didn't like this change, I realized that it was for my own good. This change let me come to terms with myself. I realized what I had completed and what I had to do to get where I wanted to get in life.

Here's what the student himself wrote in the margins:

First paragraph:
I'm giving the reader the main idea of my essay.

I'm introducing.

Second paragraph:
How I was affected by the responsibilities and privileges, competition, school.

Gives examples, reasons, and explanations.

Third paragraph:
What I think it means to be seventeen.

Use analogy to help clear up reader's interpretation.

Relates to preceding paragraph, also explaining how turning seventeen affected me.

Fourth paragraph:
How I changed, difference in values, expectations, relationship with friends.

Gives examples.

Last paragraph:
How I felt about the change and what it did for me.

Leaves the reader totally understanding my main idea.

What the student realized when he looked over his own comments was that a part of paragraph two didn't seem very different from paragraph three. As he thought back over his intentions about the essay, he realized that what he wanted to talk about was what was different about being seventeen and then how he felt about the differences. While thinking about this, he came to the conclusion that the bubble analogy would work better in the introductory paragraph. He also decided that he was satisfied with the last two paragraphs and didn't need to revise them. After several more revisions, this is what the first three paragraphs looked like:

My life changed drastically when I reached the age of seventeen. I had to adjust to the newly gained responsibilities. At seventeen, people demanded much more from me. When you turn seventeen you are really being prepared for the outside world. You are preparing to leave high school and go into a world that you have been sheltered from for seventeen years. Turning seventeen is like being in a protective bubble all of your life and each year you get bigger until finally you are too big for the bubble and you must face life without your protection.

I have had responsibilities before in my life, but I never had so much at one time before. My responsibilities ranged from taking care of the yard to more difficult tasks, like taking care of my younger brother and sister and setting a good example for them. In school, the classes became more challenging and the competition was fierce. Along with the responsibilities came new privileges. I was allowed to stay out later at night when I went to parties. The decisions that I made were not questioned as they had been when I was younger.

Now I had to make the right decisions about all those things too and
that was not easy.

   With so many new experiences occurring at the same time it was
difficult for me to adjust my life. Someone may say that every age
group has responsibilities, competition and privileges, but somehow
at seventeen all of these things seem to play a major role in a person's
life. I feel this is where the transformation from child to adult takes
place. If you do not handle your responsibilities and if you do not
live up to your expectations then you are looked upon as a failure. I
wouldn't admit it then, but I think I was scared. I began to realize
that life is unbalanced. Life starts out easy in the beginning and gets
hard as you get older. Even though I am eighteen now and I have
even more pressures I could not say that eighteen was the turning
point in my life, because at seventeen the pressures hit me without
any warning and at eighteen I expected these pressures. I know I
liked the new privileges, but sometimes I wished that someone else
would make some of the hard decisions for me.

You can see that the student basically rearranged sentences already in his original essay, but you'll note too that he added a new
thought: that he had been frightened by what was happening to him.
He said that he probably knew all along that he had been frightened,
but he had been afraid to admit it even to himself. While he was
rewriting, he said, he stopped suddenly and said to himself, "I was
scared." He realized it would be important to include this reaction
in his paper.

Naturally, we can't predict what will happen when you look at
your essay; it's possible that you won't need to make any adjustments. Even so, going through the process should make you more
aware of your essay's content and structure. Such awareness has to
be valuable.

Paragraph Length

Once you feel satisfied that your paragraph divisions suit your ideas,
you need to consider their length. One of the "rules" we've often
heard from students is that it's wrong to write a paragraph with just
one sentence. We can agree that an essay made up of a series of
one-sentence paragraphs would be odd; it would impress readers as
a series of undeveloped and unemphatic ideas. It's hard to believe
that some of these ideas wouldn't be more interrelated than others
and thus connectible to one another in longer, more cohesive paragraphs. Still, we've seen one-sentence paragraphs used effectively
both as a way to emphasize a particular idea and as a way to move
an argument or presentation from one idea to the next. The third

paragraph of the student essay on page 25 does just that. If you have any one-sentence paragraphs in your essay, you'll want to give them a closer look—especially if there are several. You can consider adding such paragraphs either to the previous one or to the following one. Your decision about whether to do either of these should be based on how the change affects your essay and not on any supposed prohibition against one-sentence paragraphs. The next time you read something, look for one-sentence paragraphs; if you find any, judge for yourself how they fit into the whole pattern set up by the writer and whether, if you were an editor, you would advise the writer to reparagraph.

Another thing to consider when paragraphing is the appearance of your essay on the page. Page after page of unindented text is visually tiresome; some variation of the pattern sustains interest. Perhaps paragraph indentations are a kind of visual breath-taking. Obviously, appearance is related to the size of the page and to whether or not text is printed in wide blocks or in fairly narrow columns. Paragraph length in newspapers is usually shorter (in actual word count) than in journals or magazines or books where blocks of print are wider than they are in newspapers. We're not saying that appearance should be the deciding factor; relationship of ideas is foremost, but appearance is a factor. And appearance (length of paragraphs, in this case) is related to a reader's ability to group ideas. If ideas keep following one another without a break, our mind tires; it, like our eyes, needs to take an occasional breather.

Writers often deliberately divide what they consider one idea into two paragraphs because they recognize their audience's need to take a mental breath. Often when a paragraph is divided, the first sentence of the newly created paragraph may need some slight revision, since it becomes less attachable to the previous sentence than it had been. Following is a fairly long paragraph from a student essay on Dryden's poem "Why Should a Foolish Marriage Vow."

> I have come to believe that this is a woman in this poem who is questioning society and actually begging for approval to end her marriage. I can sense desperation and entrapment from this grieving woman. In the first four stanzas of the poem, this woman is searching for an answer. She has introduced almost entirely her unfortunate predicament. This woman is obviously crying out for help. The following two stanzas have this woman going into a deeper explanation of her relationship with her husband. She seems extremely bitter in describing her marriage. I think that here she is emphasizing the fact that they at one time did truly love one another. Here, the rhythm changes and words are repeated. This rhythm changes where the meaning changes and goes into an explanation of why

her marriage means nothing to her anymore. This woman feels she should not have to obey her vows of love if she no longer loves. But what she also includes into the poem is that her husband no longer loves her either. She cannot understand why her husband would be jealous of a new love, when he no longer loves her. She doesn't even care that her husband had lost the love which he had once felt for her. She is just hurt that he should make it impossible for her to lead a new life, for if he had found love elsewhere she would be willing to let him go.

If you were going to split this paragraph in two, where would you end the first paragraph? The student decided to start another paragraph at: "Here, the rhythm changes." Before she made the change, the separation between this sentence and the one before it was marked by a period. After the change, the separation was marked by both a period and a paragraph indentation. To make certain that her readers continued to see the connection between the ideas in the two paragraphs, the student changed "Here" to "After the first three stanzas of the poem." Here's how it looks now:

> I have come to believe that this is a woman in this poem who is questioning society and actually begging for approval to end her marriage. I can sense desperation and entrapment from this grieving woman. In the first four stanzas of the poem, this woman is searching for an answer. She has introduced almost entirely her unfortunate predicament. This woman is obviously crying out for help. The following two stanzas have this woman going into a deeper explanation of her relationship with her husband. She seems extremely bitter in describing her marriage. I think that here she is emphasizing the fact that they at one time did truly love one another.
>
> After the first three stanzas of the poem, the rhythm changes and words are repeated. This rhythm changes where the meaning changes and goes into an explanation of why her marriage means nothing to her anymore. This woman feels she should not have to obey her vows of love if she no longer loves. But what she also includes into the poem is that her husband no longer loves her. She doesn't even care that her husband had lost the love which he had once felt for her. She is just hurt that he should make it impossible for her to lead a new life, for if he had found love elsewhere she would be willing to let him go.

Suggestions

Using one of your own papers, go through the exercise we discussed in this chapter. If, as a result, you have questions about how to divide your text into paragraphs, experiment: try different schemes, combining your ideas in different ways, and then study how each idea's relationship to the whole text is affected by each scheme. Show the different versions to other readers and use their feedback to help you decide what is effective and what isn't.

Check the length of your paragraphs. If you have a series of short paragraphs, think about whether or not ideas might be more effective if joined in larger paragraphs. If you find a very long paragraph, see if you can divide it. Remember that when you do this, you may need to make a slight adjustment in the sentence that begins any newly created paragraph.

Another suggestion some students have found helpful: imagine that you're standing before a group of people reading your paper and that your throat tends to get dry and you need, every now and then, to take a sip of water. Where would be the best places in your text for you to stop and take those sips of water without risking the audience's losing track of your idea?

And one final suggestion: paragraphing is not magical, although it can become so intuitive that it may seem magical. We don't know of anyone born with the ability to paragraph, and we suggest that if there ever has been or ever is a person who speaks beautifully but had never seen words on paper, that person will have a difficult time with paragraphs, which are visual markers of ideas just as periods and commas are. The only way for that person to learn anything about paragraphing is through reading. That's how you learned almost all you know about paragraphs. And so our final suggestion is simply to read more and, during your reading, become more consciously attentive to paragraph breaks. And perhaps the following practices will help.

Practice 2

Following is a complete essay as the student writer paragraphed it. Discuss with your classmates and teacher the appropriateness of the paragraphing and your reasons for approving or disapproving the writer's choices.

My grandfather is a man of an unusual and unique past which makes me very proud of him. My grandfather was born and raised in Poland till he was about eight years old when his parents decided to come to America. He heard so much about the New World that he could not wait to experience it for himself. Grandpa and his parents started to pack up their belongings. They were so excited about their journey that they could not wait to arrive in America to see what America had to offer them. As soon as Grandpa arrived in America, he had big plans for his future. He wanted to capture a part of the American Dream and was going to let nothing get in his way to prevent that from happening. After he settled down with his parents in a small town in New Jersey, he was doing odd jobs such as delivering meats for the butcher and grocery items for the residing neighbors. Grandfather was a very eager and anxious person. He wanted to get his life rolling. At fifteen years of age he learned many simple trades such as plumbing and carpentry which eventually led him to own his own businesses. Eight years later he met Grandma and soon married her. In order to support themselves, Grandmother became a saleslady while Grandfather became a handy man. He went around the whole town where they lived in his blue coveralls and workboots fixing clogged drains, repairing leaks and building furniture that he sold. Twenty years later when they knew that they were financially stable, Grandfather bought and operated a liquor store and a luncheonette which resulted in great prosperity for the both of them. As years went on, Grandfather was getting too old to handle and operate the stores, so he sold them. Five years later he received a job in a famous delicatessen called "Tabachniks" preparing food and making sandwiches. When he turned sixty-five years of age, he retired and started to collect Social Security. I remember as a kid I used to come visit him when he was working in Tabachniks. He would be standing behind the counter working and wearing his white apron and white paper cap. I can really be proud that my grandfather as well as my grandmother captured the American Dream just like they hoped for.

Now that my grandfather is retired and is living happily with grandmother, he did not want his life to rock away. He couldn't face the fact that he was getting old, so he became a very active person in doing things that interested him. Every day of the week he would do a different activity that occupied his time. Either he would jog around the block a couple of times or spend his day working in the back yard garden. If Grandfather had any free time he would spend it in temple. The best thing that Grandpa did that made him feel rejuvenated was coming out to Brooklyn to visit me and spend some time with me. Every time that I knew that Grandfather was coming to visit me, I was prepared for a spectacular day. When he arrived he would usually take a short nap and afterwards the fun and games began. After his nap, we walked to Coney Island to see what fun money can buy. He would supply me with quarters to play the video games and pinball machines and buy me tickets for the rides. When I was done we would take a short walk to Nathan's Famous for some hotdogs and fries. For dessert he would take me across the street for ice cream at Carvel. Most of the time we would stand there for ten minutes trying to decide what flavor ice cream to get. Grandpa's visits always bring sunshine and happiness even on the worst days of the year.

I can still remember the last time that Grandfather drove out to see me. His appearance is still embedded in my mind. He was about seventy years of age wearing wire-rimmed glasses that covered the luster of his baby-blue eyes as the light reflected off of them. He was a man of about medium height approximately 5 feet, 6 inches with a sexy build that any Grandma would kill for. His dark hair was very distinguished and was precisely combed to the right side of his head. His mustache was perfectly groomed while his high cheek bones seemed to be misfit on his round delicate face. His mustache contained many colors such as brown, grey, white, and tints of red such as a forest sheds its colors in autumn to reveal its beauty. He was wearing tan cotton twill pants with a maroon Izod shirt tightly tucked in his pants. On his large feet were a pair of brown leather loafers with a brown tweed cap on the top of his rounded head.

Grandpa today is eighty-five years of age but still in terrific shape and good health. The most heart-warming feeling I receive from him is that he never changed in personality. He still contains those special qualities that made me love him for all these past years. He is still loving, caring, and generous to me. Grandfather is still number one in my book!

Practice 3

Following is another essay as it was paragraphed by the student writer. Identify each paragraph by what it "says" and "does" and then discuss your conclusions with your classmates and teacher. Also discuss with them whether you agree or disagree with the paragraph divisions and the sequencing of them. Would you group ideas differently and put them in some different sequence if you were writing this essay?

When you say, "I like physical exercise," most people withdraw from the conversation because most people just don't like to exercise.

I look at exercise as a sigh of relief and relaxation. After exercising I can breath easily and sleep better, because my body feels strong and energized. In the morning my body feels ready to go. Some people don't like to exercise because they don't have the will power to get out there for the first time and exercise.

There are some people who don't even like to talk about exercise; those people are mainly fat. All they want to do is eat and sleep. Probably they've fallen into these habits because this is the way they've always lived their lives. These people probably do not participate in any sports.

When I look at other people who are fat, lethargic, and out of shape, I'm motivated to continue exercising. When I go to the basketball court to play, I can jump higher than most of the people I play with. My body is more physically conditioned more than theirs to do this. Just knowing that I can run farther, and do more physical activities than most out-of-shape people makes me feel good.

Physical exercise is very important to your health and mental well being. It can improve your circulation and make your heart stronger. If you are lucky not to get hit by a truck or killed in a war, you can live a stronger, longer, healthier life, by being physically fit. Mentally it can help relieve pressures that build up during the day. Physically it helps keep your body weight down, and unwanted fat off.

The problem of those who do not exercise is that they will have problems when they get older. The blood will be poorly circulated, thus leading to hardening of the arteries. A person in poor physical shape can tear muscles just by lifting a chair.

There are many kinds of good physical exercises you can do. Running is good for your heart, lifting weights is very good for your muscle groups, and basketball can help you all around. Everyone should do the exercise he most likes to do, but when you find an exercise you like, stick with it.

By continuing to exercise, and by avoiding fattening food, you will find yourself feeling, acting, and living a complete life.

Practice 4

Following is a student essay which we have printed without paragraph indentations. Discuss with your teacher and classmates where you think paragraph divisions should be.

Why shouldn't music be censored? If you listened to some of the new creations put out by supposedly called artists, one thought comes to mind, "trash." Music is an art form that is created to bring pleasure to its listeners. It is a universal form of communication with an agreeable sound that's designed to touch the soul and create a sense of euphoria. However, on the contrary, there is the nauseating heavy metal, rap and banal pop. I think if Beethoven was able to hear he would prefer to be deaf after listening to what our modern-day society refers to as music. Over the generations music has changed drastically from the enjoyable be-bop jazz of the forties and fifties to the acid rock of the sixties and seventies. Nevertheless, the music never attacked ethnic groups, such as the rap group who has been charged twice by the Jewish community because of the anti-semitic lyrics. Previously, and even in the present day and age, the songs created told a story whether it would be about the environment, or the poverty in this world or the most common subject, love. The lyrics were never offensive or criminal before, such as the song by Guns n Roses with lyrics as follows:

I used to love her,
So I had to kill her
Now she is six feet under. . . . "

With the growing rate of crime, drugs, diseases and the deterioration of the educational system, parents have enough to worry about. They shouldn't have to be concerned with the type of music their children are bringing into the home or what the radio is playing that might be inappropriate for them to listen to. Children shouldn't be exposed to music that will corrupt their minds. They already have so many negative aspects of society to deal with, they really don't need another. One might argue that censorship of the music they create or listen to is a violation of their constitutional right of freedom of expression. However, if this expression affects many others negatively, then their freedom should be curbed; they should have a limit as to what is appropriate or what is not. After all, we live in a democratic system where the needs of the majority come first and foremost. If they feel the music is improper, then they have the right to do something about its inflow into our society. Many people have stretched their liberties too far in the music they create. They have incorporated their personalities into it, whether it be destructive or serene. In a recent case, a band was charged with inserting hidden messages into their songs which led two boys to commit suicide. This was not the first time an issue such as this has arisen. Thus, with added fears such as these, parents should have the right to have the music their children listen to censored. It would be a great help to them not to have to worry about the music their child is listening to, because since it is censored they know it won't be devil-worshipping music or self-destructive subliminal messages hidden in the songs.

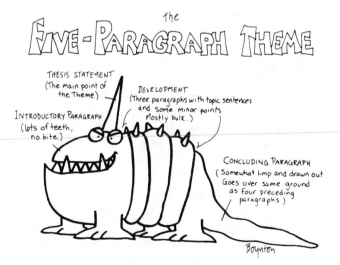

The
FIVE-PARAGRAPH THEME

THESIS STATEMENT
(The main point of the Theme.)

DEVELOPMENT
(Three paragraphs with topic sentences and some minor points Mostly bulk.)

INTRODUCTORY PARAGRAPH
(lots of teeth, no bite.)

CONCLUDING PARAGRAPH
(Somewhat limp and drawn out Goes over same ground as four preceding paragraphs)

Boynton

COLOR: Glossy rose-colored exterior, rather blue underneath Occasional theme has a blend, resulting in purple passages

Chapter Four

Sentences

Once you're satisfied with the paragraph divisions of your paper, you can begin to examine individual sentences. The first thing to consider is whether endmarks (periods, exclamation points, question marks) appear where they should: that is, only at the end of complete sentences.

Traditionally defined, a sentence is a group of words containing a complete idea, usually manifested by the presence of a subject, a verb, and, if the verb requires one, an object. A true description, perhaps, but not always a useful one. Completeness of idea may well be a philosophical issue, liable to endless debate. Nonetheless, all of us intuitively produce complete sentences and know how, in conversation, to convey that completeness to our listeners. Unfortunately, knowing how, as writers, to convey that completeness in the written language is not so easy and not so directly linked to intuition, nor do we always recognize that we haven't done it. As readers, though, we do react to the power of periods to create complete sentences; their effect on us is probably as intuitive as our ability to produce complete sentences in speech. We take periods on the printed page for granted, only recognizing their value when they disappear. As illustration, what can you make of the following?

> Architecture is a group endeavor so architects need to build with words first explaining things to their clients planners critics and each other they talk far more than they draw they conduct regular and irregular group criticisms among themselves without hesitation or special encouragement slightly reminiscent of the

consultations of the Pre-Raphaelite Brotherhood or of Hollywood story conferences these reflect and support a community of interest they occur not in actual collaboration but routinely through the ordinary fellowship of workers within the common profession and perhaps style.

Because of the syntax—the way words are grouped and the pattern and placement of these groups—you can make sense of this unpunctuated paragraph, although it isn't easy and in spots you may be unable to clear up your confusion. Notice what happens when sentence boundaries are marked.

> Architecture is a group endeavor. So architects need to build with words, first explaining things to their clients, planners, critics and each other. They talk far more than they draw. They conduct regular and irregular group criticisms among themselves. Without hesitation or special encouragement (slightly reminiscent of the consultations of the Pre-Raphaelite Brotherhood or of Hollywood story conferences), these reflect and support a community of interest; they occur not in actual collaboration, but routinely through the ordinary fellowship of workers within the common profession and, perhaps, style.

The placement of periods sets off separate ideas in grammatically satisfactory groups. However, this grouping of words into sentences in ours, not the author's. He punctuated his paragraph this way:

> Architecture is a group endeavor, so architects need to build with words first. Explaining things to their clients, planners, critics, and each other, they talk far more than they draw. They conduct regular and irregular group criticisms among themselves without hesitation or special encouragement. Slightly reminiscent of the consultations of the Pre-Raphaelite Brotherhood or of Hollywood story conferences, these reflect and support a community of interest. They occur not in actual collaboration but routinely through the ordinary fellowship of workers within the common profession and, perhaps, style.
>
> —Nathan Silver, "Architect Talk"

Our point is that you're the only one who knows exactly where you finish what you consider to be one idea and start what you consider to be another.

Run-ons

Not using appropriate punctuation to show the break between sentences creates run-on sentences. Judging from our own experience, most run-on sentences in student papers are caused by failure to punctuate properly, not by ignorance of what a sentence is. Most run-ons in student papers are really comma splices, sentences with commas where periods, semicolons, or colons should be (for more on these marks of punctuation and their relation to comma splices, see the punctuation section later in this chapter). Sometimes in student papers we find two sentences run together with no punctuation between them. We think that you can discover such errors simply by reading your essay aloud. Give a copy of your essay to a friend or classmate and ask her to follow along as you read out loud. If you concentrate on the meaning of your words as you read, your listener should easily find those spots where you have failed to mark the division between sentences. Here's a "sentence" from a student's paper on his first experiences in New York City. Read it aloud and decide where you would put periods:

> Finally, I ordered the same thing the man at the next table was eating, after dinner my sister's son and I wanted to walk along Broadway we didn't feel tired so we continued to walk around the city.

You probably had to read the excerpt twice to make your decisions, but we feel fairly confident that you, like us, put periods after "eating" and "Broadway." We also inserted a comma after "tired" because we needed to pause there as we read.

Some teachers also mark as run-ons sentences which go on and on adding one idea to another without a break. Technically, such sentences may not be run-ons (two sentences attached improperly), but they make a reader feel breathless. Because so many thoughts are bunched together, separate thoughts lack emphasis. Here's an example of that from a student paper on child movie stars:

> The parent may desperately want their child to have a prosperous future and at the same time be happy but at the same time the parent is continually disregarding the feelings of the child that they may not be right for this profession causing the child a great deal of unhappiness.

As readers, we feel the need for a break after "happy" and perhaps after "profession." We're not going to rewrite this sentence our way, though, because it's important for the writer to reassess what she's done and decide for herself which ideas to put together in sentences. Here's a similar sentence from the same paper.

> When a parent continually praises a child saying that they're the greatest it may convince the child that they are, causing then a possibility of a big letdown if they hear otherwise making the child lose all trust in their parents.

We see the possibility of three sentences here. Again, the writer needs to decide how to group her ideas; we're just going to point out to her our reaction to the sentence as she wrote it.

Fragments

Checking to see if you have used endmarks to separate groups of words into clumps which are more than one sentence is the first thing to do when you begin checking sentence division. The second thing to look for is endmarks which create sentence fragments. Run-on sentences are rarely defensible, but fragments are not by definition "bad" or "wrong." In context, they can be appropriate and—at times—stylistically superior to complete sentences. In oral language, the subject, verb, and complete meaning are not always expressed because we can use voice intonation or gesture to complete a thought; and the situation itself also contributes to meaning. Like oral language, written language too has the ability to create a context in which one or more of the elements of a complete sentence (subject, verb, and so forth) can be omitted. Another way of saying this is that all sentences, by definition, are characterized by completeness, but all the elements which create that completeness need not be explicit. Look at the following sentences from a student paper on electives in high school and see if you can supply the missing words:

> Physical education should not be changed to an elective as recently proposed because it is good for the student's social and mental growth. And, of course, for his health as he grows older.

You probably, with no extra effort, read the last group of words as a grammatically complete sentence: "And, of course, *it's also good* for his health as he grows older." Such resupplying of missing elements must require *no additional effort* on the part of a reader or listener; if he has to consciously work out what any missing elements are, communication is disrupted. We're going to say more about this excerpt farther along in this section.

Some teachers condemn all fragments; if you wish to meet the demands of such a teacher, you'll need to locate all varieties of fragments: those without subjects, those without verbs, and those which, although having both a subject and a verb, seem to lack completeness. This may sound easy, but it's not—and furthermore, coverage of all the material you need to learn in order to do this is beyond our purpose in this book. If you really decide that this work is necessary for you, we suggest that you find a good grammar book which thoroughly covers how to locate subjects and verbs. Until you know that, you can't locate every fragment you write.

The only fragments which bother us are those that confuse readers and those that *in context* distort the relative importance of ideas; that is, they divide ideas which should not be divided. We use the following as a general rule-of-thumb: if the idea expressed in a "fragment" seems *in context* to merit a separate sentence and if a reader can *easily* supply the omitted words (subject, verb, or whatever makes an idea seem whole), we're not likely to find fault with a fragment just because it's a fragment. But if the fragment expresses an idea which *in context* seems inappropriately stressed by being in a separate sentence and if the entire fragment could be attached to the preceding sentence with nothing added except, perhaps, a punctuation mark, we usually encourage a student to make that change. Look at the following excerpts and see if you can (1) locate the fragments and (2) make a decision about their appropriateness.

Our first example is the one we used above:

> Physical education should not be changed to an elective as recently proposed because it is good for the student's social and mental growth. And, of course, for his health as he grows older.

We would first ask the writer of this if she thought "health" was more important than "social and mental growth." If she said yes, then we'd advise her to keep the idea in the final group of words as a separate sentence. If she had a teacher who was fussy about fragments, we'd also suggest that she add the missing words. If she didn't consider "health" more important than the other two kinds of growth, we'd suggest that she add the final group of words to the sentence before it.

From a student paper on the relationship of politics and sports:

> There is nothing wrong with small gestures like the ones made by the two black runners in the **1976** Olympics who held out their arms with fists clenched meaning Black Power. It didn't affect anyone physically; they had a golden opportunity. And for it they were stripped of the medals, thrown out of the Olympics, never to return. In my view an unjust punishment.

The last group of words in this excerpt lacks both an explicit subject and an explicit verb. Our decision: since the idea in the last sentence seems to us important enough, in comparison to the ideas preceding it, to stand alone in its own sentence, we would not ask the student to make any changes. Notice also that most readers could easily make the complete grammar of this last sentence explicit by simply adding the words "this is" after "In my view."

From a student paper on the quality of television programs:

> The reason most people will not walk away from the TV set is
> because they have become addicted to watching it. Mostly because
> of the hypnotic trance which is created while watching the shows.

The second group of words lacks an explicit subject and verb.
Our decision: since, at first glance, "Mostly" and the words following
seem parallel in importance to the group of words beginning with
"because" in the previous sentence, we see no reason for not putting
all these words into one sentence. Notice, too, that "Mostly" and the
following words can be attached to the previous sentence with just a
comma.

The problem with this excerpt, though, goes deeper than punctuation. We would ask the student if the second *because* clause
("because of the hypnotic trance . . . ") is a second reason for people's
actions or if she means that people become addicted because of the
hypnotic trance. If she answers that the second *because* clause is a
second reason, we would suggest that she use parallel structure to
make that connection clearer (and, of course, the subject and verb
have to be made plural):

> The reasons most people will not walk away from the TV set are
> because they have become addicted to watching it, and because
> they are victims of the hypnotic trance which is created while
> watching the shows.

Punctuated like this, the passage says that there are two reasons why
people don't walk away from the TV set. If the writer answers
differently and says that the second *because* clause in an added idea,
we would suggest that she revise to make that clearer:

> The reason most people will not walk away from the TV set is
> because they have become addicted to watching it. This addiction
> results from the hypnotic trance which is created while watching
> the shows.

Punctuated like this, the passage gives a sequence of cause-and-effect
relationships: the shows create a hypnotic trance; the trance creates
addiction; the addiction causes people to sit in front of the TV sets.

Other rewritings are possible. The ones the writer herself composes would undoubtedly be better than ours since she's the one who
knows best what she wants to say. Our point is that often what
appears to be a problem of punctuation may not be eliminated by
"correcting" the punctuation. A writer may need to clarify her meaning before worrying about punctuation.

From a student paper on birth control:

> At this very confusing time of our life there are certain realities that
> we all must face. One of which is the reality of trying sex. That big
> taboo that we are afraid to ask about, yet it is this curiosity that
> cannot be cured until we know all.

Our decision: here we can't be as definite as we were in the previous
two examples. The fragment beginning with "One of which" could
be attached to the previous sentence with just a comma, but it seems
quite reasonable to us that the writer wants this idea to be in a
separate sentence; in this case she could just take out "of which," but
that would have to be her decision. "That big taboo that we are afraid
to ask about" seems a restatement of the word "sex" in the previous
sentence. Perhaps the writer could attach these words to the previous
sentence with just a comma. The remaining words could then be a
separate sentence. Here are two possible rewritings:

> At this very confusing time of our life there are certain realities that
> we all must face. One is the reality of trying sex, that big taboo that
> we are afraid to ask about. Yet it is this curiosity that cannot be
> cured until we know all.

> At this very confusing time of our life there are certain realities that
> we all must face, one of which is the reality of trying sex. This is
> the big taboo that we are afraid to ask about, yet it is this curiosity
> that cannot be cured until we know all.

Because we believe that insisting on either one of these solutions
might distort the writer's meaning, we would just point all this out
to her and suggest that she do some rethinking and decide for herself
which ideas to connect and which to leave in separate sentences.
Once she has done that, she needs to make certain that her punctuation reflects the decisions she has made.

From a student paper on developing responsibility:

> There are responsibilities to be met in college and upon entering
> college a student realizes he will have them and is forced to face up
> to them. One of the responsibilities being to do the best one can
> gradewise and to face the pressures of college as one will have to
> face the pressures of life.

The group of words starting "One of the responsibilities" is not a
grammatically complete sentence because it lacks an appropriate
verb. The topic being discussed in this sentence (its subject) is "One
of the responsibilities," but the verb following it ("being") is a participle. Alone, an -*ing* participle cannot function as the verb required
for a grammatically complete sentence; it needs the assistance of
some form of the verb *to be.* Notice that "being" has no auxiliary or

helping verb such as *is* or *are* and that adding one in this case only creates greater chaos. If the writer wants the idea in the second "sentence" to stand alone, he should change "being" to "is." The other alternative is to attach the two sentences with a comma.

From a student paper proposing a neighborhood park:

> Many communities today lack a sufficient number of recreational areas. The building of a park would enable people to meet, communicate, and interact easier with one another. Whether it may be through games or through their children's playing with someone else's.

The final group of words starting with "whether" is a fragment because its idea is incomplete. Fragments starting with *whether* or other subordinating conjunctions—such as *because* and *if* (there's a more complete list of these on page 58)—are common in student essays and not easy for writers to spot because the idea doesn't seem incomplete when read with what goes before. And, indeed, it isn't. Still, if you abstract the group of words beginning with *whether* and read it without the preceding sentence, you should recognize the grammatical incompleteness. What to do about it is—as always—the writer's decision. To us, the group of words starting with "whether" seems subordinate to the preceding sentence. However, whether to attach it to that sentence or make it into a self-sufficient sentence is up to the writer. Here are two possible rewritings:

> Many communities today lack a sufficient number of recreational areas. The building of a park would enable people to meet, communicate, and interact easier with one another, whether it may be through games or through their children's playing with someone else's.

> Many communities today lack a sufficient number of recreational areas. The building of a park would enable people to meet, communicate, and interact easier with one another. Such interaction might come about through games or through their children's playing with someone else's.

Many students come into our classes having acquired somewhere in their education a rule which forbids starting sentences with *because, and,* or *but.* We can't find this rule in any grammar book we've ever read and can only conclude that the "rule" has been created by overzealous teachers to cut down on the possibility of fragments. Most sentences beginning with these words can't be faulted; it's not the first word of a sentence that makes it a fragment. The following excerpt from a student paper is enhanced by his use of coordinators as first words in sentences:

The human mind will always have a hunger to discover and explore. And as our technological state becomes more advanced, so do the everyday things around us. Twenty years ago, arcades were full of pinball machines with clanging bells and manual scoring. Today when you walk into an arcade, you enter a totally different world, one of flashing lights, oscillating sounds, and images on screens. And as our arcades become more advanced, we are drawn to them even more—strongly hoping to leave victorious. But in order to win, one must have practice.

Not all sentences beginning with *and, but,* or *because* are as defensible as those in the excerpt we just showed you. Here are some sentences we find it difficult to defend. Compare them with those in the above excerpt and see if you agree with us.

Child movie stars receive a lot of phony praise and insincere compliments. And false friendship too.

When children don't live in the real world, they may not ever grow up to be adults who can do for themselves. Because they've never had to.

Parents who push their children into high-paying careers like modeling are not thinking of their children. But of themselves and the money.

We hope you've noticed as you read this section on fragments that they can affect style and tone. They influence the impression a piece of writing makes on a reader. Consequently, adding or deleting them is a stylistic as well as a grammatical decision.

Notice how the following published writers have used fragments:

Why should the probable and possible superiorities of the *Third New International* [*Dictionary*] be so difficult to assess, the shortcomings so easy? Because the superiorities are special, departmental and recondite, the shortcomings general and within the common grasp.

—Wilson Follett,
"Sabotage in Springfield"

There are those of us who feel very strongly that the cheapest and most indefensible way to give offense is to direct obscenities wantonly, and within the earshot of those who seek protection from that kind of thing. There will always be a certain healthy tension between Billingsgate and the convent, but in the interest of the language, neither side should win the war completely. Better a stalemate, with a DMZ that changes its bed meanderingly, like the Mississippi River.

> —William F. Buckley, Jr.,
> "On the Use of Dirty Words"

Where does it [ignorance of standards in language] all come from? Who is the chief culprit? Surely, the schools, both lower and higher, and the distemper of the times that influences them.

> —John Simon,
> "The Corruption of English"

Problems of word usage involve three areas of study. First, the study of grammatical correctness in the use of inflected forms (agreement, pronoun usage, verb usage, etc.); second, the study of the conventions of usage and of appropriateness in word choice; third, the study of vocabulary and diction as a means to a more sophisticated view of language.

> —John Warriner,
> *English Grammar and Composition*

Suggestions

We said earlier that you know intuitively, while speaking, when you reach the end of a sentence and you know by intonation patterns when someone else does. Psycholinguists who have studied the language of very young children have discovered that even before the age of two, normal children's language demonstrates that they know what a complete sentence is. What you need to do, then, is to learn to transfer the knowledge you already have onto the printed page. The best way is to read your paper aloud, concentrating on using your voice as a guide to meaning, while someone else reads along to see if the sentence breaks indicated by your voice are the same as those marked by punctuation on the paper. Such breaks can be identified by endmarks or by semicolons or colons. (For more on the use of these particular marks, see the section on punctuation, pages 92–105.)

If you can't find anyone to help you, you can always read your paper into a tape recorder and then listen to yourself and read the paper at the same time. Your own voice should help you mark sentence endings.

If you can't find someone to help and you don't have a tape recorder, you'll have to read your paper very slowly and carefully out loud—sentence by sentence. Reading your own paper just to check endmarks is not easy because it's unnatural. All of us read for meaning; once our minds become engaged in getting meaning from a text, our awareness of periods goes underground. We don't consciously see them. To overcome this difficulty, you can read your essay backwards; that way you can't attend to meaning. You do this by looking at the last punctuation mark of your essay (usually a period) and then scanning backwards until you find a capital letter. (You're not really reading backwards because that's almost impossible.) Once you have found a capital letter, you can read forward again to the period. This is a way of forcing yourself to read each sentence isolated from what goes before and what comes after. If you decide that the words you've just read can be legitimately punctuated as a sentence, you can continue the backward-reading process on the sentence immediately preceding the one you just read. Again, you start from the period (or other endmark) and scan backwards to find a capital letter. This may sound time consuming (it is), but if you have a teacher who's failing you because you write too many fragments, eliminating them will be worth the time spent.

Once you're satisfied that the endmarks you've used are adequate guides to sentence boundaries, you may—if you have a teacher who penalizes you for all fragments—need to make a final search for certain kinds of fragments which you have particular difficulty recognizing. You'll know what these are if you keep a list of all sentences in your papers which your teacher identifies as fragments. You'll probably discover that they can be grouped into just a few categories. Perhaps most of your fragments are ones that begin with *because* or other subordinators; perhaps most of them are ones with unsupported *-ing* verbs. If you make a list, you can meticulously check any paper you write for these types. Tedious, you say? Probably—but we never said a good paper appears as though through magic.

Practice 5

Read through the following excerpts from two student essays, paying particular attention to sentence boundaries. The first analyzes "Patterns," a poem by Amy Lowell; the second is the first paragraph of an essay entitled "The Art of Going Away to School." Discuss with your classmates and teacher those places where you don't agree with how these student writers have used or omitted endmarks, particularly periods.

A

The poem tells a story of a woman walking down a garden path. Her gown is very fancy and its pink and silver train that follows behind her stands out on the dull, gray gravel. Though this is supposed to be a joyful moment the woman states she is saddened. "Not a softness anywhere about me." It's just the brocaded gown and whalebone, which in those days was an underwiring for dresses. Like the garden, she too, she states is a rare pattern. The garden and its arrangement of flowers and her, a figure dressed up in this only once worn gown.

As the daffodils flutter in the breeze, she sits underneath a lime tree, daydreaming about her lover who is away in war. Then she begins to cry as a lime blossom falls in her lap it starts to rain. She thinks back and in a month they would have been husband and wife. Married in this daffodil and squill garden.

B

Senior year at Saint Margaret's Preparatory High School is deeply embedded in my mind. This would be the year that the "big decision" had to be made. The ultimate choosing of the perfect college for oneself. The SAT's, the college applications, the required essays, the college recruiters, the final choice, and the ultimate graduation from the Prep. A graduation from friends, familiar halls and classrooms, and lastly a detachment from a safe, regulated environment. An environment to be replaced by a very different one at that. My home for the next year would be at Stony Brook University. I made the decision without much hesitation. I knew I did not want to attend Queens College at home; that would mean following in my sister's footsteps—something that was taboo in my mind, and by all means to be avoided. I also wanted a change from the familiar: The familiar walls at home, the predictable actions of people, and finally an escape from the "typical" life I believed I was living. I wanted to go out and experience. I believed I was missing out on life.

Practice 6

Following is a section from a student essay in which he imagines himself as a fish in a tank. We have left out all the endmarks. Discuss with your classmates and teacher where you think endmarks should go and what these endmarks should be.

In the corner of the tank there is a plant that runs from the bottom of the tank to the top and has an orange and brown combination for a color when swimming around I notice that I can go in any direction but only for so long and then I'm stopped what stops me is the glass that surrounds the water I can travel through the glass to become a fish but I cannot leave the tank as a fish outside of the tank there is no water for me to survive as a fish.

When looking at the top of the water from inside the tank, I can see ripples due to the filter above the ripples there is a white fluorescent bulb that gives the tank a purple color because of the purple backing and rocks also filter makes a hum that runs through the water of the tank when looking at the back of the fish tank there is a heater that has an orange glow when it's on if you are cold you can squeeze between the heater and tank which is the warmest part of the tank.

In the middle of the tank there is a piece of shattered glass the glass is about two inches thick and has a pinkish color now that I look at this piece of glass I think of how it is a left over piece from another world that has crumbled in the fish tank it is a piece of glass but in an ocean it could be the only remains from a previous civilization I try to imagine what they were like and how they lived.

Sentence Structure

The most important thing about sentences as units in a particular context is that they divide ideas the way you want them divided and seem complete to your readers. Once you've decided that your sentences do that, you can begin to look at the internal structure of individual sentences. At the most basic level, sentence structure is conditioned by our seemingly innate syntactical expectations. Syntax refers to the order of words, the sense they make because of their placement in a sequence.

Few of us have been taught syntax directly: it's naturally embedded in language as we learn it. For instance no native English speaker would construct a sentence like:

Vote the I in Presidential did elections.

Rather, the necessary syntax for the same seven words as a declarative sentence is:

I did vote in the Presidential elections.

As a question, the necessary syntax would be:

Did I vote in the Presidential elections?

Ours is a language in which syntax—word order—plays a crucial role in meaning, in sense making. Not all languages create meaning in this way. Latin is generally cited as an example of those languages which rely for meaning more on word form than on syntax.

Canis momordit hominem. "The dog bit the man."

Hominem momordit canis. "The dog bit the man."

It's the ending on *can-* (the root word for *dog* and the source of our word *canine*) which determines whether it's the subject of the verb or the object of the verb. It doesn't matter where the word is placed in the sentence. In English, of course, when the words are reversed, meaning is altered.

Canis momordit hominem. "The dog bit the man."

Canem momordit homo. "The man bit the dog."

In this pair, the words are in the same order; we translate each correctly by relying on the endings of the words for *dog* and *man.*
The basic, recurrent word order in English is

Subject—Predicate/Verb—Object

or, in other words,

Actor—Action—Object/Receiver of Action

Knowing only this much about English syntax has many implications. For one, it says something about all the other components that make up sentences (i.e., prepositional phrases, adjectives, adjective phrases, adverb phrases, and so forth): they are, in a sense, extra. The many modifiers which can occur anywhere and in any number in a sentence do not influence the usual syntactic structure of English, but the usual syntactic order does put limits on the possible placement of these modifiers. We'll say more about the problem of misplaced and dangling modifiers later.

Another implication of our basic word order concerns audience: the subject-verb-object sequence is what readers have come to expect. When we sense that a new sentence is beginning (either because we hear clues in a speaker's voice or see a period and a capital letter on the printed page), we expect, before the sentence has gone on for too long, that we'll know what its subject is. Once we've heard or seen what we think is the subject, we next expect a verb which we can reasonably connect with that subject. Once we hear or see the verb, we know whether or not to expect an object (since some verbs require them and others don't). If all these expectations are not met, we're left with a feeling of incompleteness. Another way to put all this is that when a sentence begins, we identify an actor, then we listen or look for what the action of that actor is, and then we listen or look for the results of that action. For speakers of English, this order may well condition how we perceive the world around us. We expect causes (creators of action) to exist before action can occur, and we expect results to come after the action.

There exists an amusing test of the limits of our ability to hold expectations in our mind. We start with a simple subject-verb-object sentence: "The cat screeched." Now we add information: "The cat the boy held . . ." Native speakers who read this far in the sentence are still waiting for a verb to go with the subject "cat": "The cat the boy held screeched." Let's add more information: "The cat the boy the girl loved . . ." Most of us are in trouble at this point, but if someone finished the sentence with helpful voice intonation, we might be able to understand it: "The cat the boy the girl loved held screeched." Let's try one more addition: "The cat the boy the girl the man hit. . . ." Now there are four possible subjects in a row; we can link "man" and "hit," but most of us cannot complete this sentence. We'll finish it for you; see if you can read it aloud so it makes sense: "The cat the boy the girl the man hit loved held screeched." Our point in going through this demonstration is that writers cannot rely too heavily on a reader's expectations. When sentences become too complex, readers may give up. See how you do with the following sentence:

> "That little pain," she scoffed. (Although, from her own experience, which, caught in a moment of weakness for truth she has let slip, she has revealed that during my very own birth the pain was so severe she could not speak, not even to tell the midwife I had been born, and that because of the pain she was sure she would die—a thought that no doubt, under the circumstances, afforded relief. Instead, she blacked out, causing me to be almost smothered by the bedclothes.)
>   —Alice Walker "One Child of One's Own:
>   A Meaningful Digression Within the Work(s)"

Were you able to get all the way through this without frustration? If not, try it again. We admit the sentence is complex, but this one—in contrast to the cat-boy-girl-man example—is decipherable. We think—although you may not agree—that the difficulty we have reading it adds to our awareness of the pain being described: we too feel smothered.

We alter the basic subject-verb-object order of modern English on occasion, but even the alterations follow a pattern. Our deviations from the traditional order are typically predetermined. Ask yourself a question and then notice the reversal of the subject and verb (or part of the verb) in the question. Almost all questions in English which can be answered "yes" or "no" manifest subject-verb reversal; when the first word we hear or read is a verb, we expect the sentence to be an order or a question; when the second word is a noun or pronoun which can be the subject, we know the sentence is a question. When we ask questions which cannot be answered "yes" or "no" the item about which we're in doubt comes first, regardless of how that affects word order:

Which book do you want?
object-verb-subject-verb

Probably the next most common alteration of the subject-verb word order occurs in sentences beginning with "there": "There are stars in the sky." Sentences beginning with "here" have this same structure: "Here are the books I promised you."

Subject-verb reversal occurs regularly in other situations also.

He isn't going. Neither *am* I.

The movie wasn't good. Neither *was the popcorn.*

This scheme won't work, nor *will that one.*

Not only *did he* refuse the offer, he also laughed at it.

Not only *will she* challenge former champions, she will defeat them.

Never *have I* seen such conduct.

He's going. So *am I.*

The movie was good. So *was the popcorn.*

This scheme will work. So *will that one.*

So disturbed *had the couple* become that they dropped their packages.

Dangling over their heads *was a noose.*

You'll note that in a number of these sentences, the reversal is like that in some questions: only the auxiliary verb and the subject interchange; in other words, the subject comes in the middle of the verb phrase.

It's no accident that, in English, deviation from normal word order is far more likely to occur in poetry than in prose; in fact, we probably expect it in poetry: it's one of those traits that make us recognize poetry as poetry. Here are some illustrations:

> But knowledge to her eyes her ample page
> > Rich with the spoils of time did ne'er unroll
> Chill Penury repressed their noble rage,
> > And froze the genial current of the soul.
>
> Full many a gem of purest ray serene,
> > The dark unfathomed caves of ocean bear.
>
> > > — Thomas Gray, "Elegy Written in a
> > > Country Churchyard"

In the first two lines, "knowledge" is the subject of "did . . . unroll," and "page" is the object; the word order is subject-object-verb. In the final two quoted lines, "caves" is the subject of "bear" and "full many a gem of purest ray serene" is the object. The word order is object-subject-verb.

Speaking of daffodils, a poet writes:

> Continuous as the stars that shine
>   And twinkle on the milky way,
> They stretched in never-ending line
>   Along the margin of a bay:
> Ten thousand saw I at a glance,
>   Tossing their heads in sprightly dance.
>
> — William Wordsworth, "I Wandered
> Lonely as a Cloud"

In the fifth line of this stanza, the word order is object-verb-subject: the usual order for these words would be "I saw ten thousand at a glance."

Both of these poems were written well over one hundred years ago. Our failure to find much altered syntax in recent poetry suggest that modern poets tend to rely on it less than on other devices for poetic effect.

If modern poetry eschews syntactic irregularity, it's not surprising that modern prose should avoid it almost entirely. In prose, basic syntax is so very rarely altered (with the exception of the rule-determined reversals discussed previously) that we had to look long and hard for examples. We looked through pages and pages of student papers without finding any alterations of the subject-verb-object order. We did find the following ones in the Alice Walker essay we quoted from earlier:

> Am I mistaken in thinking I have never forgotten a pain in my life? Even those at parties, I remember.

In the second of these two sentences, the object comes before the subject and verb. The same word order occurs at the beginning of the following excerpt:

> But this hymn of praise I, anyhow, have heard before, and will not permit myself to repeat it, since there are, in fact, very few variations, and these have become boring and shopworn.

You understand the deviations in these sentences because they *are* deviations, because you know what the normal order is. The effect is created in each instance because you read the deviation as a contrast to what you know is normal. Disrupted syntax is one way a writer can say: "Pay attention, here's something particularly significant and unusual." If we rewrite the phrases so that normal syntax is restored, you'll probably understand better the poetic effect created by the deviations.

I remember even those at parties.

But I, anyhow, have heard before this hymn of praise . . .

Active/Passive Voice

Another implication of standard English syntax concerns the passive voice. Voice in the context of usage does not refer to tone or pitch or volume. It refers to the role a subject plays in a sentence. Sentences can be classified as active or passive depending on the construction of their main verbs. If a sentence is constructed so that its subject is the doer of the action described by the verb ("She laughs"), the sentence is said to be "active." If a sentence is constructed so that its grammatical subject is the receiver of the action of the verb, it's said to be passive ("The catcher caught the ball" vs. "The ball was caught by the catcher"). If our usual order of speech and thought places the recipient of an action last, then it's understandable why the passive voice, which places objects of actions first in the order, would create such a stir among some stylists. Yet the passive voice (i.e., "The snake was killed"), in an appropriate context, is more effective than the active voice despite the seeming lack of conformity to our expectations. Linguists have an ongoing debate among themselves about whether changing a sentence from active to passive voice alters meaning. We believe that syntax is always a factor in the creation of meaning.

Texts usually warn against the dangers of the passive voice, and there may be some justification for this warning. When sentences, especially ones that aim for a scholarly tone, take on length, the passive voice can contribute to confusion. Not only does the passive voice deaden the impact of an action, but it also tends to be wordier. Passive constructions also tend to create an impersonal tone, a tone apparent in official forms:

> This application form may *be used* when applying for loans under three programs: Guaranteed Student Loans, Auxiliary Loans to Assist Students and the NY State Supplemental Loans for Health Professions Students. If you are applying for aid under one or more of these programs, only one application has *to be completed.* When your application *is processed* by NYSHESC, your eligibility under

each of the three programs will *be determined* in the same order as listed above.

—New York State Higher Education
Services Corporation

The tone becomes more personal when we revise this excerpt to eliminate the passive voice:

> You may use this application form when applying for loans under three programs: Guaranteed Student Loans, Auxiliary Loans to Assist Students and the NY State Supplemental Loans for Health Professions Students. If you are applying for aid under one or more of these programs, you need to complete only one application. When NYSHESC processes your application, it will determine your eligibility under each of the three programs in the same order as listed above.

Of course, there may be times when you intentionally seek a distant, impersonal tone; in such cases, you may deliberately choose to use the passive, as indeed the writer of the original of our quoted passage may have done. For example, one of our students began an essay: "Someone was murdered in front of the building last night." Since the impersonality of violent death was his topic, the student's choice of the passive in his first sentence was stylistically apt.

The passive has other uses too. Sometimes the recipient of an action rather than the causer of the action is the topic under discussion. In a research paper on F. Scott Fitzgerald, a student wrote:

> Fitzgerald was, throughout his life, an avid correspondent; it appears no letter to him ever went unanswered. Luckily for us, a vast number (well over 3000) of the letters from him and a great number to him *were saved*. Many of these *were saved* by Fitzgerald himself, especially those dated later than 1930; from that time forward he wrote with the aid of a secretary and kept carbons of his letters in scrapbooks and on file.

Who saved these letters is not relevant to this student's topic; consequently, the passive is appropriate.

And certainly the passive is the better, and often the necessary, choice when the performer of an action is unknown or unknowable, as in this passage from Conrad's *Lord Jim:*

> And besides, the last word is *not said*,—probably shall never be *be said*. Are not our lives too short for that full utterance which through all our stammerings is of course our only and abiding intention? I have given up expecting those last words, whose ring, if they could only *be pronounced*, would shake both heaven and earth. There is never time to say our last word—the last word of our love, of our desire, faith, remorse, submission, revolt. The heaven and the earth must not *be shaken*.

The first sentence is passive; thus Conrad suggests through Marlow (the narrator) that who says the last word is not the significant fact here. The final sentence is also passive; again Conrad suggests that it isn't who or what shakes heaven and earth which is crucial; what is crucial is that heaven and earth should not be shaken.

And, finally, a passive construction may create a tighter link to what has gone before:

> Everything had betrayed him! He had *been tricked* into that sort of high-minded resignation which prevented him lifting as much as his little finger.
>
> —*Lord Jim*

By starting the second sentence with *he* (which necessitates a passive construction), a tighter link is created between this sentence and the first sentence, which ends with *him.*

Suggestions

When you're sharing early drafts of your writing with classmates, you should ask them if there are parts that seem dull and uninteresting, parts that suggest to them that you are bored by your own subject. You may discover that such sections contain a number of passive sentences that you can enliven by rewriting in the active voice. When you're doing your own proofreading and copyediting, look for passive verbs. (They always consist of some form of the verb *to be* followed by the past participle form of the main verb.) If you have a good reason for the construction, keep it. If not, try rewriting it in the active voice. Make certain that your decision takes into account not just the sentence itself but the context it's in, especially the sentences immediately around it, and your intentions in writing the entire piece.

In all matters of word order, the message is that if you choose to deviate syntactically, your purpose ought to be clear. Disrupted expectations are apt to cause more annoyance or confusion than insight. Readers expect word order—syntax—to contribute to meaning. They expect, except in the patterned alterations we've already mentioned, the subject to precede the verb and the object to follow it.

Subordination

So far in our discussion of internal sentence structure, we may seem to have been assuming that sentences have only one subject-verb-(object) sequence. We approached the subject in this way because it allowed us to isolate and discuss English syntax. But in truth, sentences usually combine two or more core or subject-verb-(object) groups. When such combining occurs, it produces more complex sentences whose meanings are conditioned largely by the hierarchy of ideas set up in them. In this section we're going to examine various ways of combining ideas in sentences.

DEPENDENT CLAUS

Boynton

We'll start with syntactic subordination which is a product of the structure of a sentence. Syntactic subordination usually occurs in sentences with at least one dependent clause. (A dependent clause is one which cannot stand alone as a complete sentence.) Dependent clauses are always syntactically subordinate to independent clauses. (Independent or main clauses are those which can stand alone as complete sentences.) Syntactic subordination within sentences is often accomplished by the use of connecting words that we'll call "subordinators." Although the number of words that can act as subordinators is not unlimited, it is large. The following list includes many of the most frequently used subordinators: *after, before, since, because, while, during, when, even though, in spite of, whereas, although, whether, if.* Each of these subordinators specifies a particular connection between ideas, and the placement of the subordinator determines which of the connected ideas is subordinate. Notice:

Because Sean was yelling, Doreen left the room.

The main clause here is that Doreen has left the room. The subordinate clause tells why she left.

Sean was yelling because Doreen left the room.

The main clause here is that Sean was yelling; the surbordinate clause tells why he's yelling. Obviously both of these sentences are correct, and just as obviously they don't mean the same thing.

We're sure you can produce pairs of sentences like these using some of the subordinators we listed above. You'll notice that the main clause in each of the sentences we used (the one which is *not* introduced by a subordinator) is a grammatically complete sentence; the subordinator plus the words following it are not; they leave the meaning incomplete. Subordinators can lure a writer into writing fragments since the words they introduce don't seem to express an incomplete meaning *in context.* If your teacher penalizes you for fragments, you'll need to be doubly watchful when using subordinators.

Wording indirect questions causes problems for some students. We've already talked about the reversed word order which is normal in certain kinds of questions, particularly in the kind of question which can only be answered "Yes" or "No."

John asked, "Did you read the newspaper?"

The words within the quotation marks are a direct question, a question written exactly as someone would say it. An indirect question is one in which one person is reporting what another person asked:

John asked if (or whether) you had read the newspaper.

You'll notice that in this indirect question, the subject and verb return to their usual order. The following, widely heard in conversation, is not acceptable syntax in writing:

John asked did you read the newspaper.

Another group of words, *who (ever), whom (ever), which, that,* and *whose* creates a slightly different type of subordination. Again, the subordinate element is the one introduced by the subordinator.

The man *who went to the store* has been sitting in the green chair.

The man *who has been sitting in the green chair* went to the store.

One of the things to know about this group of subordinators is that *who* and *whom* are used to refer to people ("the man" in our examples) and *which* can only be used to refer to things:

My favorite book, which I've had for years, has finally fallen apart completely.

"Which" in this sentence refers to "book." *That* and *whose,* on the other hand, can refer to people and things:

The book that I lost was a favorite of mine.

The man that I saw was wearing a green shirt.

The man whose son left is my neighbor.

The book whose spine broke belongs to me.

If you look back at the five sentences we just used as examples, you'll notice two commas in the first one, but no commas in the other four. The commas are there because the words between them—the subordinate clause introduced by *which*—are not essential to the basic meaning of the sentence; that is, if you drop them out, the sentence still has meaning. In the other four examples, the words in the subordinate clauses introduced by *that* and *whose* are essential to the meaning of the sentences they're in; so, we don't want commas cutting them off from their context. We talk more about these commas on page 99; here, we're just pointing them out.

One other thing about *that* and *which* as subordinators: Many stylists insist that *which* is only appropriate in nonessential or non-restrictive clauses. Such stylists would approve of:

The book that was on the table seems to have disappeared.

But they wouldn't approve of:

The book which was on the table seems to have disappeared.

We don't include ourselves among the stylists who make this distinction; both of these sentences are acceptable to us. And, if you take the time to notice, you'll discover that we don't always observe the distinction in this book. If, however, you have a teacher who wants you to observe this convention, you'll need to learn to see the difference.

One final thing to watch when using these subordinators (and this we do consider crucial) is their placement. In order to avoid creating a misplaced modifier (see pp. 73–79 for more on misplaced modifiers), *who, whom, which, that,* and *whose* should be as close as possible to the word or words they refer to, preferably immediately after. You'll see that all the samples we have used follow this rule.

The *that, which,* or *whom* introducing an essential or restrictive subordinate element can often be deleted without harm to the meaning.

The book ~~that~~ I lost was my favorite.

I know ~~that~~ I left it here somewhere.

The book ~~which~~ I lost was my favorite.

The woman ~~whom~~ I saw is no longer here.

If the *that* comes directly after some form of the verb *to be,* it's best not to eliminate it; most teachers would find fault with "The most important point is he's right." Some students who write the sentence this way might also put a comma after the first "is," since a pause there seems necessary. In a sense, this pause recognizes the missing word "that." You should also be careful about deleting the *that* which precedes words which might seem like possible objects of the verb preceding *that.*

He sees that the book is on the table.

Without the relative pronoun "that," a reader quite naturally reads "He sees the book" as subject-verb-object and has to readjust the meaning when she comes to the verb "is." The *that* in sentences like these helps the reader.

There's another type of sentence in which the word *that* should not be deleted.

From a student paper on boxing:

He told me that boxing has a long and respectable history and it's not just undisciplined violence.

The question here is whether "He told me" one thing or two things. If the writer means that "he told me" two things, the sentence would be better reworded either by eliminating *it* or by adding a second *that:*

He told me that boxing has a long and respectable history and isn't just undisciplined violence.

He told me that boxing has a long and respectable history and that it's not just undisciplined violence.

If the second part of the original sentence is not something "He told me" it should be made into a separate sentence:

He told me that boxing has a long and respectable history. We agreed that it's not just undisciplined violence.

The original sentence would also be problematic if *that* introduced only the second part:

He told me boxing has a long and respectable history and that it's not just undisciplined violence.

In general, it's best not to use *and that* unless you have already used the word *that* to introduce a previous, connected idea. The same restriction applies to *which, who,* and *whom.* None of these words should be used following *and* unless the same word has introduced a previous, connected idea or ideas.

Many students run into problems when writing sentences in which ideas are connected by *which.* In some such sentences—like the one you just read—the *which* is preceded by a preposition. How can you figure out when to use a preposition before the *which?* Our experience in reading student papers indicates that writers rarely leave out this preposition when it's needed, but that they may add it when it's not needed. What this means for you (if you have problems with this structure) is that you don't need to check every *which* you use to see if it needs a preposition, but you do need to check every sentence with a *which* preceded by a preposition in order to see if the preposition is necessary. We've collected some examples from student papers to show you how you might go about this double-checking.

From a student paper on high-school graduation requirements:

> Physical education cannot be compared to electives such as home economics or shop. These classes teach skills in which a person does not need.

First you need to break the second sentence into two parts. After you've done this, you'll notice that the words before "which" ("These classes teach skills") form a complete sentence without the "in." Next look at the words following "which": "a person does not need." This group of words is not a complete sentence because the verb "need" requires an object. The object is the word that "which" refers to: "skills": "A person does not need skills." This filled-out sentence has no use for "in" either. Since neither of these two parts of the sentence needs "in," it should be dropped:

> These classes teach skills which a person does not need.

From a student paper on *The Mill on the Floss:*

> Maggie is a strong girl who refuses to confirm to the pressures of society. Maggie is different from the mold in which her family is trying to shape her into.

The first part of this second sentence is: "Maggie is different from the mold." No "in" is required to complete this idea. Following the word "which" is the second part of the sentence: "her family is trying to shape her into." To complete the idea, we need to add the word that "which" refers to: "mold": "Her family is trying to shape her into the mold." This group of words does not need "in" either, so the writer should delete it. We'll get to the problem of ending a sentence with a preposition such as *into* later in this chapter.

From a student paper on fishing:

> When I arrived, Jimmy was overjoyed. I brought him a fishline in which I received the admiration and gratitude I had expected.

The first idea in the sentence, "I brought him a fishline," doesn't need an "in"; the second idea (always made up of the words after the subordinating word), "I received the admiration and gratitude I had expected," doesn't need an "in" either. In fact, this sentence is complete even without the word that "which" refers to. But, obviously the writer wanted to tie these two ideas together, so he needs to think about how the ideas relate to one another. What was it the "I" received admiration for: the fishline itself or the fact that he had brought it? We guess the latter. If so, the writer should add clarifying words to the sentence he made out of the final words of his original sentence: "I received the admiration and gratitude I had expected for bringing the fishline." The writer can now put the two ideas together. Here's one way he could do that:

> I brought him a fishline, and for bringing it, I received the admiration and gratitude I had expected.

If the writer means that he received admiration for the fishline itself, he can again try adding words: "I received the admiration and gratitude I had expected for it." Now, the writer should realize that the preposition he needs is *for,* not *in,* and he can revise his original sentence accordingly:

> I brought him a fishline for which I received the admiration and gratitude I had expected.

From a student paper on Shelley's "Ozymandias":

> My first impression on reading the poem, excluding the "obvious" impressions (of which I will discuss later), was concerned with the reason for Shelley's opening the poem with the line "I met a traveler. . . ."

The writer needs to set aside first the main part of the sentence: "My first impression on reading the poem, excluding the 'obvious' impressions, was concerned with. . . ." There's no use for "of" in this sentence. The words following "which": "I will discuss later" express an incomplete idea because the verb *discuss* requires an object; the object must be the word that "which" refers to: "impressions." "I will discuss the impressions later" is a complete idea, but it has no use for "of" either; therefore, the student should cross out the "of" in his original sentence.

Don't be discouraged if this sounds complicated. Discouragement often leads students to stop trying to combine ideas in ways which show their relationship; such students, instead, just write simple sentences, thus failing to struggle with the words and make them match their intentions. If you analyze structures like these for a while, you'll soon find yourself gaining control over them. This control will enable you to express ideas you wouldn't otherwise be able to express. In fact, some linguists think that the ability to control certain types of sentence structure makes possible the ability to think certain kinds of thoughts.

Subordination can result from certain verb forms as well as from the use of subordinators. Notice the following pair:

He listened carefully; he heard the whole conversation.

Worded this way, each of the two ideas in the sentence is in an independent clause.

Listening carefully, he heard the whole conversation.

Rewritten like this, the first idea (that he listened carefully) becomes syntactically subordinate to the second. In this case, we don't believe it's semantically subordinate; it seems to us the more important idea in the sentence. Final decision on this would depend on the context in which the sentence appeared.

Here's another set:

He was pushed aside by the crowd; he could no longer hear the conversation.

Again, this sentence structure places each idea in an independent clause.

Pushed aside by the crowd, he could no longer hear the conversation.

When the two ideas are combined this way, the first becomes syntactically subordinate to the second. Here too, though, we have doubts about whether it's semantically subordinate.

A note of warning: when you write sentences, like the second ones in each of the above pairs, which begin with either a present participle or a past participle, you need to be aware of the possibility of "dangling" your participles. We'll discuss those more fully later on in this chapter.

Writing a book such as this requires us to talk about various features of language under separate headings. The danger of this is that readers (you) may believe that any sentence we use as an example is totally explainable on the basis of the feature designated by the heading under which the sentence appears. This is usually not true. Look back at the pairs of sentences we just used. There's a different tone to each sentence in the pair. We may not describe that difference in tone the same way as you would, but that's not the issue here; the issue is that we and you will both sense a difference. Part of this difference in tone is created by the sentence structure; consequently, you need to keep yourself sensitive to tone as well as to logical subordination while you're revising. A second note of warning: altering sentence structure as we've been doing in this chapter does more than alter the relationship of ideas; it alters style. And since readers expect some harmony in the style of an essay from beginning to end, you need to be cautious when tinkering with individual sentences.

Parallel Structure

We've been discussing ways to use subordinators within sentences. But, of course, as you're checking sentences in your writing, you'll discover quite a few in which you give equal syntactic importance to two or more ideas. For this you need a different pattern, called "parallelism" in most grammar books. Parallelism allows you to coordinate (make equal) rather than subordinate ideas.

In the section in most grammar texts that addresses parallel structure, you'll find a sentence like the following one as an example of failed parallelism:

I like to ski, to swim and running.

While it's true that examples like this one are a "failure" in parallel structure, they don't appear particularly illuminating. Few people make such glaring "errors" in the first place. Moreover, parallelism is a subtler, more complex issue than the example suggests. It concerns the shape that groups of words take. These groups of words can make up sentences, paragraphs, even entire texts; in other words, parallelism may be a factor in the structure of an entire essay. Here we're concerned only with sentence-level parallelism, which can occur in clauses, phrases, or words. Here are some examples:

Coordinate clauses:

I came; I saw; I conquered.

Caesar said *that he had arrived and that Brutus had left.*

Coordinate phrases:

I looked *in the desk, under the chair,* and *behind the sofa.*

Spending money, not *making it,* is my favorite pastime.

It's more satisfying *to eat* than *to diet.*

> I would rather *pay the piper* than *suffer the punishment.*

> We can either *save the money for a summer vacation or spend it now for a new stereo.*

Coordinate words:

> I *came, saw,* and *conquered.*

> It's *love,* not *money,* which makes the world go round.

If you analyze these sentences, you'll notice the basic principle behind parallel structure: once you have begun to use a particular form, it's best to stick with it. Think of how confusing it would be if signs along a road you had never traveled appeared in no predictable places or sizes. Like regularly placed and scaled road signs, parallel structures allow readers to make headway through language to meaning.

Following are some examples of problems caused by a failure to observe strict parallelism.

From a student paper on making tuition rates fair:

> I feel that different tuition rates are a bad idea. I cannot see two people going to the same school but have to pay different prices.

Since the person writing this is saying that there are two things she can't see, she could make the structure of her sentence aid her meaning better by changing "have" to "having."

From a student paper on choosing a college:

> She should first decide which is more important to her, being more independent or abide by her parents' rules and continue to live with them.

We suspect that if the writer read this sentence aloud, she would almost automatically change "abide" to "abiding" and "continue" to "continuing." Presenting her two alternatives in parallel form will make clearer to her readers that the alternatives are equally valid. The structure of this sentence could be made parallel in the following way also:

> She should first decide which is more important to her: to be more independent or to abide by her parents' rules and continue to live with them.

Parallel structure is also essential when using phrases like "as much . . . as" and paired words like "more . . . than" and "either . . . or" to compare or contrast ideas. Paired words which do this are called "correlatives," defined as words which "correlate" or show the relationship of ideas to one another.

As much-as:

He's *as much* ready as he is willing.

Both-and:

He was both *ready (to go)* and *willing to go.*

Either-or:

He was either *unprepared (to go)* or *unwilling to go.*

Neither-nor:

He was neither *prepared (to go)* nor *willing to go.*

Whether-or:

He couldn't decide whether *to go* or *to stay.*

Not only-but (also):

He was not only *ready (to go)* but (also) *willing to go.*

Whether to use the words in parentheses in these examples is a matter of style; the structures are parallel with or without the enclosed words.

One thing to keep in mind when using correlatives is that the word or words directly following each member of a pair of correlatives should designate whatever is being coordinated, compared, or contrasted. For example, neither of the following sentences is as clear as its partner in our previous samples.

He either was unprepared (to go) or unwilling to go.

He not only was ready (to go) but (also) willing to go.

Correlatives make possible the clear expression of certain kinds of relationships. If you don't use these structures, practice writing sentences with them. Once you feel comfortable with the structures, you'll be glad to have them available to you. Don't misinterpret us: we're not saying that you should deliberately find a way to include such sentences in your writing. What we are saying is that if you become comfortable with the way correlatives structure ideas, you'll know how to use them if the opportunity arises. And, if some linguists are right, understanding the way correlatives structure meaning may actually make you able to think in ways which are best expressed by the correlatives.

You'll notice that parallel structure often requires repetition of words. We'll say more about repetition later in the section on word choice; what's important to say here is that the repetition sometimes connected to parallel structure is useful because it makes clear to readers which ideas are parallel to one another. Judge which of the following you consider more effective:

> You should give that one to Janet, not me.

> You should give that one to Janet, not to me.

The first of these two sentences might be ambiguous (although context should prevent that) but the second isn't. In the second we've set up a contrast which is made clearer by an awareness of small details. In the next section, we're going to talk more about the importance of attending to small details when making comparisons.

Comparisons

Some students run into problems when comparing or contrasting things, ideas, concepts, or people. If, while you're checking through your paper, you come across sentences which compare or contrast, it's wise to give them a bit of extra attention. The first question you should ask yourself is if comparable things are being compared or contrasted. As illustration, here's an excerpt from an ad for gas appliances:

> Dry your clothes with less money than electricity.

"Money" and "electricity" are being contrasted here, but they're not comparable. We're sure that the gas company is comparing gas and electricity as energy sources. We'd suggest that the ad be rewritten to say:

> Dry your clothes for less with gas.

We suspect, though, that the ad writer wanted to get the word *electricity* in the ad—and, of course, in context, the sentence probably makes sense even if, out of context, it conjures up images of fueling a fire with quarters or hanging clothes on a line and fanning them with dollar bills.

Comparisons are always potentially tricky, but the trickiness goes beyond adhering to what some might think are nitpicking usage rules. When meaning can be compromised by a failure to word statements clearly, all of us need to be concerned. We repeat what we said in the previous paragraph: when you make a comparison, make certain you're comparing the comparable. "The skins of oranges are like lemons." Think about that. How can the skin of an orange be like a lemon? Faulting this sentence may seem picky to you, and perhaps it is, but not observing the principle violated by this sentence can lead us to say puzzling things. This excerpt is from a student's paper on a poem by Frost:

> When all the memos are received, and the red tape is straightened out, the job is done and gone forever. The humanless interaction between people is like the dead ants that are systematically buried and forgotten.

"Interaction" is not comparable to "ants." This student needs to think about what he's comparing. We can't be sure (this is not as easy as the oranges and lemons), but we would guess that the student wants to compare "the humanless interaction between people" to the same sort of interaction among ants: "The humanless interaction between people is like the interaction between dead ants." But then, we ask, how can "dead ants" have any kind of "interaction"? Possibly the writer means that whatever the interaction is between ants, it leads to their dying and being forgotten. Perhaps he means that the interaction between ants is such that they bury their dead and forget about them. All we can do is pose all this to the writer; he's going to have to do the rewriting since only he knows what he wants to say.

Here's another sentence from a different student's paper:

> The death of Baby Jane Doe can be compared to mayflies who only live for a day because that's their fate. Perhaps it was her fate to live a short life also.

On first reading this sentence, one might conclude that the writer was comparing the death of Baby Jane Doe to the death of a mayfly, even though he uses the plural of *mayfly* and never mentions their death. Readers seek meaning from a text and are willing to overlook flaws in a sentence if they can extract from it a logical meaning. Readers may decide, if they give the sentence a second glance, that the writer would have been more precise if he had written: "The death of Baby Jane Doe can be compared to the death of a mayfly." Now comparable things are being compared. However, this reading of the sentence doesn't make sense within the context of the writer's argument. He isn't really comparing Baby Jane Doe's death to anything; he is, in fact, leading up to a statement about a necessary acceptance of the shortness of her life. It's the shortness of her life which he should, logically, compare to the length of a mayfly's life. Because the reader is forced to work this out on her own, she may become irritated with the writer or the text. If the writer had focused on the terms of his comparison, he might have avoided annoying the reader. Here's one possible rewording:

> The shortness of Baby Jane Doe's life can be compared to the shortness of a mayfly's life; it only lives for a day because that's it fate.

(Notice that we had to restructure the sentence to eliminate "who" because there was no satisfactory place for it; we can't say "a mayfly's life who" because *life* cannot be referred to as *who*.) Another possible rewording:

> The shortness of Baby Jane Doe's life can be compared to that of a mayfly's life which only lasts for a day because that's its fate.

We could have used "that" instead of "the shortness" in our first rewording also.

Some students don't fully understand the function of *that of* (or *those of*) in sentences such as this and begin to insert it into comparisons where it has no function:

> Life doesn't treat everyone the same. Some people have more misfortunes than those of other people.

"Those" in the second sentence seems to refer to "misfortunes"; if so, the sentence might read:

> Some people have more misfortunes than the misfortunes of other people.

Now it's easier to see the illogic of this sentence since we can't compare "misfortunes" to "misfortunes." What's intended for comparison here is the number of misfortunes people have. One way to reward the sentence would be to remove "those of":

> Some people have more misfortunes than other people have.

We added the second "have" because we think it makes the idea clearer.

Here's another sentence with "those of":

> The ideas in my essay became so complicated that I didn't realize how difficult they were for others to understand. I decided to get rid of unclear ideas and replace them with those of ideas which were clearer.

In the second sentence, we can't figure out what "those" refers to; the sentence is complete without "those of."

We can't be certain that we made the proper assumptions about the meaning of the sentences we were just discussing. We can't tell a writer what we think he means; he has to tell us. Our point is that we shouldn't have to make too many assumptions. You can probably get away with saying things similar to: "The skin of an orange is like a lemon" because readers will know immediately what you're comparing. But understanding why it's better to say: "The skin of an orange is like a lemon's" will be a benefit to you when your ideas get more complex and readers have trouble making the correct assumptions.

One more picky thing about comparisons. It isn't, in a strict sense, logical to say: "He's taller than any boy in the class" because he's one of the boys in the class and he can hardly be taller than himself. Strict logic is better served if you say: "He's than any *other* boy in the class." We don't consider this particularly serious because we don't see how anyone could possibly think the first of these means that the boy is taller than himself. But some teachers are fussy about this and perhaps we all should be; learning to read exactly what your words say extends your control over your ideas. Poor reading of your own text may not matter much on this issue, but it's bound to matter at some other spot in your text.

Practice 7

Read the following excerpts from student essays and discuss with your classmates and teacher any problems you see in the use of the passive, the subordination of ideas, parallel structure, and the construction of comparisons.

This excerpt is from an essay analyzing an article on abortion:

A

To get into her argument, the author explained the situation, that results in abortion, is one of an unexpected and unplanned pregnancy. Then the next thing she did was to give reasons why and circumstances when she believes abortion is wrong. Abortion is made the easiest thing to do by a young woman in this situation. The woman is prompted by the inconvenience of the situation to take the easy way out without really considering all the details and not looking at other choices and those of other alternatives. When the writer felt abortion is wrong, that is the main reason she gave.

The writer then went on to explain a situation in which she felt that abortion might be the right choice and to get one would be almost inevitable. She felt that abortion could be understandable when having the child could be a life-or-death situation for the mother or it concerned the health of the child. If it's known that the fetus is already severely sick and will be for the rest of its life, then that alternative must be considered or done.

To understand the arguments that the writer gave, the reader had to read between the lines too much. She sometimes wrote like a short story where a reader expects to fill in some of what happens. But since she was writing an essay, she should have been a lot more clearer when giving her reasons and with her counter reasons. When she was explaining the situations in which she thought abortion was right or wrong, she left a lot of questions unanswered. For example, she should have asked how did the woman get pregnant? If she had asked and answered this question, this is the sort of question of whose answer would help readers see the argument more clearly. The piece was concluded by the author by leaving the issue with a question mark for the reader to decide the best outcome in the situations that were given.

This excerpt is a continuation of essay (B) in Practice 5.

B

The decision was made, and the application was sent out in February. The notice of acceptance to the SUNY school was received in April. I was enrolled in the school, to begin the academic school year on August 27th. The whole summer was spent thinking, worrying, dreaming, imagining, and crying over the thought of my choice. I guess I was getting cold feet. Yes, I believed my toes were frozen; they were frozen for the entire summer. The week before I was to go up they were beginning to thaw out. I was actually doing it. Going away to school was always something everyone else did, but me, I was more conventional.

Though the decision to leave home was frightening, yet at the same time it was challenging and exciting. What I have learned from my semester at Stony Brook composes the rest of this essay. I hope to paint a comprehensive look at what it's really like to go away. You see, it is not that simple. There is a science, a type of art, to it. I believe that you can say the best title for this essay would be the "Art of Going Away to School."

It was a pretty warm day but beautiful and sunny when I left for the Brook. The entire ride up was spent reading the sentimental message in a card from my best girlfriend, someone who had been a better friend to me than any one I've ever known. Everyone was silent in the car, silent like the lives of shadows. It was my time to contemplate on my four years of high school, and what my first semester would prove to be like. After finding the building assigned to me, we began to unload the car and promptly the dorm room was found. Wow, time certainly went fast! Yet, it seems so long ago since that day in August. So much has happened, so much has been learned.

This excerpt is from an essay entitled "Conservation of Wildlife, Is It Important?"

C

I think that the conservation of wildlife is very important. There are so many animals in this world that are not only beautiful but they also are important to our survival. If we do not try to preserve our wild kingdom, the whole balance of nature will be thrown off.

As we expand across the world's frontiers, many animal species are being forced to move and they have to find new homes. The problem is, the animals are running out of places to go. We are like a plague which spreads to every corner of the world and which cannot be stopped.

The California coyote, for example, has been pushed from its home but has no place to go. This is because people are killing them because they raid their garbage and have been known to kill small pets. Blame for this cannot be placed on the coyotes of which it is not their fault. After all, it is we who are invading on their territory, not the other way around.

The beautiful and graceful bald eagle is also an endangered species. This creature can be compared to the courage and power of a lion. We have chosen it to represent our country and yet they are senselessly slaughtered. A law has been passed which centers around the way in which I think the bald eagle should be protected, but which hasn't stopped people from killing them anyway. Fishermen are the main group to which we have to attach blame.

Every culture and time period have characteristics unique to themselves but also from which future culture will build on. We're not leaving future culture what we should leave though—a beautiful range of beautiful animals and birds.

Misplaced Modifiers and Dangling Participles

We've talked so far in this chapter about structuring certain elements of a sentence so that your readers can follow the connections you're making between ideas. Other sentence components, known as modifiers, also demand your close attention.

A modifier is any word or group of words which gives us additional information about one of the three basic parts of a sentence (subject, verb, or object). In traditional terminology, a modifier which qualifies in some way the meaning of a subject or object is called an adjective; a modifier which qualifies the meaning of a verb or an adjective is called an adverb. Adverbs also have the ability to modify other adverbs. When any modifier is removed so far from what it modifies that a reader isn't sure *what* it modifies, it's said to be "misplaced." When a modifier is in a sentence in which it has nothing logical to modify, it's said to "dangle."

For some reason, the term "dangling participle" has come to be symbolic of the mysteriousness of grammar and the complexity of its rules. As such, it often makes its appearance in jokes. One Saturday Night Live regular whispers slyly to another as he slips off the stage, "I'm going to dangle some participles." The *Oxford English Dictionary* gives as one definition of the verb "dangle": "to hang after or about any one, especially as a loosely detached follower" and cites as one of its examples an 1861 source in which a character says, "I am very happy that I have no dangling neighbors."

What is a dangling participle? Let's start with "participle." A participle is a verb form ending in -*ing* (present participle) or -*ed* (past participle). Many past participles are irregular in form; for example, *broken, sung,* and *done* are all past participles. (For a list of irregular past participles, see pp. 161–65.) Participles can be used as adjectives ("a *broken* chair," "a *singing* bird") or as parts of a verb phrase ("I have *broken* the chair"; "The bird is *singing*"). Present participles can also be used as nouns: "*Singing* is more productive than *breaking* chairs." Such participles are called gerunds. Only a participle used as an adjective—or more broadly, a modifier—can dangle; in the words of the *OED,* it is "loosely detached." Here's what that looks like (with apologies to Robert Frost):

> Stopping by the woods on a snowy eve, the trees glistened in the moonlight.

The present participle here is "stopping"; the problem is that there's no reasonable thing for it to modify. Since we expect modifiers to be close to what they modify, we may try to connect "stopping" to "trees," the first word which is not linked to "stopping" by a preposition. Being reasonable people, we reject that connection—unless, of course, the sentence is in the context of a paragraph about walking trees. But, of course, that's just the point. All sentences, including those with "dangling participles," exist and gain meaning from context. If, in context, a reader cannot tell who or what is doing the "stopping," you need to rewrite. In the process, your dangling participle will probably disappear.

Many examples of dangling participles in grammar books are humorous (or at least they're humorous to linguistic purists): "Flying over Washington, the Capitol looked like . . ."; "driving down the road, a huge snake suddenly appeared." For the linguistic purist (apparently) these sentences evoke images of a winged Capitol building and a motoring snake. Most of us would understand these sentences differently because we're focusing on meaning as the writer is moving from sentence to sentence. We are *not* advocating that participles should be dangled; what we *are* advocating is clarity.

Having said all that, we recognize that you may have a teacher who's fussy about *all* dangling participles and not just those which confuse readers. In this case, if you're a writer of dangling participles, you'll need to work carefully to eliminate them. Here are some guidelines:

First (and probably most difficult), you need to identify the participles in your writing. You do this by finding all regular verbs ending with *-ing* and *-ed* and all irregular past participles. You can eliminate from your list (1) all which are parts of verb phrases (they'll be paired with forms of *to be* or *to have*); and (2) all *-ing* forms which are subjects or objects.

Second, look for the word each participle modifies—the noun or pronoun which is performing the action of the participle. If the word designating whatever the participle modifies is not explicit, you'll need to add it.

Third, rewrite the sentence so that the word you've added or the word you've identified as being modified is as close as possible to the participle.

Here are some sentences to give you practice.

From a student paper on the merit of various grading systems:

> A pass/fail system would be a lower standard of grading that would bring a decaying educational environment. By only grading students according to their ability to pass or fail, there would not be a distinction between accelerated students and barely passing students.

We don't need to worry about "grading" in the first sentence because it's the object of the preposition "of." We do need to ask about "decaying" in the first sentence and about "grading," "accelerated," and "passing" in the second sentence. "Decaying," "accelerated," and "passing" are as close as they can get to the words they modify (that is, to the words which specify who or what is performing their actions): "environment," "students," and "students," respectively. This leaves us with only "grading" in the second sentence, and we conclude that it "dangles" because it has nothing to modify; obviously, professors are doing the grading, but the word *professors* is not explicit. One possible rewriting of the last sentence would be:

> By only grading students according to their ability to pass or fail, professors would not be distinguishing between accelerated students and barely passing students.

From a student paper on the value of sports:

> However, I feel that on a boring Sunday afternoon, sports programs give you something to do. They are exciting and fun to watch. While watching them, these sports programs create a feeling of suspense in your mind.

"Boring" is as close as it can get to "afternoon," and "exciting" is as close as it can get to "They." "Watching," however, is a problem. We would guess that it modifies "you," a word not present in the sentence. We don't see any confusion of meaning, but here are two possible "corrections":

> As you watch them, these sports programs create a feeling of suspense in your mind.

> While watching them, you may get a feeling of suspense in your mind.

From a student paper on boxing:

> Stunned by the blow, his opponent easily knocked him out.

"Stunned" can't modify "his opponent" since that would contradict the meaning of the sentence. And yet readers will connect these words and expect the sentence to be something like:

> Stunned by the blow, his opponent was no longer a threat.

Possible rewritings would be:

> Since he was stunned by the blow, his opponent easily knocked him out.

> Stunned by the blow, he was easily knocked out by his opponent.

Despite the anathema heaped on dangling participles, they have a way of appearing in the writing of the well-known as well as in the writing of students:

> Moving through and over the West Riding landscape with my father in his car, the hills were sculptures; the roads defined forms.
>
> —Barbara Hepworth,
> *A Pictorial Autobiography*

It's hard for us to believe that anyone would read this to mean that the hills were moving through the landscape, but technically "moving" is a dangling participle. Here's another:

> The great stucco movie theatres of the thirties had been given over to X-rated films; freckle-faced young couples watched them holding hands and eating popcorn.
>
> —John Updike, "The Other"

"Holding" is closer to "them" than to "couples," and perhaps there are those who might read this sentence to mean that the films are holding hands. Although we don't read it this way, here are two rewritings that eliminate the dangling participle:

> The great stucco movie theatres of the thirties had been given over to X-rated films; holding hands and eating popcorn, freckle-faced young couples watched them.

> The great stucco movie theatres of the thirties had been given over to X-rated films which freckle-faced young couples watched while holding hands.

We like Updike's version better, although we think it would read better with a comma before "holding."

Teachers and stylists with martinet tendencies frown on "dangling" infinitive phrases also. (An infinitive phrase is a group of words introduced by the infinitive form of the verb.) Here's an example:

> To sell newspapers over the telephone, persistence is necessary.

Those who object would insist that the above be "corrected" to read:

> To sell newspapers over the telephone, one needs persistence.

We don't believe that so-called dangling infinitives usually lead to misreading. Both of the following taken from instruction manuals may be frowned on by some language purists:

> To prevent vertical uplift of pilings by the winter ice sheet, a styrofoam wrapping can be placed around the pier supports.

> To record with a tape deck, this switch must be set to the "origin" position.

We find both of these sentences acceptable.

Modifiers other than participles can cause problems for readers also. The basis for such problems lies in syntax. Our syntactical expectations condition us to expect all modifiers of the subject to be close to the subject, all modifiers of the verb to be close to the verb, and all modifiers of the object to be close to the object. Such placement aids reading. Most modifiers which are not clearly associated by sentence structure or word choice with what they modify are "misplaced." Such "errors" can be serious if they cause misreading—even if that misreading is only temporary. Notice the following from the introduction to a book on sentence combining:

> One way to enrich your supply is through sentence modeling—that
> is, the practice of imitating patterns in books and magazines that
> you like but don't ordinarily use.

What does the writer mean? That you don't ordinarily use the books
and magazines or don't ordinarily use the patterns? Probably the
latter; but on first reading, a reader can be confused, and once a writer
confuses a reader, he risks losing her attention. Here's another example from a software advertisement:

> If the cost is acceptable and the technical staff approves the method
> of solution, the executive has all the information she needs to make
> a decision on one page.

A reader's first reaction to this sentence is probably puzzlement. How
can someone make a decision on a page? The reader probably looks
at the sentence a second time and realizes that "on one page" belongs
elsewhere in the sentence—perhaps rewording it for herself: "the
executive has on one page all the. . . ." However the reader copes
with her momentary confusion, she may suffer some loss of trust in
the text she's reading.

> They wouldn't cancel my traffic ticket which was another example
> of bureaucratic pettiness.

What's an example of bureaucratic pettiness: the ticket or the fact that
they wouldn't cancel it? Probably the latter, but again a reader may
be confused (and possibly even annoyed) by the writer's seeming lack
of interest in making meaning clear. As we said before, clarity is
promoted when a writer keeps all modifiers as close as possible to
what they modify.

Not all word-order problems are totally solvable on the basis of
the principle that modifiers should be as close as possible to what
they modify. This is particularly true when a noun (an object or a
subject in a sentence) is modified by more than one word or group
of words. Let's look more closely at a sentence we reproduced earlier:

> One way to enrich your supply is through sentence modeling—that
> is, the practice of imitating patterns in books and magazines that
> you like but don't ordinarily use.

The relative clause "that you like but don't ordinarily use" modifies
"patterns," but "in books and magazines" also modifies "patterns."
Merely reversing the modifiers doesn't solve the problem:

> One way to enrich your supply is through sentence modeling—that
> is, the practice of imitating patterns that you like but don't ordinar-
> ily use in books and magazines.

What to do? One solution is simply to reword:

> One way to enrich your supply is through sentence modeling—that is, the practice of imitating patterns that you like but don't ordinarily use. You can find models in books and magazines.

Here's another sentence from a news story in *The New York Times:*

> The Interior Ministry predicted that the Greek Communist Party, a small Eurocommunist party, would be the only new group in Parliament, with a single seat.

The meaning of this sentence would be quite different without the final comma. We can only wonder if the writer tried other arrangements. Let's see what the sentence would look like if the final prepositional phrase were moved:

> The Interior Ministry predicted that the Greek Communist Party, a small Eurocommunist party, with a single seat, would be the only new group in Parliament.

Worded in this way, it seems as though the Party already has a single seat, and that's illogical in terms of what the whole sentence is saying. The writer may have found the best solution when she wrote it as she did and used the comma. If you run into structures like these while you're writing, you'll probably need to try several versions; the one you end up choosing may simply be the least unsatisfactory one.

Sentence-ending Prepositions

We're not sure exactly what category this "problem" fits into, so we're putting it here since it does have some connection to sentence structure. The prohibition against ending sentences with a preposition is a genuine myth which, for some reason, has become a symbol of language correctness. There are several structures which can create sentences ending with prepositions. One of the most common is questions of the following form:

> Who did you give the book to?

Purists would insist on:

> To whom did you give the book?

But we suspect that even purists would not insist on the latter structure except in the most formal contexts.

Another structure which leads to sentence-ending prepositions looks like the following:

That's the person I came with.

He's the man I spoke to.

You could say: "That's the person with whom I came" and "He's the man to whom I spoke," but very few teachers are going to insist on these changes.

The last sentence type that can push prepositions to the end is really a product of a particular kind of verb, called by some linguists a two-word verb. They would call the second word an adverb, not a preposition.

The house burned up.

I called him up.

We can't get rid of these prepositions because "the house burned" doesn't mean the same thing as "the house burned up" and "I called him" doesn't mean the same thing as "I called him up."

The truth is that there is absolutely nothing wrong with ending a sentence with a preposition; the prohibition against it is one you don't have to put up with.

Variety

Up to this point in your copyediting activities, we've been asking you to check your sentences for possible flawed structures. Now we're going to ask you to do something a bit different: analyze the structure of individual sentences just to see what sorts of structures you use.

In speaking of syntax, we've said that all sentences in English require a subject and a verb and, depending on the verb, an object.

But sentences often contain elements other than a subject, verb, and object. The placement of these elements, particularly adjectives, is determined by the subject-verb-object word order. Other modifiers have more freedom: they can come before, in the middle of, or after the main part of the sentence. If modifying elements precede the main idea, we can call the sentence left-branching:

Before noon, he left.

If modifying elements follow the main idea, we can call the sentence right-branching:

He left before noon.

If modifying elements appear within the subject-verb-object sequence, we say the sentence is characterized by embedding:

The man, leaning against a tree, whistled softly to himself.

Right-branching sentences are the most common ones, particularly in speech. Their predominance isn't surprising, since it's natural in a word-order language to build as one goes along. It's probably for this reason that left-branching sentences and sentences with embedded elements sound more formal than right-branching sentences; that is, they often sound like written rather than spoken sentences.

Sentences can also be classified as active or passive (a distinction we've already discussed on pp. 55–57), and as declarative, interrogative, or imperative. A declarative sentence makes a statement:

She's leaving now.

Interrogative sentences ask questions:

Is she leaving now?

or

Who's leaving now?

Imperative sentences give orders:

Leave.

In some styles of English, a subjunctive mood is used, although its use seems currently to be declining. Those of you who have studied foreign languages have probably had problems with the subjunctive; it can cause problems in English also. One use of the subjunctive is to express ideas which are contrary to fact:

I wish I *were* a tree.

If I *were* a tree, I'd be green.

You'll notice two things happening in these sentences: first, there's a plural verb (*were*) where you'd expect the singular (*was*), and second, the subjunctive verb is in the past tense form even though the speaker is making a statement about the present. If the speaker wanted to say something about the past, she would say:

I wish I *had been* a tree.

If I *had been* a tree, I would have been green.

The subjunctive also appears in certain expressions which convey a degree of compulsion:

She demanded that we *be* silent.

He recommended that Joan *leave*.

If these sentences sound strange to you, that's only proof of our earlier statement that the use of the subjunctive in English is declining.

You may find it interesting to analyze a piece of your own writing to discover what sorts of sentences you use most often. The predominant sentence type in a piece of writing is one of the elements which create individual style. Following are two excerpts from two separate pieces of student writing. Before you look at the analysis of the excerpts, try to get a "feel" for the style of each. Ask yourself which of the two excerpts you prefer and which of the two you think your teacher would prefer.

From an essay on heterogeneous vs. homogeneous educational grouping:

Excerpt 1

The latter educational philosophy is the better of the two. It is more realistic in that it acknowledges the fact that there is a distinction in the level that individuals are able to learn at. Not everyone can learn at the same rate, and to develop a system around the belief that everyone is intellectually equal is a wasteful process.

To teach a group of people at the same level will hold back those who are capable of an accelerated learning rate. Those with the potential of this accelerated learning rate will never be put to their limit of education, and in this way are being cheated of their full possibilities. This cannot be remedied by offering diversified levels of learning after high school, because the greatest capability of a person to learn occurs at an early age. Study habits, expectations, and self image are all formed in these years, and by not encouraging true potential, the level of output cannot be improved substantially. This situation can be compared to that of a child who is not fed properly during childhood. The child will not be able to attain its true mental and physical levels, even if after a few years it receives a properly balanced diet. The damage is done, and for the most part is irreversible.

From a paper on the Olympic games:

Excerpt 2

The Olympic games have put hopes and dreams into the hearts of all young athletes throughout the world, and nothing should be allowed to ruin this. Opposers say politics should have nothing to do with the Olympics, but they do. It started with the Israeli episode a few years ago when Israeli athletes were held hostage and later killed. Then, the Russians moved into Afghanistan, and we boycotted the games. Now, we go and move into Grenada, and we don't know what will happen. The chances of the Russians boycotting the games are slim, but there is talk of trouble brewing. Now, they're tightening up security and hoping for the best. Some say if something happens this could be the last Olympics. I certainly hope not. Now, you can see what a heavy hand politics play in any world competition.

Aside from the obvious reasons why the Olympics are important to us, there is another one. The Olympics make the major world powers compete on the playing field rather than the battlefield. In my opinion, this could stop us from having a war. Common sense tells us that the best way to get rid of hatred and anger toward another person is to compete, to prove who's the best. The Olympics do this. The Olympics have brought us some of the fiercest competition between the world powers that we could expect.

These two excerpts are of approximately the same length, but average sentence length is close to twenty-two in the first excerpt and about fourteen and a half in the second excerpt. In the first excerpt, there are ten sentences. In the second excerpt, there are sixteen sentences. In the first excerpt, there's one left-branching main clause: "by not encouraging true potential, the level. . . ." In addition, the one compound sentence in this first excerpt contains embedding in the second main clause: "to develop a system around the belief *that everyone is intellectually equal* is a wasteful process." The second excerpt has five left-branching sentences: four of these start with a single word ("now," "then") and one with the phrase "In my opinion." This second excerpt contains no sentences with embedded elements. The first excerpt contains seven passive verbs, concentrated toward the end of the excerpt: "are being cheated," "cannot be remedied," "are all formed," "cannot be improved," "can be compared," "is not fed," "is done." In the second excerpt, there are only two passive verbs: "should be allowed" and "were held."

The overall impression these two excerpts make on you is partially a result of these features we've pointed out. A piece of writing dominated by simple and compound sentences, such as the second excerpt, is quite different in style from a piece of writing dominated by complex sentences. Sentence length and the number of passives also affect style. Other factors, such as word choice, degree of intimacy, and level of formality, condition our sense of a writer's style too.

What makes a writer have the style she does? We can't answer that question. Certainly, a writer's subject affects her style. If the writers of the two excerpts had exchanged subjects, probably their styles would have changed somewhat also. No one sits down and says to herself: "I'm going to write longer-than-average sentences, use passive verbs, and produce left-branching sentences." A writer's purpose as she writes is to create meaning, first for herself, and then usually for others too. The influences at work on a writer as she writes are subconscious and intuitive; when she revises, her attention to matters of style can be conscious. Still, we believe that all of us are better off if we work to make our personal styles as effective as possible while we're revising rather than trying to write in some way foreign to us. We don't believe that any one style is, by its nature, better than any other style. This doesn't mean that we don't have preferences just as your teachers do, but we recognize that these are personal preferences that have nothing to do with what's "right" or "wrong." One of the traits of a piece of writing that makes us rate it highly is a harmony of style and subject matter.

We suggest that you do this exercise on a piece of your writing, not to find out what's "wrong" with how you write, but simply to become more knowledgeable about the characteristics of your natural style. We think this knowledge can help you develop your own style to its fullest potential, just as analysis of her forehand stroke can help a tennis player improve her play. And just as a tennis player might decide to try a different way to see how it works for her, you might decide to try some different sentence types to see how they work for you. One of the best ways to do this is to select a piece of prose written by someone else, read it to get a sense of its style, and then try to imitate that style. But remember our tennis analogy: no tennis player is going to try a new stroke in the Wimbledon finals unless she has made it a part of her natural style of playing; you should not try out a new sentence type in a paper being submitted for grading unless you have been able to make it a part of your natural style through practice.

If you've read through the past few pages, you've seen that English has built into its grammatical structure the potential for great variety. In fact, one of the most amazing properties of all languages is their potential variety. Native speakers and writers of a language have the ability to create an infinite number of sentences out of seemingly finite resources. Grammar textbooks usually speak approvingly of "variety" and encourage writers to deliberately vary sentence structure and length. Sentence form is, however, related to sentence meaning and style. Consequently, it isn't wise to tinker with form alone. In Chapter 1, we talked a bit about the tendency of some grammar books to glorify certain kinds of sentence structures—particularly those which use relative clauses and those which combine shorter sentences into longer ones. We don't always agree, but we suspect that if you looked at the excerpts we analyzed above, you'd expect most of your teachers to prefer the first to the second; and it does have longer, more complex sentences. There's nothing wrong with that preference provided it stays away from labeling one style as "right" and the other as "wrong."

We suggest that after writing something, you read it aloud, either to yourself or to others. If you sense a singsong, invariant pattern in your sentence structures, you need to consider possible causes. The most likely one is that your subject doesn't interest you. In that case, you'd be wide to abandon it (if that's an alternative) or (if it isn't) to seek a different approach to it which will be more stimulating to you. It's almost always possible to tell when a writer is bored with his own subject.

Sometimes, however, writers purposefully choose not to vary their sentences. Ernest Hemingway is famous for his direct and simple style. Carolyn Forché, a poet, chose to use simple sentences when writing about El Salvador:

The Colonel

What you have heard is true. I was in his house. His wife carried a tray of coffee and sugar. His daughter filed her nails, his son went out for the night. There were daily papers, pet dogs, a pistol on the cushion beside him. The moon swung bare on its black cord over the house. On the television was a cop show. It was in English. . . .

In most instances, variety stimulates reader interest. Just as the eye tires of being exposed to the same visual pattern, the mind tires of repetitious written formulas. But variety is more than cosmetic; its presence or absence conveys meaning. If you look back at the excerpt from Carolyn Forché and question yourself about the speaker's state of mind, you'll probably agree with us that the sameness of sentence structure makes the speaker seem to be numb or in a state of shock, unable to express anything but the simplest observations.

A student writer recalls her childhood in sentences animated by a variety of sentence structures.

Long before I started school, I learned my way around the maze of miner's paths over the Southern mountains. I would hike to high clearings where I could look down at the postcard-perfect little town with the white church and neat rows of houses. Miners on their way home in the afternoons stopped as well, to sit on the rocks, smoke their pipes, and gaze out at the scenery below. Green in summer, white in winter, views from the mountain always drew passersby for at least a moment or two. But autumn was my favorite season for traveling the pathways; the village and surrounding valley would then be framed by the blazing foliage of October.

This narrator gives the impression that she is alert and responsive to her environment; she is not numb. Her choice of words and her sentence structure together convey that responsiveness.

One of the traits of a good piece of writing that we need not be consciously aware of, though it certainly affects us, is a harmony of content and form. As we said in Chapter 1, content and form are inseparable. As a writer revises, both form and content change; she struggles with both at the same time. Following is an excerpt in which the harmony of content and form is particularly evident:

> The plain fact is that Mondale was not a thematic politician, and resisted attempts to make him one. A thematic campaign calls for a kind of repetition and discipline that are not in Mondale's nature: if there was something he wanted to talk about, he went out and talked about it. He had a curious and far-ranging mind, and if he thought something was important—and he thought a lot of things were important—he wanted to say so. He often talked about fairness and compassion—and did it passionately—but he talked about many other things as well. Mondale's suspicion of uplifting rhetoric—he called it "words" or "dawnism" (as in "the dawn of a new era")—lasted until almost the end of his campaign. He is a highly intelligent, well-informed, serious (but not humorless) man who believed to the end that the issues mattered. Mondale sees the complexity of things and talks about them in a complicated manner; Reagan sees simple truths and delivers a simple message.
>
> —Elizabeth Drew, "A Political Journal,"
> *The New Yorker* (Dec. 3, 1984), p. 115.

What we notice here is the complexity of the sentence structure the author uses while talking about a man she considers complex, and the simplicity she uses in the last sentence when talking about a man who "sees simple truths." This, added to the obviously greater space devoted to the complex man, creates a parallelism of structure and idea which reenforces the writer's main point.

Another potential source of sentence variety is sentence length. The following excerpt from an article in *The New York Times Magazine* gains force by a contrast in sentence length:

> Call it racewalking, powerwalking, exercisewalking, aerobicwalking or healthwalking—Americans, some 50 million of them, are now taking physical fitness in stride. They walk.
>
> —Deborah Blumenthal,
> "Taking Fitness in Stride"

If you're revising a section of a draft which seems dull and lifeless to you or to your readers, you might want to examine sentence length.

One sentence after another of approximately the same number of words can create a monotonous rhythm. But varying just to vary sentence length is not usually productive. Still, it's hard for us to believe that anyone can regularly express most of what they want to say in sentences of almost the same length and structure most of the time. We suggest that you experiment.

We suspect that most textbooks and teachers when they encourage sentence variety are reacting to what they consider immature style characterized by childish-sounding structures. Young children do tend to use short sentences, mainly unmodified subject-verb-object sequences. The research of psycholinguists demonstrates that the creation of complex sentences (those which contain at least one subordinate clause) is a result of maturation. Textbooks thus conclude that simple sentence structure is a reflection of immaturity. We're not so sure the logic can be reversed in this way; we've seen many simple sentences which are far from immature.

Certain sentence structures are almost never found in spoken language; as a result such sentence structures probably do indicate that the writer of them is an experienced writer and reader. We don't deny that; in fact, we think that practice in combining ideas (an exercise called sentence-combining) can be effective—but only to a certain extent. What writers need to learn to do is to put their own ideas together—not someone else's. We're going to talk about a method for doing that now.

Major Surgery ("Awk")

We've spent some time during the past few years observing how students use grammar books. What we've noticed is that they have great difficulty finding anything useful in them unless they already know what's wrong with their essays. Also, during the past few years, we've made several attempts to categorize the errors students make. For the most part, we find that the errors don't fit into neat little categories. This is another reason why students are often frustrated by grammar books.

Up to this point, we've put language problems or potential problems into categories and suggested that you examine your writing to see where these categories might apply to what you've written. We hope you've found that some of the categories match your problems. But we're quite sure that you're still left with some sentences you're dissatisfied with, but don't know why. We often find faulty sentences in student's papers that we can't explain on the basis of what we've said so far. It's sentences like these that your teachers are likely to label "awkward." Your teachers could rewrite these for you and get rid of the awkwardness, but this isn't helpful to you. The rewriting may produce a satisfactory sentence in terms of structure and usage, but the sentence may not say what *you* want it to say. You need a way to cope with these "awkward" sentences on your own. And the truth is that general rules aren't always useful; each sentence has to be considered as a special case. It's for your problem sentences that we recommend our method of Major Surgery.

To perform major surgery on a sentence, you must break it down into parts. Once you've done that, you can make each part into a separate sentence. Your next task is to examine these separate sentences and their relationship to one another. Then you can recombine those which you think should be recombined. You may have seen or even used sentence-combining textbooks. We don't recommend them, though, for two reasons. Many of them suggest that long, complex sentences are better than short, simple ones, and we don't think that's necessarily true. Secondly, we're not convinced that learning how to control sentences written by someone else helps a writer combine her own sentences. You need to work with sentences which express your ideas, not someone else's.

Following are illustrations showing both the decombining and the recombining efforts of two of our students:

From a student's paper on modern heroes:

I think that a hero should have as much qualifications and characteristics that he could understand and handle.

The student broke her sentence down into separate ideas and made each of these into a sentence:

I have some ideas about heroes.

There are many qualifications for being a hero.

Heroes have certain characteristics.

Heroes must understand their own qualifications.

Heroes must be able to handle their own special powers.

You'll notice that the student used the verbs in her original sentence as a guide to the creation of separate units. She rewrote as follows:

Heroes are people who have special qualifications and characteristics that they've come to understand and handle.

From a student paper on careers:

Just as you would apply for any job your background, lifestyle, and hobbies are all included in the determination of your capability for the job.

The student broke this sentence down into these units:

You apply for a job.

You have the skills and education for the job.

Your background is important.

Your lifestyle is important.

Your hobbies are important.

All this determines your capability for a job.

The student rewrote as follows:

When you apply for a job, you need to have the skills and education for it. But your background, lifestyle and hobbies also determine your capability for a job.

After you've performed major surgery on several of your own sentences, you'll begin to realize that what's important about the process is that it forces you to think about what you're saying. This is the key to clearing up writing problems: as you struggle to write out each element of a sentence, you begin to see more clearly what you want to say.

This is a bit of an aside, but this seems like a good spot to remind you of something we said earlier. We've been talking in this chapter about revising individual sentences. One of the pitfalls of this practice is that you may forget that sentences need to sound all right when read with what goes before and what comes after. We suggest that you develop the practical habit of rereading (preferably aloud) any paragraph in which you have revised sentences—even if it's only one sentence. This will help you decide whether or not your newly rewritten sentences integrate smoothly into their surroundings. If not, you'll have to do more readjusting.

We're going to ask you to try a little experiment. You've been doing rewriting of sentences in this section. You may discover that no matter how many ways you rewrite a particular sentence, you're still unhappy with it. One possible reason for this is that the sentences surrounding it seem to become worse as the sentence itself gets better. You may feel a paragraph disintegrating. If that's the case, you need to do major surgery on the paragraph also.

Read over carefully the paragraph you're unhappy with. Once you've done that, set it aside where you won't be tempted to look at it. Now, on another sheet of paper, jot down what the major ideas of this paragraph are or should be. Next, rewrite the paragraph completely—don't even look back at the way you wrote it previously. As you write, don't think directly about the words or the sentence structure; just think about what you need to say. Focus solely on meaning as you write. Every intention to write something down starts with an impulse containing potential meaning. As we write, the meaning becomes realized; we struggle with that meaning until it matches our original feeling about its original potential. When it does that, we know we've got it right. If as you're struggling, you find yourself blocked because you can't think of the word you want, just put in an X and continue. When you've finished, compare your new paragraph to the old one and see what the differences are and which you prefer. Even if you decide to stay with that original paragraph, we hope you'll realize you've got some choices. We should warn you that if you like your new paragraph, you may want to rewrite several other paragraphs too. All elements of a paper work together. There's no way of isolating a sentence or a paragraph from its context.

For the exercise we just described, one of our students selected the following paragraph from an essay on parents and teenagers:

> Parents want to cut their teenagers' wastefulness to show them how to conduct themselves in a more mature way. To make their children aware, they complain to their children. Their complaints are not directed towards their children's activities. Parents just wish to protect them against social evils that could arise when they have excess time and money. Parents are there to advise them. Even though you might say they are living their lives, they are not. They're just watching out for them. When their children deviate from a safe and accepted path someone close should step in and redirect them. This is not living their children's lives, it is just helping them. They're helping them see their mistakes before they happen. Even though they have the right to make mistakes and learn from them, they suffer less when they recognize mistakes and don't fall flat.

We'll talk about the pronouns in this passage in the next section. The writer recognized the problem she was having with the pronouns and tried unsuccessfully to rewrite a few sentences. She finally gave up and agreed to try our exercise. She reread the paragraph and then wrote down the following as the main points she had in mind:

1. Parents want to help children grow up.
2. They also want to protect them.
3. That's why they control children's time and money.

4. Parents don't want their children to suffer because they make mistakes.

She rewrote the paragraph as follows:

> Parents want to help children grow up, but they also want to protect them. This is why parents need to exercise some control over their children's excess time and money. When teenagers have too much time on their hands and too much money to spend, they may get into trouble. In our age, that trouble will probably be drugs, or girls may get pregnant. When parents step in and try to limit their teenagers' free time and extra money, it's because they want to keep them from the suffering that these activities can cause. Sometimes teenagers don't think about the results of their actions, so they need someone to step in and warn them. Young people have the right to learn from their mistakes, but if someone who loves them, like a parent, steps in and controls them a little bit, they'll suffer less. In this way, children will learn to be somewhat independent but they'll be safer while they're learning.

She liked her rewritten paragraph better and so do we; ideas seem to come after one another here in a way that makes it possible for us to follow her main idea as it develops from one sentence to the next.

If all of this sounds like work, it is and should be. The miracle of good writing is that it sounds effortless, as though it flowed from the writer's pen (or onto the word-processor screen) like magic. The truth is usually quite different; smoothly flowing, spontaneous-sounding sentences are usually products of many revisions that are based on refining our natural language production to make our usage acceptable for our purposes and our ideas clear to our intended audience.

Practice 8

The following student essay contains a number of errors in sentence structure. Locate and discuss these errors with your classmates and teacher. You can also benefit by discussing the structure of sentences which you particularly like.

> If I had to select one object which best represents my culture which is America to people of other countries is our flag. I choose this item because of the symbolism and because of the unification of my people it represents. It has evolved into an object with which our society has trouble surviving without. By looking at this object would help others understand my society.
>
> The symbolism of the flag which is most profound are the colors Red, White, and Blue. It's Betsy Ross we give the credit to. The flag

in which she founded states that the color red displays the hardiness and courage of all our ancestors that was shed throughout the centuries of this country. The color white displays the purity of innocence, and the color blue represents the vigilance, perseverance and justice of our motherland in which my pride comes from.

By being divided into stars and stripes, we can see some of the history of our wonderful land. The fifty stars show only that there are fifty separate states. When the flag was first made, there were only thirteen stars because there were only thirteen states. One star was added each time a new state came into being. At first a stripe for each new state was added, but soon came the realization that lots of stripes would not look good and so the official flag went back to just the original thirteen stripes. The American flag has flown in many battles which men and women have given their lives for freedom in America and for their families. Hung from our porches and houses, we can rejoice in our beautiful national emblem.

The unification in which the flag represents is that everyone of whatever descent must unify. This must be stressed emphatically with the children because America invites everyone in. Our children must understand that we have strength in numbers. They must also understand that every individual is different. Just because you are of one country does not mean that you have to get along with everyone of your country, but there is a commonality that we as a people share. Our flag helps us understand what the American Dream is all about.

Punctuation

So far, we've avoided saying anything about punctuation except for the periods necessary to mark sentence endings. You've probably inserted some punctuation other than periods as you were writing and revising, but now that you've finished those tasks, you need to focus on punctuation. It affects your readers' ability to deduce meaning from your words. And since punctuation marks are a visible sign of sentence structure, we think you should check them as soon as you're satisfied with your sentence structure. In fact, you probably found yourself doing that *while* you were revising sentences. It seems almost impossible not to.

All written languages developed and established themselves without an elaborate system of punctuation, almost without any punctuation at all. The Rosetta Stone doesn't contain a single punctuation mark in any of the three languages inscribed on it. The earliest surviving manuscripts of the Bible, in Greek and Latin, have no punctuation. Some languages (such as Persian, Armenian, and Japanese) didn't even put spaces between words until recently. In some Old English manuscripts there are marks, called points, which seem to mark off words in rhythmic patterns.

It was movable type, invented in the fifteenth century, and the concomitant increase in printed books and literacy that made punctuation desirable and necessary, just to make reading easier. But, back then, punctuation seems to have been a guide to reading aloud. A number of books even equate punctuation marks with musical notation. It wasn't until the eighteenth and nineteenth centuries that editors at publishing houses began to standardize punctuation.

In the *Oxford English Dictionary* (OED) the earliest references to the period, comma, and paragraph show that these were used to mark breaks in the ideas of a text. The Greek ancestors of our words *comma* and *colon,* in fact, designated not marks of punctuation, but the groups of words made into a cluster by the comma or colon. Other marks, like the dash and semicolon, refine our abilities to show the relationship between ideas. Yet always, punctuation has developed with the needs of a reader in mind, a reader who needs to have some way of breaking strings of words into logical groupings. It should not surprise you that, as average sentence length has decreased over the past two hundred years, so has the use of punctuation marks. As sentences get shorter, punctuation gets simpler. We today punctuate far less frequently than seventeenth-century writers whose sentences might go on for a full page or more.

Since punctuation is integral to meaning, most of us use the marks fairly automatically as we write (even if most of them in our early drafts look like dashes!). During the early stages of writing you'll still be too involved in developing the ideas to worry whether you should use a comma or a semicolon. Only at the editing stage does the choice of a particular mark become crucial. When you're ready for that final stage, try to enlist the aid of a friend or classmate to listen as you read your piece aloud. Whenever she hears you pause between words, she can mark the text in some way—with a red *X* for example. Then, still with her help if she's willing (you can always return the favor), and with the guidance we give, you can look at each red *X* and decide whether a punctuation mark is needed and if so, which one. If you have to do this task on your own, you can tape yourself reading and then replay the tape and mark your text for yourself.

Instead of first advising you about how to use periods, commas, and other punctuation marks in your writing, we decided to talk to a colleague of ours about punctuation. After transcribing the interview, we had our colleague check the punctuation. The following extracts from the interview with her cover a few of the more troublesome marks. As you read through, noticing how the marks have been

used will clue you in to possible ways to use them in your own
writing. (As a matter of fact, the best way to develop a sense of
punctuation is through extensive reading. Whether you consciously
analyze the punctuation is irrelevant.)

1   These days, the most commonly used punctuation
2   mark is the period, though some people like to use commas.
3   Most writers, I think, are just too frightened to use any-
4   thing but commas and periods. They're not the type to
5   flout convention, and convention says: "Every sentence
6   must have a period." Convention doesn't say anything
7   about anything else, really, not when you get right down to
8   what you *have* to have. Sentences don't even have to have
9   commas, you know; you could just write "and and and" all
10 the time. [laughs] But it would take nerve to do that,
11 wouldn't it? . . .
12   I feel sorry for commas, you know? They're overworked.
13 They have to carry so much responsibility—separating
14 clauses, or things in a series, or whatever. I'd like to invent
15 different kinds of commas, so that this one is only for
16 using in quotations, and that one is only for separating
17 clauses, and other ones for all the rest. It's not like periods,
18 which can only end sentences. Commas have to do a lot of
19 different things. . . .
20   About four years ago I went through a phase of being
21 infatuated with the dash—I still use it a lot, but not as
22 much as I used to. My editor flipped out when I gave her
23 the manuscript for "The Period Shop." But when I told her
24 to have a look at Emily Dickinson's poems—that is, at the
25 way they were printed before editors got hold of them—and
26 to look at how she [Dickinson] used the dash all the time, I
27 figured that would calm her [the editor] down a little. For
28 me, the dash is a way to set off information; it's like
29 parentheses. But, you know, parentheses sort of say to me,
30 "This isn't really important, but I wanted to put it in
31 anyway." Dashes say, "Hey, take a look at this." They
32 really stand out on a page—and they connect ideas a lot
33 better than a semicolon. I've always been a geometry nut; I
34 wish there was some way I could include more Euclidean
35 diagrams in my writing. The closest I can get is a dash.
36 [pause] But I've calmed down a bit. Now I'm into slashes.
37   I really hate the way semicolons look, but I like using
38 them. They remind me of certain words that are very ugly
39 sounding, yet very effective. Like "screech" and "pusil-
40 lanimous." You know what I mean? So when I use punctu-
41 ation, I'd rather be effective than beautiful, so I use semi-
42 colons. They help me set up hierarchies, levels of importance.
43 I'll give you an example. Let's say I've got two ideas that

44 seem to me to go together; I don't want to separate them
45 with a period because that would make them too separate;
46 but a comma makes them too close. "And" is completely
47 out of the question; in poetry, you know, you can't go
48 around adding words after, just to help you punctuate. A
49 semicolon is perfect. It says, "Wait; there's more; don't stop
50 yet." You know the best poem with lots of semicolons? It's
51 "The Second Coming" by Yeats. Listen:
52   Things fall apart; the centre cannot hold;
53   Mere anarchy is loosed upon the world,
54 That poem has twenty-two lines but only five sentences;
55 and he uses six semicolons!
56   I don't use colons very much—they're very formal and
57 don't often fit into what I write. I remember one time I used
58 a lot of them: it was in a poem that had lots of lists. A
59 colon came before each list. But I was very revolutionary
60 in that poem [laughs] because there were no words before
61 the colons. I mean, it went "colon something something
62 something, new line, colon something something." Like
63 that. That poem is still in my file; it never got out of my
64 apartment. . . .
65   How did I learn to punctuate? I guess I read a lot and
66 I experimented a lot. My sister-in-law—she helped too: I'd
67 give her a poem and we'd talk about the ideas. Then I'd
68 make her tell me how she reacted to the punctuation since
69 it's so crucial in poetry: you can't waste anything; nothing's
70 superfluous. I think my style—the way I use punctuation, I
71 mean—developed more from her reactions than from any
72 reading I did. But I may be wrong.

Our colleague's attitude toward punctuation may seem cavalier, but she at least feels secure about what she does and is not afraid to experiment—her security comes from knowing what the punctuation marks can do and what they can't do. The marks our colleague didn't mention—apostrophes, hyphens, underlines, and quotation marks— shouldn't be forgotten. They each are important, and for some writers they're confusing.

But before we talk about the marks she didn't mention, let's look more closely at those she did and see how well the way we punctuated her words measures up to what the words say. We've numbered the lines of the transcript so we can go back now and look at the punctuation we used.

Periods

Our colleague speaks first of the period and the absolute need for it at the end of a sentence. We're only going to speak of the period briefly here since we covered the importance of marking sentence endings earlier in this chapter. We talked there of the relations between the speaking voice and the end of sentences. Let's see how that works here in the first sentence of the transcript. If you read that sentence and the following one aloud as they're punctuated, or listen to someone else read them aloud, you'll notice that there's a slight pause after *days* and a more definite one after *period.* After *commas,* the pause will probably be even more obvious, but, in addition, you'll hear an emphasis on *most,* the first word of the second sentence. The combination of the pause and the emphasis signals the sentence break. Now pretend there's a period instead of a comma after *period* and read the first sentence aloud again. This time, you'll notice that in addition to the pause after *period,* there's an emphasis on the word *though,* which now seems to begin another sentence. If it weren't for the seven words after *period,* we could end the sentence there. However, if we punctuated the next seven words as if they formed a sentence, what we'd have would be a fragment. You'll notice that *though* is one of the subordinators we listed above in our section on subordination; this word added to the six following it creates a sense of incompleteness. Within these seven words there's a subject (*people*) and a verb (*like*), but the sense is incomplete without the words preceding *though.* That's why we didn't punctuate these seven words as a sentence.

Commas

Let's look now at the comma, probably the mark of punctuation most difficult to pin down. As our colleague notes, it does many different things. The first she mentions is separating clauses (line 13). A clause is a group of words with a subject and a verb; if it can stand alone, we call it an independent clause or a main clause; if it can't stand alone (like the seven words we were just talking about in the previous paragraph), we call it a dependent or subordinate clause. One of the traditional uses of the comma is before the conjunction that connects two independent clauses. The comma and this conjunction called a coordinating conjunction, create the link between the two sentences. You'll notice this sort of comma in line 5 of the transcript before the conjunction *and.* Notice that you could, if you wanted to, read the words before the comma as a complete sentence and the words after the *and* as a complete sentence. In line 30, the comma is also used this way. This time the conjunction is *but,* not *and.* (These are the two most common conjunctions; others are *or, nor, yet*—when it means *but*—*so,* and *for*— when it means *because.*) Notice again that you can read the words before this comma (the one in line 30) as a complete sentence and the words after it and the conjunction as a complete sentence. The comma used in this way, to separate independent clauses connected by a con-junction, appears additionally in line **41** (before *so*). Whether or not to put a comma before a coordinating conjunction can be a matter of sen-tence length, of style, or of the way you hear the words. We didn't use a comma in line 65 or line 67, though in both places there's a conjunc-tion connecting two complete independent clauses. We think these sentences read better without pauses—but we recognize that they could be read *with* pauses also.

The second use of the comma our colleague mentions is to separate "things in a series" (line **14**). A series is a list of things longer than two items. We hope you noticed that lines 13 and **14** present a series: the three items are "clauses," "things in a series," and "whatever." Another series occurs in the next sentence: the items this time are "this one is only for using in quotations," "that one is only for separating clauses," and "other ones for all the rest." Almost any sort of language grouping can be used in a series, provided all the items are basically the same type of language grouping (this is a form of parallelism). A series can be made up of clauses ("The reporter asked her when she wrote the first draft, why she revised it, and how she changed it for the final version"), phrases ("I ran down the street, around the corner, and into the alley"), and words ("A series can be composed of clauses, phrases, or words"). In all the examples of series we've given here, there are three items, but a series can be composed, at least theoretically, of an unlimited number of items, although we must warn you that if you produce a series that just keeps going on, and on, and on, and on, and on, you may lose your reader. This series comma is almost mandatory; without it a reader would be hard pressed to tell where one item in a series ends and an-other begins. The more important a comma is to clarity of meaning, the less likely a writer is to forget to use it. Commas in a series are so integral to meaning that writers, even inexperienced ones, rarely have diffi-culty putting them in the right places. But the final comma in a series, the one before the conjunction, is optional, since the conjunction itself shows that another item follows. If there's any reason why the final item in a series and the one that precedes it could together be one item, you should use the comma. As an example, figure out how many re-ports are listed in this sentence from a student's paper about his course of study as a political science major:

> During the semester we wrote reports on democracy, communism, totalitarianism and fascism, socialism, monarchy and autocracy.

If you as a writer regularly omit the comma before the final *and* in a series, your reader cannot be certain whether there was a report on monarchy and a report on autocracy, or one report on both. If, however, you regularly use a comma before the final conjunction, your readers will know what you mean. For clarity, though, we would suggest that the writer of this sentence rearrange the items in this list—unless, of course, he has a reason for this particular order. The important thing is for you to be consistent about the comma before the conjunction: either use the final comma or don't use it.

Sometimes descriptive words, adjectives, occur in a series before the word they modify: "The tall, dark, handsome one is a vampire." In constructions like these, a comma is used even if there are only two terms: "The tall, dark one is a vampire." Sometimes the final descriptive word in a series like this seems so much a part of the noun that the comma before it is omitted: "The tall, dark, handsome young woman is a vampire too." If you write a sentence in which a series of adjectives precedes a noun, you're going to have to rely on your intuition when deciding about the commas. "Young" doesn't always join so closely with a noun: "The tall, dark, handsome, young sky-diver waved at the vampires."

Commas perform other tasks too, tasks which we assume our speaker included within the word *whatever* in our transcript. These other uses have the same essential function as the two we've already talked about: they group words into units of meaning. Since, in speaking, short pauses within sentences also serve to group words into meaning, it isn't surprising that commas appear in sentences just at those points where our voices would pause if we read the sentences aloud. Essentially, commas such as these set apart words which are not an integral part of the structure of the main or independent clause in a sentence. This is the overall rule which can be subdivided into more and more specialized rules. (Back in the 1800s, grammar books often had as many as 98 rules for the use of the comma!) First, commas are often used to show where the introductory words in a sentence end and the main part of the sentence begins. (In the section on sentence variety, we called these "left-branching" sentences.) You'll see this sort of use of the comma in our transcript in lines 1, 26, 28, 29, 31, 41, 47 and 61. The next time you do some extended reading, pay some attention to authors' use of the "introductory" comma. In fact, pay some attention to ours! You'll probably find authors equally divided between those who would write: "In 1941, the war began in earnest" and those who would write: "In 1941 the war began in earnest." If you look at line 20, you'll see that we could have put a comma after "ago," but we decided that the speaker had not paused here and that she didn't really have to.

Many teachers who are flexible about the comma in sentences which begin with short phrases are not so flexible about the comma that follows longer introductory units such as introductory subordinate clauses; they may insist on the comma in such cases. The commas in lines 26 and 41 of our transcript follow such clauses. The introductory unit in the first of these is quite long. It stands to reason that the longer an introductory element is, the more likely it will be that a comma will be useful.

We're not finished yet with commas. It isn't only introductory words that are not integral parts of the main idea, the subject-verb (-object) core, of a sentence. Sometimes that main idea is interrupted *in medias res* (that's Latin for "in the middle of things"—you may have heard it used to describe how epics traditionally begin). Some of these interruptions are like asides in a play; you'll see commas used like this in our transcript in lines 3, 7, 9, 29, and 47. Sometimes the words which interrupt a main clause make up a nonessential dependent or subordinate clause: "My handwriting, *which has never endeared me to teachers,* sometimes confuses even me." You'll notice that you can omit the words between the commas in this sentence and not lose the basic meaning of the sentence. If you write a dependent clause in this position that *is* essential to the meaning of the sentence, don't put commas around it: "The one thing *that has never endeared me to teachers* is my handwriting."

One final word about using a comma wherever you would pause in an oral reading. If you examine recently written texts, you may notice that some writers don't use commas where there would be a pause. You'll also notice that the omission of the comma usually causes you no trouble as you read *if the structure of the sentence dictates a pause even without the guidance of a punctuation mark.* Observe:

> After Jim had waited hours for everyone to leave he got annoyed and drove off alone.

This sentence contains an introductory clause, but the break in sense between "leave" and "he" is so apparent that the lack of a comma causes no reading difficulties.

> ~~After he had waited hours for everyone to leave, Jim got annoyed~~ and drove off alone.

As readers, we need the comma in this sentence to keep us from reading "Jim" as the object of "leave." Many teachers, though, are going to insist on commas in both versions of this sentence. We can't really quarrel with that since commas are a useful way of visually grouping words on a page so that visual groups coincide with grammatical structure.

Sometimes, though, if you use a comma to mark off every structural unit in a sentence, regardless of its length, you're likely, we think, to annoy your reader and, in the long run, undermine your own, well-intended, carefully planned efforts.

Semicolons and Colons

In the transcript, our colleague talks about the way semicolons work; they connect two ideas which the writer wants to state separately but yet link. The sentence that begins in line 43 and ends in line 46 uses two semicolons; we wanted to keep the three ideas in this sentence somewhat separate, but still considered them related enough to be kept in one sentence. Our colleague also speaks of colons and the formality they connote, noting that she once used them often to introduce lists of items. This is indeed one of the conventional uses of colons, although they're usually omitted if the list starts after a verb or a preposition. Colons can also serve as the equivalent of the words "that is": a way to introduce a restatement or an explanation. Serving this function, they can replace semicolons that come between independent clauses: they then carry the same weight as semicolons.

Back in the sixteenth century, when printers first became interested in formulating rules about the use of various punctuation marks so that the printing industry would have some standards, one authority compared punctuation marks to symbols used in music. He equated a period with a full rest, a colon with a three-quarters rest, a semicolon with a half rest, and a comma with a quarter rest. Of course rest marks in music are a way of marking off a segment of time, not a way of measuring degrees of relationship. Still, it may be useful to think of punctuation marks in this way since it may help you understand better the relative values of the period, colon, semicolon, and comma. This relative value becomes more apparent in sentences which contain a number of items subdivided into smaller units; in such sentences, a writer needs a way to keep the items properly distinguished. Here's how that might look:

> Receiving special awards were Jane Doe, 777 Smith Street; John Smith, 888 Jones Street; Jill Jones, 999 Miller Street; and Jonathan Miller, 111 Brown Street.

The semicolons show divisions between units which themselves are subdivided by commas. This principle has another possible application, particularly in compound sentences. We said earlier that commas usually appear in compound sentences connected by a conjunction:

> The provost herself made a list of all students who had received special awards, but she neglected to include addresses.

If, in one or both of the independent clauses in a compound sentence, commas are used, the comma showing the division between the clauses themselves can be "promoted" to a semicolon.

> The provost herself, annoyed at the inefficiency of her office staff, made a list of all students who had received special awards; but, because she was rushed, she neglected to include addresses.

In a sentence like this one, the relative strength of the comma and semicolon helps a reader group words into units of meaning.

Remember those run-on sentences earlier in this chapter? Let's see if we can fix them up by using semicolons and commas. The originals of these are on page 40.

> Finally, I ordered the same thing the man at the next table was eating; after dinner, my sister's son and I wanted to walk along Broadway; we didn't feel tired, so we continued to walk around the city.

> The parent may desperately want their child to have a prosperous future and at the same time be happy; but, at the same time, the parent is continually disregarding the feelings of the child that they may not be right for the profession, causing the child a great deal of unhappiness.

> When a parent continually praises a child, saying that they're the greatest, it may convince the child that they are, causing them a possibility of a big letdown if they hear otherwise, making the child lose all trust in the parents.

So you see that, even though we usually use periods to show where one segment of thought ends and another begins, we can also use semicolons and colons if we don't want to divide our thoughts up as absolutely as periods do. Indicating the points of division between grammatical units is crucial to comprehension; as a result, some grammarians frown on using commas to do so. They call such use a "comma splice." "Splice," as used in this term, means "connect": a comma which splices is one which connects. What is connected by comma splices is two complete sentences. Over the past few years, we've noticed that the frequency of comma splices in student prose has increased. Generally, if the sentence structure is otherwise effective, comma splices do not cause difficulties for a reader. If the sentence structure is already confusing, comma splices can certainly add to that confusion. Teachers—especially English teachers—who are on the lookout for comma splices will probably find yours. Other readers will probably not be much aware of them unless they become puzzled about what you're saying. However, in all fairness to you, we must warn you that we think a high percentage of your teachers consider them "wrong." If you examine edited prose in newspapers and books, you'll discover, as we did, that comma splices are rare. They're rare because they can mislead readers.

Despite these warnings, whether to use a comma, semicolon, colon, or period between two complete sentences can be a matter of style and meaning. Consider these sentences:

> When we were children we wanted to talk to animals and struggled to understand why this was impossible. Slowly we gave up the attempt as we grew up into the solitary world of human adulthood; the rabbit was left on the lawn, the dog was relegated to his kennel.
>
> —Loren Eiseley,
> *The Unexpected Universe*

There are four grammatically complete sentences in this excerpt. Eiseley places a period after two of them, a semicolon after one, and a comma after one. We think he knew what he was doing.

Isak Dinesen is another author whose punctuation, while not always following the strictest rules, serves her meaning:

> But towards the West, deep down, lies the dry, moon-like landscape of the African low country. The brown desert is irregularly dotted with the little marks of the thornbushes, the winding river-beds are drawn up with crooked dark-green trails; those are the woods of the mighty, wide-branching Mimosa-trees, with thorns like spikes; the cactus grows here, and here is the home of the Giraffe and the Rhino.
>
> —*Out of Africa*

She wrote six grammatically complete sentences here, but uses only two periods; after two of the sentences she uses commas, once with a conjunction and once without; after the other two sentences, she uses semicolons. The semicolons create segments within the larger unit which begins with a capital and ends with a period; within each of the units marked off by semicolons, the commas create smaller divisions.

Probably what bothers teachers (including us) about comma splices is that they are often visual signs of a writer's failure to set up hierarchies. One sentence marches after another like a line of ducks. In a sense, a succession of sentences connected by commas is equivalent to a paper with only one paragraph: there's no grouping of ideas into larger units, no emphasis of one idea over another. We're not suggesting that you just change all your commas to semicolons or periods; we're suggesting that you examine your prose to discover the best way to set off small units, group these into larger units, and then group these into still larger units. Writing which does this can have a richness of texture—it's like the difference between looking at ruffled and unruffled water in a pond. There may be order in the unruffled water, but we can't see it; ruffled water has a pattern, and patterns appeal to the human need for structure, which enables us to make meaning. And, when we see structure in a piece of writing, we sense an ordered mind behind it and are more likely to grant authority to the words before us.

Punctuation marks are conventional devices for grouping words into chunks of meaning. Think of them as traffic signs. Traffic signs are governed by convention also; in terms of logic, there's really no reason why "red" should mean stop and "green" go. The reason they do is that most of us live in a world that uses them this way. If suddenly one day the colors were reversed, accidents would probably make our highways impassable. For most of us, stopping at a red light is second nature. To a reader, a period says: "Stop here a minute." If some sort of completion of meaning doesn't occur at the spot marked by the period, a reader becomes disoriented (metaphorically speaking, she has an accident). Our expectations about semicolons, colons, and commas are not quite so strong, but they do exist. Furthermore, these expectations exist relative to the whole system of punctuation. Think about this as you read the following excerpt from a student's paper on grading systems:

> Another negative side to the pass/fail system would be a lack of competition among students. This would in the end result in a lack of interest within the student body to compete for grades, therefore academic standards would drop considerably with students not caring how their class rank would stand but just being satisfied with passing their courses.

The one comma here is technically a comma splice since there's a complete sentence before it and a complete sentence after it. According to strict current convention, *therefore* is not a coordinate conjunction and cannot connect sentences with just a comma. The comma splice in this sentence doesn't give us difficulties, but other problems in this sentence may affect our advice about this particular comma splice. We had difficulty reading the second sentence because we first read: "This would in the end result" as a unit of meaning and then realized we couldn't do that. When we went back to the beginning of the sentence, we realized that "in the end" was a little segment and that "result" was a verb, not the object of the preposition "in"; the writer could have forestalled our misreading by putting commas before and after "in the end." We would also advise the writer to think about other spots in the second sentence which might be candidates for commas—particularly after "considerably" and "stand." The lack of resting points in this sentence makes us feel a bit breathless. Once the writer inserts additional commas in this long sentence, she might consider changing the comma before "therefore" to a semicolon. In this way, she will maintain the hierarchy of ideas she started out with.

We've noticed in our students' papers that the lack of commas is usually not as disruptive to reading as the presence of commas which seem to fragment ideas. Metaphorically speaking again, it's as though someone put a stop sign in the middle of the block—quite disconcerting! So when you check your papers for punctuation, be sure you pause wherever you've put commas. That's what your readers will do almost instinctively; years of reading have trained us all to do that. We've culled some examples from student papers to show you how misplaced and omitted commas affect us as readers.

From a paper on sex education:

> Then again some parents are more understanding and can accept the fact, that their child is using birth control to prevent unwanted children.

We find it difficult to read this sentence with a pause after "fact": the pause interrupts the idea unnecessarily.

From the same paper:

> Passing a law like that, should be declared unconstitutional.

We have no problem reading this sentence with a pause after "that," but (and here's another convention) many teachers, especially English teachers, frown on commas which come between the subject and the verb in a sentence. (The subject in this sentence is "passing a law like that," and the verb is "should be declared.") Depending on the nature of the words between the commas, it's acceptable to have two commas between the subject and the verb:

> What he did, passing a law like that, should be declared unconstitutional.

Summary Table

Comma

To separate items in a series	She bought apples, pears, and oranges.

	He said he would not listen, he would not speak, and he would not move.
To separate adjectives preceding a noun	The small, green, unadorned box holds a treasure.
To set off introductory phrases	In spite of the rain, she decided to water the lawn. When speaking, he never looked directly at the audience.
To set off introductory clauses	Before you leave, please turn off the lights.
To set off nonessential words, phrases, and clauses	She is, in fact, not at all interested. He will not, therefore, try to sell her the picture. I awakened my brother, who is a light sleeper, and asked him to go with me.

Colon

To precede a list or emphasize a point (but not usually directly after a verb or preposition)	She stocked up on supplies: apples, cereal, butter, bread, hamburger, eggs, marshmallows. He's motivated by one thing: political power.
To separate complete sentences, especially when the second sentence restates or explains the first	Let's eat, drink, and be merry: life is too short for sorrow. He is deferential: he shows respect to his elders.
To introduce a formal quotation	He said: "I will not go."

Semicolon

To separate independent clauses	I dance; I sing.
To separate word groups already divided by commas	When we interviewed him, his life sounded so serious; and yet, when he spoke about acting, he came across as funny and down-to-earth.

Practice 9

Following are two excerpts from student essays. Discuss each of the punctuation marks in these excerpts with your classmates and teacher and decide whether it is appropriate. In addition, look for spots where you think the students should have inserted punctuation and did not.

A

Violent crimes have become commonplace in our society. Murders and rapes have become an everyday affair in most, if not all, of the large cities in the U.S. The criminal justice system has attempted to intervene and handle the problem in the best way possible. For many of the crimes, those which have been judged to be "less serious", the parole system has been established. Plea bargaining is also very common in all courtrooms, offenders who would normally be charged with a felony can, with the help of an astute attorney, bargain with the D.A. and settle for, say a misdemeanor. But, let us examine the "serious" crimes, those that are considered wrong by all members of society; how has the criminal justice system handled them? Life sentences are one way but after a pre-established number of years the inmate can be released on parole; a system made to lessen the burden of the prison population. Thus, we have a convicted criminal back out on the streets because of parole and there is nothing to prevent him from committing other crimes. For those crimes which have been labeled as serious, such as murder and rape, capital punishment should be the solution. Capital justice would be, in effect, a deterrant because it would lessen society's burden of prison expenses and would rectify the present criminal justice system which has proven itself to be inadequate.

B

The presence of violence, nudity and sex on TV programs has long concerned viewers especially parents of young children. Cable television shows many more movies with such elements than regular television. Groups who oppose sex and violence on regular television, have therefore begun to direct their attacks against cable television demanding that the government regulate more strictly the kinds of shows shown. Although I can sympathize with these groups in their feelings about regular television I cannot agree with their desire, to restrict cable television.

At one time someone might have been able to argue, that if you did not like what was on television, you did not have to buy one. That seems like a weak argument now since television is so much a part of everyone's life. Television provides immediate news, culture and education programs, and sports events, which educate and entertain people with no ill effects. If when someone went into a book store they had to buy all the books in the store in order to get the one they wanted, I could understand censorship of books. But no one has to do that, you do have to do that when you buy a television set though. You in a sense bring all its programs into your house. And since it is unreasonable to assume that parents can supervise their children's viewing all the time I can understand, why parents are opposed to sex and violence on regular television. It does not seem fair to tell such parents to give up all television programs, not only are many of them informative, they also make all of us, including children better citizens.

Practice 10

Following are excerpts from published works. Discuss with your classmates the appropriateness of the punctuation in each.

A

It is important to recognise that medieval artists generally shunned innovation, preferring to copy from an authoritative source; and that, even when we do not know what model an artist used, we can recognise in the fall of a garment or placing of a limb that the artist was working within the convention of his day.

> —Gale R. Owen-Crocker, *Dress in
> Anglo-Saxon England* (Manchester
> University Press, 1986), pp. 15-16.

B

Hence, according to Havelock, Greek culture gradually took on the stylistic and cognitive characteristics of literacy as opposed to orality: hypotaxis, the subordination of one idea to another in logical hierarchies; generalizations that appeal to reason and text-assisted memory for validation; and a questioning relationship to authority and custom, encouraging, in place of agonistic combat, the disinterested criticism of ideas.

> —Patricia Bizzell and Bruce Herzberg,
> *The Rhetorical Tradition* (Boston:
> St. Martin's Press, 1990), p. 20.

C

We're not suggesting that you should be satisfied with your current vocabulary; you should try using new words, since this is the only way you're going to add them to your vocabulary. Experiment with words during your early drafts of a piece of writing; this will help develop that intuitive sense of context which you need to have in order to use words properly. However, if the word or words you choose to experiment with are not a part of your vocabulary, you'd be wise to ask your teacher about them before using them in a paper you're planning to submit for grading.

> —Pat Belanoff, Betsy Rorschach, Mia
> Rakijas, Chris Millis, The Right
> Handbook, First Edition
> (Portsmouth, NH: Boynton/Cook, 1986), 168.

D

The campus also contains, by definition, a high concentration of bright and interesting people. Some of these people will become your close friends for a lifetime; others you will admire from a distance as they dazzle the place with their charm and their learning. One definition of a university is "a place where people come together for the precise purpose of disagreeing with one another." College is not just the cornucopia of information and the laboratory of research; it is also the arena of ideas.

> —John N. Gardner and A. Jerome Jewler, eds.
> College is Only the Beginning: A Student
> Guide to Higher Education. 2nd ed.
> (Belmont, CA: Wadsworth, 1989), 26.

E

A family of screeches lives in Axl Rose's throat. One sounds like a chainsaw hitting a railroad spike; another slides and catches like a car alarm on a deserted street; another yowls like a tomcat locked out of a fish store. There's a ratchety quaver, a narrow-eyed low growl, a strangled shriek, a decadent cackle. His voice, the voice of Guns 'n' Roses, is never pretty or endearing; it's a constant irritant. The band would rather stick in the craw than tickle the ear.

> —Jon Pareles, "Guns 'n' Roses Against the
> (Expletive) World," The New York Times
> (Sept. 15, 1991): Section 2, p. 28, Col. 1.

Dashes, Parentheses, and Brackets

Dashes, parentheses, and brackets also set off parts of sentences, but their effect on meaning is different from the effect of commas. (On the typewriter you make a dash with two hyphens.) Dashes say: "Here's some more information which may or may not be essential to my subject right at this moment; in fact, it may even be related to it only tangentially, but it's essential to me that you not skip over this information—look at it!" Dashes may, for example, be used instead of commas if you wish to emphasize what's between them: "He asked—without recognizing the irony of his request—if I could see him." It's also best to use dashes when the group of words delimited by them interrupts natural syntax: "He asked—what an ironic question—if I could see him." Parentheses say: "Here's a bit of extra information on my subject (parentheses) which isn't essential to what I'm saying in this sentence, but it may help you understand me better." We used no parentheses in the transcript since none of the speaker's comments sounded to us like asides (parenthetical remarks). There are, however, brackets around comments we made— the brackets "say" that the comments are ours and not hers.

In the preceding paragraph we used three sets of parentheses to set off asides which acted as explanations (of dashes, of our subject, and of asides). In our transcript you'll notice both dashes and brackets. In line 21, the dash introduces a change in the author's practice— a change she wants to emphasize. In lines 24 and 25, the dashes set off an idea which the speaker doesn't want us to miss. These words were spoken with a slightly sarcastic tone. In line 32, the dash says: "See, notice this." What you'll notice is that the dash here does what the speaker says: it connects the two ideas in this sentence better than a semicolon or comma would. Several sets of brackets in the transcript serve as editorial comments, that is, comments inserted by us (the editors) into the transcript as a way to express what was not said. In lines 10 and 60, the speaker laughs; and in line 36, she pauses. In line 26, the brackets explain who the "she" is; and in line 27, they explain who the "her" is. (You'll notice that just four lines earlier we used parentheses instead of brackets to explain the referent of a pronoun. In this case, we aren't in the middle of quoting someone else and thus don't need brackets to indicate that a different person is expressing the idea. It's still us talking. In the transcript, the context is different.)

Be careful about dashes and parentheses. If you use too many dashes, your readers may feel as though they are being constantly bombarded; and if you use too many parentheses and brackets your readers may become so frustrated they'll be unable to concentrate on your main point since most of your text will be in the form of asides. In the following excerpt, we see problems with the dashes:

> In the first paragraph Gibson, who—as the architext of the 1987 mayoral campaign, when Baltimore elected a black mayor, Kurt L. Schmoke, for the first time in its two hundred-and-sixty-two-year history—is now widely regarded around Baltimore as the city's most influential political strategist, tells a story from an older Baltimore: the Baltimore of the early nineteen-sixties.
>
> —Tony Hiss, "Annals of Place,"
> *The New Yorker* (Apr. 29, 1991), p.40.

Apostrophes

A number of other punctuation conventions also affect meaning— though usually not as drastically as periods, semicolons, colons, and commas. Chief among these are the apostrophe and the hyphen.

The apostrophe is a relative newcomer to our current set of punctuation marks. It performs three functions in written English. The first is to indicate where letters have been omitted in contractions: does not = doesn't; I would = I'd; he is = he's. The second is to show plurals of letters, numbers, symbols, and words used as words: the word *possession* has four *s*'s; Europeans write *7*'s differently from Americans; don't overuse *-*'s; don't capitalize *and*'s in titles; the 1990's will surely be different from the 1980's. (It's also correct not to use the apostrophe in some of these last examples: *7s, ands, 1990s.*) The third function of the apostrophe (and the one which causes writers the most problems) is to show possession. In Old English, possession was indicated by adding an ending to nouns; that ending might have been an *-es,* an *-a,* or an *-ena;* gradually the *-es* ending became the regular sign of possession. Since this represents the same sound that indicates a plural, we can't tell by sound alone the difference between *horses* and *horse's* in the spoken language; we tell the difference by understanding the meaning of a particular sentence, by attending to context. According to the *OED,* in the early part of the eighteenth century the *-e* of the *-es* possessive ending began to be dropped by printers who then used the apostrophe to indicate the omission. As a result, the apostrophe came to represent possession. Others dispute this history, claiming that our apostrophe results from a shortening of the word *his.* In Shakespeare's time, possessive expressions often took the form of "the king his daughter" which meant "the king's daughter." According to this theory the *his* was shortened to an *'s,* and the apostrophe was born. In its original use, then, the apostrophe was what it is today in contractions: an indication of missing letters.

The rule governing the use of the "apostrophe s" is quite simple: if a word representing the person or thing that possesses ends in an *s,* only the apostrophe is added; if the word does not end in an *s,* an *'s* is added. Consequently, we get: the dog's collar = the collar of the dog; the man's umbrella = the umbrella of the man; the men's umbrellas = the umbrellas of the men; the children's toys = the toys of the children; the doctors' office = the office of the doctors, but the doctor's office = the office of the doctor. The only exception to this general rule is for singular words—like *boss*—ending in an *s:* the boss's office = the office of the boss; the bosses' office = the office of the bosses. If you listen to yourself say these two phrases, you'll probably not hear any difference. Since most of us do add an extra *s* in speech when saying "the boss's office," it makes sense to add one in our writing also.

You may have heard, as we have, the -'s used at the end of quite long constructions: for example, "the boy around the corner's sister." Such constructions are much more widely accepted than they were even a few years ago. We suspect that English teachers are not accepting them, but we could be wrong. You might want to try one of these out on your teacher and see what his reaction is. Once you know that, you can decide what to do when you find yourself wanting to write one. You can always say: "The sister of the boy around the corner."

In order to be totally honest with you about the "possessive s" ending, we must admit that it's used in expressions which don't exactly show possession. "A child's unhappiness" means "the child is unhappy," but "a week's unhappiness" doesn't mean "the week is unhappy"; "my daughter's picture" may mean "a picture of my daughter," but it could mean "the picture (of, say, the Grand Canyon) that belongs to my daughter"; and "the man's executioner" certainly does not mean "the man possesses an executioner." We're just pointing this out to you as information; you're not likely to be confused about these expressions since the only other thing the-*s* ending could be on these words is a sign of the plural and that's clearly impossible.

Apostrophes are not "heard" in speech; we hear only the *s* sound; another way of saying this is that apostrophes are solely visual. They signal possession to a reader. This being so, it's not surprising that more and more we see the apostrophe on possessive words where traditionally they were not present: *yours, hers, ours, its, theirs.* Since in each of these forms there's a meaningful word before the *s,* writers (keeping in mind the -'s on nouns) may write *your's, her's, our's, it's, their's.* But we've yet to see *hi's,* and the reason is that *hi* cannot be seen as a word in any context where *his* would be appropriate. The only logical explanation for all this seeming illogic lies in the historical development of the language. Apart from that, "The book is your's" certainly seems as logical as "The book is Janet's." The truth is that language features are often quite arbitrary—at least to a nonlinguist. What you need to do is not use apostrophes on personal pronouns to show possession; save them for your nouns.

This books philosophy (context determines usage) should lead to the conclusion that possessive apostrophes are unnecessary in writing because context will indicate, as it does in speech, whether the -s is a plural or a possessive. (Did you have any trouble in the previous sentence figuring out the difference in meaning between the -s on book and the -s on apostrophe?) Such a conclusion is a logical one, but it isn't a conclusion we're going to make just yet, although we predict that the language is going that way. (As further evidence of the increasing instability in this feature of language, think about the number of signs and advertisements you've seen recently in which 's is used to make a word plural.) We know any number of teachers who consider the omission of the possessive apostrophe to be only a minor sin, but we know of none who approve. And, furthermore, we know many teachers who become indignant when students don't visibly indicate that they know the difference between *its* and *it's,* even though it's a difference which context readily clarifies. And one further thought on this: since we assume that all writing is meant to be read, we need to satisfy a reader's expectations, and almost all readers are accustomed to seeing apostrophes. When they're omitted, a reader may become distracted from what you're saying.

Hyphens

Hyphens and their relation to compound words and phrases can be problems. None of us have difficulty with "sister-in-law," but what about "straitlaced/strait-laced"? You'll see this last one both ways, although current usage is leaning more toward the first form. The only exception to the general trend of combining rather than hyphenating is in words which have a prefix ending with a vowel and a main word beginning with one, although even here practice varies. Consider these: "pre-existing" or "preexisting," "re-enforcement" or "reenforcement"? We've seen all of these forms in print. The only advice we can give you is to use a good dictionary and be consistent. If you don't find a particular combination in your dictionary, chances are you should keep the words separate. But don't be surprised if major dictionaries disagree on some words.

Two-word adjectives (as distinct from those with one word and a prefix) present a slightly different problem. Notice "two-word"; although there are two words, only one thing is being said about the adjectives. This hyphen helps us read correctly; the lack of an *s* on *word* probably helps also. It's highly unlikely that you'll ever see printed "twoword adjectives" or "oneway street." Where misreading is unlikely to occur, the hyphen may disappear: "lefthanded writer," "bluenosed dolphin." Many two-word adjectives, however, are ones joined only rarely: "correction-fluid bottle," "red-handled bicycle." Consider this: the velvet-lined coat may not look the same as the velvet, lined coat. In speech, the way you pronounce this expression will clue your listener into what you mean. A good scheme to help you make decisions requires only that you pay close attention to meaning: is the coat lined with velvet or is it velvet and lined? In other words, do you have one descriptive term or two? If it's only one, the hyphen will help your reader realize that quickly. You can use the dictionary to help you make decisions here also, but obviously the dictionary can't have all combinations. You may find "red-handed" or "redhanded," depending on the dictionary, but you won't find "red-handled" or "redhandled." You're going to have to make your own decision in many cases.

One other, perhaps strange-to-you, use of the hyphen appears in writing. What do you do if you want to write about adjectives made up of two words *and* adjectives made up of three words? Here's how that works: "two- and three-word adjectives." The unconnected hyphen after "two" signals that it's connected to "word" the same way "three" is. You can avoid this peculiarity by writing: "adjectives made up of two or three words." We mention this construction because sometimes you can't avoid it and sometimes you may find it useful (and, besides, we've used it a number of times in this book). Perhaps you will too in one of the four-, five-, or six-page essays you're writing this semester.

Failure to use a hyphen in "two-word" probably won't bother most readers under any circumstances. Still, we think that awareness of the difference between a velvet, lined coat and a velvet-lined coat is valuable because it makes you attentive to a reader's needs. This convention applies also to adjectives made up of more than two words: "Her devil-may-care attitude will get her into trouble some day; it's almost as bad as his I-don't-give-a-damn attitude"; and to fractions before nouns: "a one-third share of the profits." Compound numbers from twenty-one to ninety-nine also require the hyphen. Numbers above that are usually written as numbers, not words.

We've been talking so far about two-word-or-more adjectives that come directly before the nouns they modify. If, instead, the adjectives follow a verb, you don't need the hyphen: "The coat is velvet lined"; we're not likely to read this to mean that the coat is velvet *and* lined. Still, many writers keep this hyphen even though most grammar books don't advise it. The hyphen in a fraction usually disappears too when the fraction is the subject of a sentence: "One third of the profit belongs to me."

Underlining (Italics)

Since here we're mainly concerned with conventions that offer writers choices, we've covered most uses of italics (underlining in typing) in Chapter 7, "Mechanics." We don't have any choice about whether to underline a title. The underlining that we can choose to use or not use is the underlining which serves to create emphasis. We've done that (italicized) in a number of places in this book. To see an example, look back at line 8 in our transcript on page 94:

> Convention doesn't say anything about anything else, really, not when you get right down to what you *have* to have.

We italicized the verb *have* to give it emphasis because we heard the speaker say it with exceptional stress. Sometimes when we "hear" what we're writing (in our inner ear), we also feel the stress on certain words. Here's a sentence from our discussion on fragments on page 41:

> Such resupplying of missing elements must require *no additional effort* on the part of a reader or listener; if he has to consciously work out what any missing elements are, communication is disrupted.

Needless to say, we need to be stingy about such use: underlining (italicizing) *can* be used for *emphasis,* but when *overused* it *obviously* becomes *ineffective.*

Quotation Marks

Most of the rules governing the use of quotation marks, like those governing italicizing (underlining), allow us no choices. You can read about these uses in Chapter 7. Here, we'll concern ourselves only with quotation marks that affect meaning. Their most common use is to show where an exact quotation begins and ends. Quoted words can be introduced by a comma or a colon; the colon suggests that what follows is a formal or crucial statement. Notice the colon in line 5 of our transcript at the beginning of this chapter:

> Convention says: "Every sentence must have a period."

If you don't want the quoted words to seem too formal or decisive, a comma is better. You'll see this in line 29 of the transcript:

> But, you know, parentheses sort of say to me, "This isn't really important. . . ."

If quoted words flow easily into the sentence which holds them, they don't need any punctuation mark to introduce them:

> The judge called the crime "pernicious, atrocious, and abhorrent."

For more on integrating quoted words into your writing and examples of doing so, see Chapter 9, "Research."

Punctuation marks following quotations are governed by quite arbitrary rules. American stylebooks recommend that periods appear inside quotation marks, but you've probably read, as we have, books in which periods appear outside quotation marks, which are single, rather than double. This is the style used by the British. If you opt for the latter, be consistent—and check with your teacher first. Question marks and exclamation points go inside quotation marks only if they're part of what is being quoted; otherwise they belong outside. If the structure of your sentence requires a semicolon or a colon that is not part of the quoted material, it belongs outside the quotation marks. If the structure of your sentence as you write it calls for a comma at the end of a quotation, you have the same choice as you have with a period, but we recommend, as American stylebooks do, that you keep them inside. Again, whatever you do, be consistent.

Another use of quotation marks that is more integral to meaning is their use to indicate to a reader that the word or words within them are either too formal or too informal for their context. The quotation marks show that the writer knows this, but cannot find—or doesn't believe there is—an effective substitute. In practice, we've noticed that most students enclose in quotation marks, not formal words, but informal words, words they consider slang. We're not opposed to this stratagem; sometimes there's no other word or words which can create the desired effect. But it's mind-stretching to try to find substitutes on occasion. You may discover that the attempt to do so forces you to get closer to your meaning. One of our students, in a paper about *The Mill on the Floss,* wrote:

> Maggie's desire for knowledge has subsequently engaged her in a difficult situation. She is constantly being criticized for her action. She is not precocious but her manner is obviously "out of sync" with her society's norms.

The writer recognized that "out of sync" is inappropriate for its context. She tried rewriting the sentence in several ways:

> She is not precocious but her manner is obviously out of place in her society.

> She is not precocious but her manner is obviously not in tune with her times.

> She is not precocious but her manner is obviously unacceptable to her society.

> She is not precocious but her behavior is obviously uncoordinated with the norms of her society.

She finally decided on the following replacement:

> She is not precocious, but her behavior cannot be understood by others because it doesn't follow society's norms.

This sentence, in addition to being stylistically in keeping with its context, actually says more than the sentence it replaced.

Quotation marks can also serve to identify words you don't want the reader to take in their usual sense because their usual meaning is, to you, not valid in their present context. Consider: the government selected an "impartial" jury. The quotation marks tell a reader that this is a so-called impartial jury, that someone else might consider it impartial, but the writer doesn't.

Suggestions

We suggested at the beginning of this section that you get someone to mark your text as you read it aloud. Now that you've identified all the possible spots for punctuation marks and made decisions about which, if any, marks to use, you need to read your paper aloud again. Let your reading be guided by the punctuation you've inserted. If you have problems doing this, you'll have more thinking to do. We believe that a semester—maybe less—of looking at punctuation this way will result in better instinctive use of punctuation as you write. Eventually, you should only have to check carefully those features of punctuation use which you have come to recognize as most troublesome to you—comma splices or apostrophes, for example.

We believe (and there's research which supports our belief) that if a piece of writing actively engages a reader's mind so that her sole interest is to follow the train of thought being presented by a writer, she becomes unaware of the niceties of punctuation. She then accepts almost any style of punctuation which doesn't disrupt her attention to meaning. If, however, someone—usually an English teacher—reads your paper just to assess technical features (such as punctuation, subject-verb agreement, and spelling), you're going to have to deal with that teacher in some way. That may mean becoming quite attentive to punctuation while you're proofreading. But don't misinterpret us; we're not saying "Anything goes." Becoming aware of how punctuation affects the meaning of what you write will improve your punctuation skills, but—more importantly—it will improve your ability to communicate meaning. You probably have figured out yourself while going through the examples we've given you that what starts out looking like a need to alter punctuation ends up being a need to rewrite. It's in this sense that "rules" can actually be heuristic: they stimulate additional thought.

Practice 11

Read the following excerpts from students' papers and discuss with your classmates and teacher all the apostrophes. You should also look for places where the writers should have used apostrophes and didn't.

A

It is a cloudy day in Clarksville, but the sun has managed to peek through the opening of the great cotton cloud wall. It's rays filter through the leaves of the noble trees which ramble on endlessly over the rolling hills.

B

Regarding the matter of Socrates's atheism, it is within the vested powers of this court to hold a citizen guilty of blasphemy as defined by the publics' denunciation of the existence of the gods.

C

Instead of going to parties, I find myself cooking. Instead of talking on the phone I find myself cleaning my apartment that is downstairs in the basement of my parent's house.

D

I've been a father for a month's time now. I start to realize how much the birth of James' has changed my life.

E

Even your avid golfer is unaware of the charm golf courses' retain during off-peak hours. I always enjoy lounging on the lush Kentucky Bluegrass turf, perhaps Long Island's finest lawn.

F

The station is pretty empty. A man is asleep on a bench against the wall. Two women are talking about that days' shopping. . . . My feet ache under the pressure of my body, more after a hard days work. I look to the left across the tracks, to the downtown trains' platform.

G

However, as strange as it may seem, I would willingly repeat the most difficult episode of my life while enjoying its every second.

H

In the first two months, we had to live in my mother's friend's house since we could not find any house for rent until two months' later.

I

My parents divorced when I was a year and a half old. At the time I was too young to understand why it was happening or who's fault it was.

J

The first thing I would consider when looking at a neighborhood is location. My neighborhood is found in the very clean, safe area of Anderson Township. Near doctors offices, hospitals, grocery stores, a large shopping mall, and a variety of churches, my neighborhood would be considered to be very convenient.

K

When I first wrote this paper it was a one-on-one dialogue. The paper gave the impression that Richie was a real klutz, maybe even a dingbat. As I revised the paper, I justified some of the reasons why Rickie sometimes acted the way he did. In the revision I also added outsiders' opinions toward different situations.

L

It sits at the departure gate like a giant bird. It's motionless as its being serviced by the work crew. The plane seems like it's some kind of god, or protector, and the work crew is worshipping it through this ritual. The luster of its' sleek, large body shines as the sun glitters off it. The Concord's engines are the largest on any jumbo jet in the world, making its predecessors' engines seem small and weak.

M

When one is little, dance is for fun and for the love of it. When one becomes older, dancing becomes time consuming and competitive. One becomes so involved in dancing that nothing else matters. One's life is dance; its all that matters. When dance becomes competitive, its joy goes.

Practice 12

Read the following excerpts (some from student papers, some from published pieces) and discuss with your teacher and classmates the appropriateness of the punctuation— particularly the dashes, parentheses, brackets, apostrophes, hyphens, and quotation marks.

A

The primary focus in my culture today is money whether people admit it or not. Everything in my culture revolves around money. It is not sufficient to say that people in my culture value money as a means of obtaining the "necessities" of life—food, clothing, and shelter. People value money as a means of obtaining the modern-day "necessities"—an expensive sports' car, an elaborate summer home, or designer clothes. People abuse money and feel that without it, they cannot be happy, popular, or successful. Money has turned my culture into a power-hunger culture where money is the root of all evil.

—from a student paper

B

In the tradition of pulp science fiction the galaxy of Captain Kirk was full of women, and he went for all of them. He romanced courtesans in parallel universes and Joan Collins in earth's past (she was a decorous young social worker during the Depression). He fell for a pretty young android, and didn't even care when he found out what she was. And he cast his eye on attractive yeomen (yeowomen, actually, but Kirk, in naval tradition, I suppose, liked to call them mister) in a way that would clearly be considered sexual harassment on "The Next Generation."

Not that the new show is without sex. For instance: Why does the zaftig counselor Deanna Troi wear such a low-cut uniform? (This may also come under the heading of pajamas.) To be more precise, and Spock-like, let me say that I do understand the principle of low-cut dresses; my question is: Why is the *shrink* the only crew member with decolletage?

> —James Gorman,
> "'Star Trek': It's a Wonderful Galaxy,"
> *The New York Times* (September 15, 1991):
> Section 2, p. 29, Col. 1-2.

C

In his initial "obsession" with Mangan's sister, it is apparent to the narrator that he has found true-love—even though he is more "in love with her sanctified image" than with her actual self, "doting" over his "inamorata". Watching her door and waiting by her window, he seems *truly* in love with her, a love which he feels is genuine. His foster father [or more accurately his uncle]—even though he had been reminded several times of his nephew's desire to go to the bazarre, replies curtly, and obviously does not listen and cares very little about the narrator's wishes.

> —from a student paper

D

Our Chesterfield sofa from Old Hickory Tannery of North Carolina is an authentic 18th century reproduction. Made with eight-way, hand tied construction and fully padded frame, covered in the finest aniline-dyed leather that will actually improve with age and that's soft to the touch. Handtailored by expert craftsmen, the rolled arms, deep-button tufting and brass nail-head trim create a classic look that has stood the test of time.

> —from an advertising brochure for
> The Horchow Home Collection,
> Volume X891, p. 4.

E

Even if the St. Louis Cardinals, the masterly users of that user-unfriendly ball park on the banks of the Mississippi, change their turf, so to speak, Joe Torre promises they won't change their modus operandi.

—Claire Smith, "On Baseball,"
The New York Times (Aug. 21, 1991),
p. B13, col. 1.

F

The student notes from David Masson's course, for example, do not vary over thirty years by more than an occasional word or two. Robert Schmitz tells the story of students who were following Masson's lecture from sets of previous years' notes. They objected to changes in the lectures and when Masson deviated from their copies, they would shuffle their feet in protest, whereupon Masson, rising, would remark: "Gentlemen . . . , as I have been in the habit of saying" and would return to his previous years' notes. J. D. Comrie writes about the lectures delivered by the three Munros—father, son, and grandson—who held the Chair of Anatomy at the University of Edinburgh for 150 years.

—Winifred Bryan Horner,
"Writing Instruction in Great Britain:
Eighteenth and Nineteenth
Centuries," in *A Short History of
Writing Instruction* (Davis, CA:
Hermagoras Press, 1990), p. 142.

G

When the narrator of *Njal's Saga* says of Hallgerd that she is impetuous and willful, he is giving us simply and directly the keys to her character. All her later actions are derived from these two principles of impetuosity and willfulness plus her tendency to dishonesty which is also presented simply and directly through a character named Hrut (who is, we are told, "always reliable in matters of importance"). Hrut remarks in the opening passage of the saga that Hallgerd has "thief's eyes." These attributes, together with a crucial physical detail—her long, blond hair—are all we need for apprehending her character completely.

—Robert Scholes and Robert Kellogg,
The Nature of Narrative (New York:
Oxford UP, 1966), pp. 171–72.

H

Strawberry, responding to the biggest challenge of his first year with Los Angeles, had a bat—or feet—in each of the first four runs the

Dodgers scored tonight as they defeated Atlanta, 5–2, and leap-frogged back into first place in the National League West. After a three-day stay in first, the Braves slipped half a game behind the Dodgers, their winning streak ended at seven games.

This was the first game of the first of a pair of consecutive-weekend three-game series between the contenders, and it was as dramatic as a pennant-race game should be.

—Murray Chass,
"Dar-ryl, Dar-ryl Puts on a Show for
Braves' Fans," *The New York
Times* (September 14, 1991): p. 27,
col. 5.

Chapter Five

Phrases

If you've got your sentence endings marked, the punctuation aptly placed, and segments of the sentence arranged in an order which helps develop your meaning clearly, you can begin to consider some features which interfere very little with meaning but loom large in most readers' awareness. The first of these is subject-verb agreement.

Subject-Verb Agreement

What is usually meant by agreement is that singular subjects belong with singular verbs, and plural subjects belong with plural verbs. That sounds simple, perhaps, but it isn't quite that simple. For example: *I* is certainly a singular subject, and *we* and *they* are certainly plural subjects, but usage demands that all be followed by the same form: *I jump; we jump; they jump. You* can either be singular or plural, but it's always followed by the same verb form regardless of whether it represents one person or more: *you jump.* The only singular subjects which are followed by a different present-tense verb form are words for which *it, he,* or *she* can be substituted: *the dog jumps, the boy jumps, the girl jumps.*

You probably have realized yourself that the *-s* (or *-es*) ending is not necessary for meaning; and, in fact, it's virtually nonexistent in certain speech communities in the United States. The disappearance of this suffix would be in keeping with previous language change. Whatever the fate of this *-s* in the future, its nonpresence (as in *the girl jump*) is still considered nonstandard by most teachers and probably by most other speakers of English in this country. If you're a member of one of those speech communities who don't use this -*s*, and if you want to adhere in writing to standard usage, be sure to get someone outside your speech community (or someone inside it who has found a way to alter his speech if he wishes) to proofread your papers. Once that person has added the *s*'s, read your paper out loud giving unnatural stress to the added *s* sounds; in this way you may be able to train your ear; it's your ear that will eventually guide you in adding the *s*'s yourself. You can't be thinking about this suffix and writing at the same time; the mind can only focus on meaning while writing. You'll have to check the need for the *s*'s after you write.

Those who don't use an -*s* on verbs are speakers of a dialect which varies verb form only to show past tense and to create participles. The invariant form in the present tense has no *s* ending; therefore, third-person singular and plural forms are the same. Consonant with this rule, a number of irregular verbs also are the same for third-person singular and plural subjects. Deviation from standard usage is particularly evident in three heavily used verbs in our language: *have, do,* and *go.* Members of this speech community may write "she do," "she go," and "she have" rather than "she does," "she goes," and "she has." Correcting such deviations from standard usage takes close reading. If you're a member of this speech community, you'll need to locate every use of *do, go,* and *have* in your writing and check to make certain the subject in each case is plural. Again, reading the corrected sentences aloud—perhaps several times—will begin training your ear to catch these linkages.

Quite a few of the subject-verb problems we're going to talk about can be avoided by rewriting. The -*s* (or -*es*) ending can't be avoided. It simply isn't possible to write very much of anything in our language without using a third-person singular verb. Therefore, if you have this problem, this is what you should concentrate on in terms of conforming, when you wish, your usage to standard usage. It will also probably be the hardest adjustment you'll need to make. Don't be discouraged if it takes time to learn to use the standard forms in your writing; it's difficult for anyone to alter something as basic as verb forms in his native speech. But these verb forms are ones you're going to need to use often, so the extra effort you exert to master them is worth it. Eventually, you'll be able to switch back and forth whenever you wish from your native-dialect forms to standard forms.

The most concise rule for standard English usage in the matter of subject-verb agreement is that, in the present tense, all English verbs, except modal verbs, end in an *s* when the subject is third-person singular. Modal verbs are invariant in form: *can, may, might, would, will, could, shall, should, must.*

Indefinite Pronouns

Sometimes, however, it isn't easy to decide whether a subject is singular or plural.

A number of indefinite pronouns (some, any, most, all, none) can be singular or plural depending on whether it's some, for example, of a single unit or some of a group of countable items or people. If you've used one of these words and are trying to decide whether to use a singular or a plural verb, look first to see if your indefinite pronoun is followed by an of phrase. Then look at the noun at the end of that phrase to see whether it's singular or plural. Even though this noun is not technically the subject of the verb, it can tell you whether the verb should be singular or plural.

Some of the people are here.	None of the people are here.
Some of the soup has been eaten.	None of the soup has been eaten.

If an of phrase is not explicit, you'll have to determine the form of the verb on the basis of what the indefinite pronoun refers to. If you can't decide what that is, you can stop worrying about the verb form and focus directly on clarifying your meaning. Usually, of course, you'll know whether the indefinite pronoun refers to something singular or plural.

Some have been eaten.	None have been eaten.
Some has been eaten.	None has been eaten.

All the sentences are correct. In the first of each pair we assume that what has been eaten (or not eaten) is countable—bananas, perhaps, or cookies, or carrots; in the second, we assume that the writer has in mind a single unit—like a pie or an apple. If our assumptions don't suit the context, we're going to be puzzled.

Other indefinite pronouns, in current usage, are always connected to singular verbs. (None used to be in this group; some teachers and writers still place it here.) These include each, every, everyone, either, neither, one. How can you remember these and keep them separate from the group we talked about in the last paragraph? You can try memorizing or you can just keep this book handy. Some of our students say that creating an acronym (SAMAN) out of the first group has helped them. Another clue: This second group of words can be used only before singular words: each letter, either word, neither sentence, one paragraph, every essay. In fact, the force of every is so strongly singular (think about the logic of that!) that we've all heard the expression: "Every man, woman, and child is. . . ."

Obviously many people are being referred to, but the verb is still singular. The words in the SAMAN group, with one exception— *none*—can appear before plural words: *some letters, any syllables, most phrases, all essays.* This distinction helps explain why *none* (a shortening of *no one*) was originally a member of group two: we can say *no one person,* but not *no one persons.* (Now that we've brought this up, *no one* belongs in the *each* group of indefinite pronouns.)

Collective Nouns

We related the problem we discuss in the last paragraph to pronouns, but certain nouns also cause a similar kind of subject-verb problem. We call these nouns "collective nouns": nouns which are singular in form (they have no-s ending) but plural in meaning; *class, troop, committee* are some samples. When choosing a verb to go with these, base your decision on form, not meaning; in other words, use a singular verb.

> A group of us goes to the beach every Sunday.

> The jury has come to a decision.

Other collective nouns pose the same sort of ambiguity as indefinite pronouns. For example:

> A majority of the class is passing.

> A majority of the people are satisfied.

Notice that in making a decision here, you can again look at the word in the *of* phrase and use it as a guide. If your sentence has no *of* phrase, simply ask yourself: "What is this a majority of?" If your answer is a singular word, use the singular verb; if your answer is a plural word, use the plural verb. If you have no answer, you have a different problem.

Neither-nor; Either-or

When *neither* is used with *nor,* and *either* with *or,* a special usage rule takes over:

> Neither he nor they are rational.

> Neither they nor he is rational.

The rule is that the verb should be linked to the part of the subject closer to it. *They* is closer in the first example and *he* in the second.

Perhaps it's simpler for you to ignore the *nor* (or *or*) and all the words before it and rely upon your ear. Your ear will reject *they is rational* and *he are rational*. So you see, there's something rational about this rule after all.

There, Where in Subject Position

In fact, your ear is usually a good guide to accepted usage. Continuous oral exposure to standard language leads us to expect certain verb forms after certain subject forms. At times, though, our ear can betray us into nonstandard usage. This occurs usually when verbs and subjects are not in their usual order or are widely separated. We said many pages ago that in *there* constructions the verb comes before the subject. Since in sentences such as these, our ear has not yet heard a subject (it has heard only the word *there* which has a singular air to it), we often follow *there* by the singular form *is*. Such sentences as: "There is my sister and brother" or, what's more likely: "There's my sister and brother," may well not disturb your ear at all—in which case you'll feel no need for correction. Those of you who discover via your teacher's comments that he looks for this error may need to proofread very carefully, specifically looking for the word *there* and then checking the agreement of subject and verb. Sentences which start with *here* may cause errors also. In fact, any sentence—other than questions or orders—in which the verb precedes the subject may muddle your natural language ability. We're used to hearing subjects and creating expectations for verb forms as a result. When we don't hear a subject, our expectations may lead us to the wrong conclusions. This is probably the reason why one of our students started a sentence: "Not only does my brother and sister argue all the time. . . ." In questions, *where* can create the problem: "Where's your mother and father?" instead of "Where are your mother and father?"

WHAT in Subject Position

Sentences or clauses that begin with *what* also have a way of tricking our ears and causing us to question whether verbs which follow the *what* should be singular or plural. Unlike *there* and *here* which are adverbs, *what* is a pronoun and *can* act as subject of a sentence. Used as a subject, *what* is always singular—unless the sentence gives us clues otherwise. Ordinarily this causes no confusion at all:

What's (what is) for dinner?

What are your reasons for not wanting to go?

Of course, we could also say:

> What is your reason for not wanting to go?

When *what* introduces a clause which then serves as the subject of a following verb, problems can occur. In fact we uncovered just such a problem as we revised the first edition of this handbook. In the section on comma splices (page 101), we had written:

> What are connected by comma splices are two complete sentences.

We have corrected this sentence in this second edition to read:

> What is connected by comma splices is two complete sentences.

The subject of the first *is* in the sentence is *what* and, as we stated above, convention dictates that *what* be singular almost all the time. The subject of the second *is* is the whole clause *what is connected by comma splices* and, since this is one clause, it has to be singular.

Here's a published example of this same convention:

> What stirred the Tories into action in 1987 was three things.
>
> —Julian Barnes, *The New Yorker*
> (Jan. 7, 1991): 62.

Compound Subjects

In general, sentences with a compound subject require a plural verb: "Tom and Jerry are animals." (A compound subject is made up of two or more subjects connected by *and.*) Certain combinations of words, although having the form of a compound subject, are singular in sense. With these, standard usage allows a singular verb: "Peanut butter and jelly is my favorite sandwich at lunch"; "Duty and devotion to country is admirable." If compound subjects like these are singular in meaning to you, you'll use a singular verb. Chances are, if your sentence is otherwise satisfactory, no one—except the strictest of eagle-eyed grammarians—will notice. In an interpretation of a folktale, one of our students wrote:

> As for the lesson or message being conveyed, complete conformity
> and dependency on any institution is dangerous and deprives one
> of individuality.

The subject is compound; the verbs are singular. Most readers will not question either *is* or *deprives.*

The following sentence from a student paper exemplifies a similar error:

The constant reminder of a disaster and the mention of the records of floods in the past gives us enough warning so we are not surprised at the ending.

By the time the writer wrote "gives," she had forgotten (apparently) that she had started the sentence with a compound subject. The subject-verb-object core of this sentence is: "reminder . . . and . . . mention . . . gives . . . warning." Later on in the same paper the student wrote:

The image of the boat floating down the river and the illusion of departing souls in death expresses what happens to the characters in the flood.

See if you can locate the subject-verb-object core of this sentence and make the necessary correction. Once you've made the correction, think about what might have caused the writer to make the error. If you discover that you make similar errors, you're going to have to be attentive to all your *and*'s.

Your ear can also mislead you into a usage error when the verb doesn't follow the subject immediately—the farther away it is, the less likely your ear can help. In the following sentence, taken from a student paper about *Jude the Obscure*, the subject is separated from its verb by twelve words:

The continuous warnings in the beginning of the story about something bad happening to Jude accounts for our sense of foreboding doom.

Perhaps because several singular words come between the subject and verb, the student's sense of the pluralness of the subject faded by the time he got to the verb, "accounts." If you make this sort of usage error, you're going to have to do meticulous proofreading. First, you'll need to locate the subject of each sentence. Second, you'll need to see if a verb directly follows it. If it does (and you're a native speaker), it will probably be correct. If the verb doesn't follow immediately, you'll need to look for it. Once you've found it, you can check agreement. We've spoken often in this book of the importance of the subject-verb unit. Listeners and readers expect sentences to have both. Once they've heard or seen a word which they think is a subject, they hold this word somewhere in their memory, waiting for the verb that goes with it. If a verb occurs which doesn't fit with the subject, these listeners or readers are apt to be puzzled—at least, momentarily. And even momentary puzzlement on the part of your audience can interrupt communication.

Compound Verbs

Also leading to slips in usage is a slightly different kind of subject-verb separation, one created when a subject performs more than one action, as in this sentence:

> The young man next enters all the stores on the east side of the block and purchase one item.

Perhaps by the time the writer wrote "and," he lost the sense of singular in "man," and so wrote "purchase." This violates standard usage. Finding such usage errors requires close reading—perhaps you'll simply have to look for all verbs which follow and and and consciously match them to their subjects.

Dependent Clauses with Relative Pronouns

Verbs in dependent clauses which have relative pronouns as subjects must agree with the antecedent of the relative pronoun (the word to which the pronoun refers).

> Here are the papers which need editing.

The antecedent of "which" (the subject of the dependent clause) is "papers" and, since "papers" is plural, the verb "need" must be plural also. Probably the only time you'll make a usage error in this construction is if the word one is used.

> This is one of the papers which need editing.

"One" is not the antecedent of "which"; "papers" is. Think about it. How many papers need editing? One or more? When the word only sneaks into this sort of construction, the verb must change.

> This is the only one of the papers which needs editing.

In the following sentence from a paper on decision-making, the student got into trouble with a verb in a relative clause because the clause is separated by intervening words from what it modifies:

> The kid should make his own decision because he is the one and not his parents who are going to have to live with it.

The relative clause ("who are going to have to live with it") modifies "one," not "parents"; therefore, the verb in the relative clause should be "is," not "are."

If you find yourself unable to make a decision about a verb form because your particular sentence doesn't seem to be like any of the samples we've used, you have two choices: you can ask a friendly reader or you can rewrite your sentence in some way that makes the decision easier to make or no longer necessary.

Double Negatives

Subject-verb agreement mandates that you notice how two or more words work together in a sentence; negation—the addition of any word which reverses the meaning of what it's added to—also requires that you attend to how two words work together. Current academic usage supports the view that two negatives shouldn't be used together unless the speaker or writer intends a positive statement, as in "It's not unlikely that . . ." (a stuffy way to say "It's possible that . . ."). But, if you applied this mathematical rule strictly to all double negatives, you'd conclude that "Don't you never do that to me again!" means the speaker wants the person addressed to do "that" again—yet it's highly unlikely anyone would understand these words that way.

Such a prohibition has only been in existence since the middle of the eighteenth century. The following lines from Shakespeare's *Twelfth Night* demonstrate that he had no qualms about multiple negatives:

> I have one heart, one bosom and one truth,
> And that no woman has; nor never none
> Shall mistress be of it.

Although we suspect that most teachers still frown on double negatives, we also suspect that their disapproval is not based on a belief that such usage actually confuses meaning. Few of us would misinterpret the following "double negative" which appeared in a student's paper about the minimum wage:

> It wouldn't decrease unemployment among students neither.

The negatives serve here as those did in the Shakespearean line: they intensify the inaction. Despite the fact that none of us are going to misread this sentence, none of us are going to consider it acceptable in academic writing either.

Sentences which contain a number of negatives are difficult to read even if technically they do not contain a "double negative." See how you do with deciphering the following sentences:

> Not only did he not speak up in support of me, he did not even appear at the hearing.

No one is not going to speak up in defense of negating an increased emphasis on arms build-up.

Those who are not going to the picnic should not pick up travel directions.

Now, we know that none of these sentences may be inappropriate (that is, each may be appropriate) in context, but they *are* difficult to understand at first reading. Our advice is to be aware of the risk you may be taking when you expect your readers to do too many about-faces: they may think you're saying the opposite of what you mean to say. This isn't to say that you should never write sentences like the three we used as examples; after all, readers need to do some work also. And, besides, sometimes the negatively worded sentence is the most effective one: if someone is worried about whether there are enough copies of travel directions and if he's speaking to a group which includes some people who are *not* going to the picnic, he will probably say:

Those who are not going to the picnic should not pick up travel directions.

Writers get into trouble with negatives mostly when they use the words *nothing* or *none* or *no one.* If you have been criticized by teachers for using double negatives, we advise you to be particularly aware of these words. The best advice we can give is to use the words *anything* or *any* or *anyone* if you've already used a negative in a sentence. "I don't want nothing" becomes "I don't want anything"; "He didn't want no one to inspect the records" becomes "He didn't want anyone to inspect the records." Naturally, there are many other combinations of words that create double negatives, so you'll have to inspect what you write carefully in order to find all such slips. Two other words to be particularly on guard against are *hardly* and *scarcely,* since these are negatives also: "I hardly bought nothing" and "He scarcely never gives me help." These sentences should be corrected to: "I hardly bought anything " and "He scarcely ever gives me help."

Double Comparisons

Something else current usage frowns on is the "double comparison." In English we can show degrees of modification by using *-er* and *-est* endings: "He is taller; she is tallest"; or *more* and *most:* "He is more confident; she is most confident." In general, current usage prefers that -*er* and -*est* be used on one- or two-syllable words; with other words *more* and *most* are preferred. Notice the examples we used in this paragraph; they follow these principles. Current usage is far more dictatorial when it comes to forbidding the use of both methods at the same time: "He is more happier." Again, such a prohibition was not always in effect. Witness another line by Shakespeare, from The Tempest:

> nor that I am more better / than Prospero

One other academic preference in this matter: most teachers prefer that writers use -*er* and *more* when two people or things are being compared and -*est* and *most* when more than two are compared: "The sky is blu*er* than the ocean." "Of the three of them, she's the strong*est.*" Strict grammarians will probably also expect you to complete comparisons: "The grass is greener here *than on the other side of the fence.*" "He is better dressed *than most young men.*" Some teachers extend this rule to include expressions which contain *too* or *so:* "It's too hot *to stay in the sun.*" "It's so hot *that I can't stay in the sun.*"

Split Infinitives

Our attitude toward split infinitives is the same as our attitude toward ending sentences with a preposition: we don't understand why anyone would care, since we can think of no way in which either affects anyone's ability to communicate written meaning. So, all we're going to do here is tell you what a split infinitive is. An infinitive is the base form of a verb (the verb with no ending) preceded by the word *to: to see, to feel, to believe,* and so forth. To split an infinitive is to, according to purists, wrongly insert a word or words between the *to* and the base verb. Here's a nice one embedded in words which may be familiar to some of you:

> Space—the final frontier. These are the voyages of the spaceship Enterprise—its five-year mission to explore strange new worlds, to

seek out new civilizations, *to boldly go* where no one has gone before.

Perhaps the writer of this could have said "boldly to go" or "to go boldly," but we don't think either is as effective as "to boldly go."

Sometimes infinitives have to be split or else meaning will be sacrificed:

> They tried *to further encourage* successful encounters between rival gangs.

Moving the word *further* distorts the meaning of the sentence:

> They tried *further to encourage* successful encounters between rival gangs.

> They tried *to encourage further* successful encounters between rival gangs.

Here's another where the infinitive cannot be unsplit:

> He wants *to fully uncover* secret activities.

Moving the adverb would give us sentences which don't mean the same thing as our sentence with the split:

> He wants *fully to uncover* secret activities.

> He wants *to uncover fully* secret activities.

Most of the time, though, judgments on split infinitives reflect personal preferences. We think the following sound awful:

> He asked me *to hurriedly depart.*

> All candidates prefer *to, if possible, advertize* during prime time.

But these don't bother us at all:

> Some rules are difficult *to fully understand.*

> We need *to firmly establish* the ground rules.

The truth about split infinitives is that you're not likely to write ones that seem awful to you. But if you need to satisfy a teacher who penalizes you for all split infinitives, you'll have to track them down. Our suggestion is that if you don't like what your sentence sounds like after you unsplit the infinitive, rewrite the entire sentence.

Practice 13

Following are excerpts from students' writing. Read them and discuss with your classmates and teacher those spots which you think contain errors in standard English.

A

My childhood was very different from most kids. When I was born, my lungs wasn't really developed, so I was in and out of hospitals till I was 7. I couldn't scarcely walk until I was almost four and had to mostly stay in a respirator even at home. I attended a grammar school called St. Brendan's from grades one through eight. I didn't hardly mind that I was in a catholic school though the neighborhood kids all went to public school and seemed to have more fun than me. It was particularly hard for me as a boy who was small and weak for so many years. I always remember the school playground as a place where the weak are exploited, made fun of, and even beaten by the strong who wants to maintain superiority.

B

I learned some hard lessons when I dropped out of high school and hung around with the wrong people. As an almost school dropout, it would be necessary to mention a commentary on problems faced by dropouts such as drug use and unemployment which play such a crucial role in the course of one's life. . . . The average mom and dad today holds two jobs just to make ends meet; it doesn't help none when one of their kids is unemployed and out of school. Our culture believes that dropping out of school, welfare, and stealing is wrong. My dad's a great guy who kept me from those things; even though I didn't do nothing right for months, he stuck by me. For a while, he tried to talk me into going into the army. I almost did that; after all the soldier and the flag is what has made this country so great. But I finally decided I'd rather go to college. I'm luckier that way than lots of other kids I know. Now I'm working hard to slowly improve my grades and looking forward to graduation.

C

In Bloom's book, *The Closing of The American Mind*, on young people and books, he made several points based on his own observations and beliefs. For example, one of his points were, " . . . students have lost the practice of and the taste for reading. They have not learned how to read, nor do they have the expectation of delight or improvement form reading." On the surface, Blooms' arguments and reasoning sounds plausible, but, when examined fully, flaws and generalizations are seen.

D

Each vendor is an expert in their field and are prepared to provide goods which meet the highest standards. One of those vendors who have agreed to participate in the show manufactures the best-selling product in their field.

E

Contemporary plays are indicative of the thinking of the times. They give insight into the problems, interests, concerns, and controversies of modern society. Contemporary plays also reveal much about our humanity. They not only reveal our dark sides, but also expose our positive nature, and the source and form of our humor. Where we stand on the issues of good and evil are also exposed through the theater.

Pronouns

Proper choice of pronouns also requires, in most instances, that you understand the interaction of words in what you write and that you read *exactly* what you write. But pronouns are much trickier than the other choices we've discussed so far in this section, as you can see in the sentence below (from a faculty memo):

> Faculty that has been employed at the college on a fulltime basis for 2 years or more has a choice of 50% of their courses being evaluated, and are notified by mail and/or telephone and asked to choose.

At first, the writer used *faculty* as a singular noun ("Faculty . . . *has*"), but the plural meaning of *their* influenced her next verb choice so that *faculty* suddenly shifts into plural ("and *are*"). The writer may have been trying to avoid sexist language (*their* instead of *she* or *he*), but her choice here controlled her next decision, despite what she'd done at the beginning of the sentence. If she had carefully reread her memo, she'd have noticed the shift and then figured out a less confusing way to phrase her meaning.

Certain choices involving pronouns receive a lot of unwarranted concern and attention. Should you say "This is I" or "This is me"? At the beginning of the book, if you remember, we spoke of the number of letters "Dear Abby" has gotten about this choice. Should you say "Who are you going with?" or "Whom are you going with?" A strict grammarian would argue for *I* in the first of these pairs and *whom* in the second. The reason is somewhat complicated, but boils down to the idea that certain pronouns, as a result of their linguistic history, serve as subjects in sentences while others serve as objects. However, what is considered proper is evolving, so that many handbooks now recognize both alternatives in the illustrations here as equally legitimate. (Actually, the strictest grammarians would probably frown on the final preposition and insist on: "With whom are you going?")

Language experts disagree about how to define what a pronoun is. The traditional definition is that it's a word which replaces a noun; recently, experts have defined it as a word which fits into sentences in the same places nouns do. Since neither of these definitions is totally adequate, we're going to avoid definitions and simply talk in this section about a group of words which have been conventionally labeled as pronouns.

In this book, we've used *we* and *you* quite often. *We* refers to the authors of this book; *you* refers to the reader. Both *we* and *you* are personal pronouns. Other personal pronouns are *I, me, us, she, her, he, him, it, they,* and *them.* All of these personal pronouns can be paired with possessive pronouns: *my* and *mine, our* and *ours, your* and *yours, her* and *hers, his, its, their* and *theirs.* There's also a whole set of matching reflexive pronouns: *myself, ourselves, yourself, yourselves, herself, himself, itself,* and *themselves.*

More sets of pronouns exist. First, there are interrogative pronouns: *who, whom, what, whose,* and *which.* We use these to ask questions: "Who's there? Whom did you speak to? What's that? Whose is that? Which do you want?" *Who, whom, which, what, whose,* and *that* are relative pronouns, that is, pronouns which create subordination: "The child who cried was sick; the boy whom I spoke to laughed; the table that broke was an antique; I agree with what you said; I spoke to the boy whose life was saved; I like poetry that doesn't rhyme." *Which, what,* and *whose* are also interrogative adjectives: "Which table broke? What book do you want? Whose car is that?" Other pronouns are demonstrative adjectives; that is, they point to the noun being talked about: "This book is green; that book is red; these books are black; those books are white." All four of these can be used with no nouns following: "This is green; that is red; these are black; those are white." Another group of pronouns is created by the suffix *ever: whoever, whomever, whichever, whatever.* Indefinite pronouns make up another group: *some, someone, any, anyone, many, all, each, none, one, neither, either, every, everyone, everybody, somebody, anybody,* and so forth.

First-person pronouns are all those which a speaker or writer uses to refer to himself or to himself plus others (*I, me, we,* and so forth). Second-person pronouns are all those which a speaker or writer uses to refer to the person or persons he's speaking to (*you, yourself, yours,* and so forth). Third-person pronouns are all those which a speaker or writer uses to refer to both a thing or things he's talking about (*it, them,* and so forth) and to a person or people other than himself or the person he's speaking to (*he, she, they,* and so forth). Another way to group these same pronouns is by function or case. Pronouns which can function as subjects of verbs are in the nominative case; these are *I, he, she, we,* and *they.* Pronouns which can function as objects of verbs or prepositions are in the objective case; these are *me, him, her, us,* and *them. You* and *it* can function in both capacities. Even this brief overview of the pronoun system of modern English should convince you of its complexity. But don't let its complexity mislead you into thinking you can't master pronoun use. If you're a native speaker, you've already mastered most of it. What you need to give conscious attention to are a few minor kinks in the system.

Perhaps you've been advised not to use *I* or *me* in academic papers. The reason for this "rule" is probably that some people think the presence of the first-person pronoun lessens the sense of objectivity they consider desirable in a scholarly paper. Recently this preference for impersonal prose has been changing, to the extent that the American Psychological Association noted in the second edition of its publication manual that: "An experienced writer can use the first person . . . without dominating the communication and without sacrificing the objectivity of the research." Inexperienced writers can also use *I* and *me* without jeopardizing the objectivity of their work, but they may need to rely much more on reactions of readers to tell them when these pronouns are "dominating the communication."

In some cases, even scientific ones, whether to use *you* in your writing depends upon the degree of formality you're aiming at, that is, upon the closeness you wish to create between yourself and your reader. In a less formal context, you might feel free to refer directly to your reader by using *you,* as we've done throughout this book. In a more formal context you may prefer to use *one* (the formal version of *you*) and *we* or *this writer* (the formal versions of *I*). Being sensitive to varying expectations in the matter of usage is part of what it means to be aware of your audience. Our purpose, for example, in using *you* rather than *one* in this book is to create a direct link to you, making you feel that we are speaking directly to you, which we are.

The context in which *you* causes the most trouble is where it is being used as informal *one*—being used, that is, to refer to people in general. Some teachers forbid such use altogether. We're not among such teachers, but we do agree that *you* must maintain a consistent reference throughout a piece of writing.

The greatest confusion in the reference of *you* usually results when a writer uses the second-person *you* to refer to himself or herself or to people in general, but then switches to a third-person pronoun to do the same thing:

> You learn a lot about people at school, and it is through these interactions that one also gets in closer contact with his "true self."

Notice how the following writer switches her pronoun references:

> Often in life one creates situations that yield physical pain. Whether it was just a mere scratch, a fall or a really painful experience like a broken limb, the incident is not easily forgotten. Physical pain lasting only for a moment can linger on in memory for your entire life.
>
> It really doesn't matter how one does it; the fact still remains the same that painful physical experiences that happen in just a few seconds can leave an imprint in your mind for the rest of your life.

If *you* seems at times to refer to just the reader and at other times to refer to humans in general, your reader may begin to feel somewhat disoriented without exactly understanding why. Here's a student talking about grading systems:

> Due to the grading system, students are made to strive for a goal. Whether that goal is to receive an "A" or "B," it is still an aim. I believe that if you change that system, you will lose that ambition to learn.

The first "you" can legitimately refer to a teacher-reader, but the second one can't: after all, the teacher isn't going to lose her ambition to learn. The second "you" must be a generalized "you" meant to refer to society in general. No matter what the second "you" refers to, it doesn't have the same referent as the first one. Had the writer been attentive to his use of *you,* he would have decided to rewrite this sentence.

Another problem in the use of *you* relates even more directly to the point of view set up by a piece of writing. Every writer establishes a point of view on his subject. If he seems to be talking to a reader about other people and then suddenly by shifting to *you* seems to be talking about the reader, his text becomes confusing. Here's another sentence from that same student's paper about grading systems:

> When he is graded with letters, it seems to produce a sense of competition within the individual to better himself. This

competition is important because it doesn't stop when you get your diploma. Competition is what business and industry thrive on.

At first this writer seems to be talking to the reader about a particular student as a representative of his group. When the reader comes to the "you" in the second sentence, he can be confused because "you," whether meant as a generalized pronoun or a specific one, is a sudden switch from "he." The following sentence from a student paper on maturity is another illustration of the problems caused by switching pronouns:

I would recommend this friend to leave home on good terms with his family, especially his parents, and to consider them as friends who can help you if you are facing problems later on.

At the beginning of the sentence, the student is talking *about* the friend, and at the end of the sentence, she is talking *to* him. Here, too, the writer needs to be sensitive to the *you*'s she's using in her text because she's causing confusing with them.

The choice to use or not use *I* and *you* is a matter of the degree of intimacy an author wishes to establish with his reader. For students, the choice may also depend upon their teachers' preferences. Third-person pronouns present much trickier problems. In conversation, a speaker can use gestures or intonation to make clear what his pronouns refer to and may not need to make the referents explicit. These extra-linguistic aids are unavailable in the written language. For writing to be coherent, readers must be able to determine what noun (called an antecedent) is being referred to by every pronoun. *I* and *you* used carefully cause no confusion because their antecedents are unambiguous. But because antecedents for third-person pronouns can be ambiguous, they must be in the text or a reader will have problems trying to understand it. Even if a writer begins a text with "he," as in the paragraph below, the reader isn't confused about the antecedent, since throughout this paragraph "he" refers to the same subject:

He stood at the hall door turning the ring, turning the heavy signet ring upon his little finger while his glance travelled coolly, deliberately, over the round tables and basket chairs scattered about the glassed-in verandah. He pursed his lips—he might have been going to whistle—but he did not whistle—only turned the ring— turned the ring on his pink, freshly washed hands.

—Katherine Mansfield,
"The Man Without a Temperament"

The pronouns in the next paragraph, however, cause a great deal of confusion:

Parents want to cut their teenagers' wastefulness to show them how to conduct themselves in a more mature way. To make their children aware, they complain to their children. Their complaints are not directed towards their children's activities. Parents just wish to protect them against social evils that could arise when they have excess time and money. Parents are there to advise them. Even though you might say they are living their lives, they are not. They're just watching out for them. When their children deviate from a safe and accepted path someone close should step in and redirect them. This is not living their children's lives; it is just helping them. They're helping them to see their mistakes before they happen. Even though they have the right to make mistakes and learn from them, they suffer less when they recognize mistakes and don't fall flat.

Keeping track of all the *they*'s, *their*'s, *them*'s and what or whom they refer to in this excerpt is no small task.

In order to help a reader make the needed connections, a writer needs to use pronouns which point a reader to the proper antecedent. In general, this means that when an antecedent is one female, a writer uses *her* and *she;* when an antecedent is one male, a writer uses *him* and *he;* when an antecedent is one thing, a writer uses *it;* and when an antecedent is more than one thing or one person, a writer uses *they* and *them.* Generally, all this causes no problems for a writer. All she needs to do is to make certain that the antecedent is unambiguous and not too far away from its pronoun.

Problems do arise, though, when we use an indefinite pronoun such as *anyone* or *everyone* as an antecedent because we usually mean *anyone* and *everyone* regardless of gender. These pronouns are singular in form; that is, we use a verb in the singular form with them ("anyone who *has* shares can vote; everyone *has* a vote"), but usually plural in meaning: that is, we think of them as referring to more than one person. Because these indefinite pronouns are singular in form, many teachers and some handbooks insist that singular pronouns be used to point to them. But there's the problem: the only singular pronouns we have to refer to people are either masculine or feminine; which should we use? If the sex of the *anyone*'s and *everyone*'s is the same, we have no problem; we can pick the pronoun to use. But if we don't know or if the group is mixed, we can create misunderstanding by using either a masculine or feminine pronoun. Instead, since *anyone* and *everyone* both refer to more than one person, we can use third-person plural pronouns: *they, them,* and *their:*

Everyone trusts themselves to deal fairly with their challengers.

Everyone left the party because they were bored.

Other antecedents which can cause the same difficulty are *each, no one, nobody, anybody, somebody, someone.*

Although *they, them,* and *their* have been used with antecedents which are singular in form (like *everyone)* for at least 600 years, over 150 years ago an alternative practice developed, which hardened into a usage rule that found its way into almost all grammar books. This rule stated that pronouns must agree in number with the form of the antecedent; thus agreement in number takes precedence over agreement in gender. So, although *everyone* is plural in meaning, since it's singular in form, it must be followed by a singular pronoun. Adherence to this usage led to the following correction of the first sample sentence we used earlier:

> Everyone who truly believes in himself trusts himself to deal fairly with his challengers.

Assuming the original sentence meant to include males and females, the revision alters its meaning. Correcting the second of our examples leads to distortion of meaning also:

> Everyone left the party early because he was bored.

Now, in addition to the possibility that there may have been women who left also, this revision sounds as though "he" has the power to ruin everyone's fun which was not the meaning of the original sentence.

Despite these problems, this matter became such an issue that in 1850 the English Parliament passed an act which legislated that the singular masculine pronoun (*he, his, him*) should be used as a pseudo-generic. This meant that the masculine pronouns could be used whenever the antecedent's gender was unknown or mixed. In addition to sentences like that above, therefore, this Act of Parliament also implies that sentences such as the following are correct:

> (A doctor is) . . . a physician . . . licensed to practice his profession. . . .
>
> — *Webster's New Collegiate Dictionary*

> Just as the chemist draws his deductions from the results of laboratory experiments, the biologist from his observations of forms of life, and the astronomer from his telescope, so must students of language draw their deductions from an observation of the facts of language.
>
> —Robert C. Pooley,
> *Teaching English Usage*

Sentences like these are difficult to make nonsexist because the antecedents of *he* and *his* in each case are not plural, but the antecedents are not necessarily male either. (For a linguistic point of view on the sociological causes of the rules against using *they* and *them* with singular antecedents, see Ann Bodine, "Androcentrism in prescriptive grammar: singular 'they', sex-indefinite 'he or she', *Language in Society* 4 (1975): 129–146. The writer connects the 1850 Act of Parliament to explicit statements about the necessity for women to be subservient to men.)

For these cases, and for your sake if you have a teacher who insists on a singular pronoun to refer to a singular-in-form antecedent, we offer the following suggestions. There is, in fact, no one solution; when trying to resolve a particular problem, you should be guided primarily by your context, by the meaning you wish to communicate within that context, and by how your sentence sounds.

Suggestion 1 Make the whole expression plural.

> Just as chemists draw their deductions from the results of laboratory experiments, biologists from their observations of forms of life, and astronomers from their . . .

The problem with this solution is that singular expressions have, at times, a special force of their own which seems to be lost when they're made plural. For example:

> Each member of this jury must be able to look himself straight in the eye tomorrow morning.

Compare this to:

> All jury members must be able to look themselves straight in the eyes tomorrow morning.

Use of the plurals weakens the sense, inherent within the singular, that the statement applies to each and every one of us. In the plural version, the jury is responsible; in the singular, each member of the jury is responsible.

Suggestion 2 Include both masculine and feminine pronoun forms.

> A doctor is a physician licensed to practice his or her (his/her) profession.

The problem with this solution is that it can become annoying to many readers, particularly when sentences are long and structures complex, as in:

> Anyone who honestly asks herself/himself what his/her objections really are may recognize that she/he is being irrational.

Several sentences like this in one paragraph irritate most readers; the sounds begin to overwhelm the sense.

Suggestion 3: Let typography help you.

> Anyone who says s/he will deal fairly with opponents is probably prevaricating.

This solution was popular for a short time, but seems to be losing favor. The problem, of course, is that it does not help with her/him, hers/his, or herself/himself. And, too, how does one read s/he aloud?

Suggestion 4: Alternate using feminine and masculine forms. In sentences such as those above, you can sometimes write:

> Anyone who says she will deal fairly with opponents is probably prevaricating.

Some authors write books in which they use *he* throughout one chapter or paragraph and *she* throughout the next chapter or paragraph. This is the method we've chosen to use in this book though you'll probably find slips here and there.

Suggestion 5: Acknowledge the problem and do as you wish.

The way you solve the problem will depend ultimately on the context of what you're writing. What you need to be sensitive to is that it's just as logical to designate all persons as *she* as it is to designate them as *he*. This whole problem of pronoun use is one created by the nature of our language; the fact that it *is* a problem has created unstable use.

A related problem occurs with the use of *man* and *mankind* to refer to people of both sexes. When Ben Franklin said "Early to bed and early to rise makes a man healthy, wealthy, and wise," did he mean women too? We know that women were not included in these familiar words: "We hold these truths to be self-evident, that all men are created equal." (Remember, women weren't able to vote then.) But of whom was ex-President Reagan speaking when, in proclaiming National Bible Week, he said: "In the Bible is the solution to all men's problems"?

In order to create clarity, you should use *mankind* and *man/men* when you speak of male members of the human race, and *womankind* and *woman/women* when you speak of female members of the human race, and *humanity* and *humankind* when you want to include both sexes in your meaning. All of us need to be sure that our language reflects reality. Those of you who are Star Trek devotees probably know that the quote we used back on page 133–34 used to say " . . . where no man has gone before." The new series "Star Trek: The Next Generation" recognized the inappropriateness of man and replaced it with "no one."

Before the 1960s most nurses and elementary-school teachers were women and most police and electricians were men. (Proctor and Gamble created a successful ad campaign by casting a woman as a plumber, thus drawing attention to their product through an unexpected characterization.) These sexual distinctions are disappearing, and writers who use them risk resurrecting stereotypes about the world. Language has also changed as a result of new perceptions of the world, but—paradoxically—language has the power to create perceptions too. We've heard the argument of language conservatives that: "Everyone knows *man* includes women too." We can hardly accept that statement since it isn't true for us; and we know many others for whom it isn't true either. And, of course, if *men* had meant *men and women* in the Declaration of Independence, the Nineteenth Amendment, giving women the right to vote, would have been unnecessary. (The Thirteenth Amendment, abolishing slavery, would also have been unnecessary.)

Deciding whether to use object or subject forms of pronouns is rarely difficult for native speakers. There is one construction, however, which does confuse some students, as illustrated in the following sentence from a student paper about friendship:

> Jim and I started playing tennis at the same time, but I never played as well as him.

Since the pronoun at the end of this sentence is really the subject of the understood verb "did," it should be "he" instead of "him":

> Jim and I started playing tennis at the same time, but I never played as well as he.

Comparisons using *than* cause the same problem:

> He plays better than me.

Again, there's an understood verb at the end of the sentence and the pronoun is serving as the subject of that verb. Standard usage thus requires rewording:

> He plays better than I.

These two sentences we've used as examples will not be misread regardless of the pronoun form, but this isn't always the case, as you can see in the following:

> Jezebel was a greater threat to Samson than him.

Does this sentence mean that two people were threatened or that two people were threatening Samson? In other words, does it mean:

> Jezebel was a greater threat to Samson than he (was)
>
> or
>
> Jezebel was a greater threat to Samson than to him?

So even though the choice between the object and subject form of the pronoun may not matter most of the time, it will matter some of the time. Consequently, it's best to adhere to standard usage in this construction, at least in your written work. (For more on comparisons, see pages 68–71, 132–33.)

Making the choice between object and subject forms of pronouns comes up in other constructions too. Is it standard usage to say "between you and I" or "between you and me"? To make this choice, you need to realize that the pronouns in this phrase are functioning as objects of the preposition "between." "You" can serve as both an object and subject form, so you only need to choose between "I" and "me." Since "me" is the object form, the correct phrase is "between you and me." You can use your ear to help you make this choice by turning this compound expression around and deciding which sounds better: "between I and you" or "between me and you." Very few of us would say "between I and you." What you need to realize is that if "between me and you" sounds correct to you, the reverse is also correct: "between you and me." Current standards of politeness require that you not mention yourself before others, so when you say or write this phrase, it's best to keep it in the form "between you and me." We suspect that the current prevalence of "between you and I" in speech and writing is evidence of a phenomenon which linguists call "overcorrectness." We'll talk about this farther along, in our discussion of the choice between *who* and *whom*.

When a compound expression with one or more pronouns serves as the subject of a sentence, a similar problem needs to be solved:

> She/Her and Jane had an argument.

You can reverse the parts of the compound subject here too and ask yourself whether "Jane and her had an argument" sounds correct to you. But you can also test the pronouns separately; does "Her had an argument" sound correct to you? We suspect it doesn't. "She had an argument" will sound much better. And if "She had an argument" sounds right to you, then choose "she" in the compound expression also: "She and Jane had an argument." When the compound nature of the subject is not influencing you, you'll make the choice required by standard usage. For instance, we suspect that those of you who might say "José and them are going to the party" or "Him and Shin

Li went to the opera" would *not* say "Them are going to the party" or "Him went to the opera."

We're going to say just a brief word about reflexive pronouns (the ones that end with *self* or *selves*) before we get on to another difficult point. Reflexive pronouns refer back to the subject of the sentence:

The doctor cured himself.

They paid themselves well.

Reflexive pronouns also serve as intensifiers, emphasizers of meaning:

The doctor herself didn't feel well.

I myself don't like it.

These are the only uses of the reflexive in standard English. You've probably heard, as we have quite often, *myself* used as a subject or object:

Karen and myself went to the wedding.

It was written by John and myself.

This seems to serve as a way to avert the implication of egotism caused by a frequent use of *I*. Such use has found its way into quite a few people's informal speech style. Two other forms often heard in certain dialects are *hisself* and *theirselves*. These are forms created on the analogy of other reflexives which use the possessive form as the basis of the reflexive. Remember that the standard forms are *himself* and *themselves*. You'll notice, just by looking at these last two words, that whether or not *self* is singular or plural depends on the pronoun it's attached to. It's only in the reflexive pronoun, in fact, that we know by the form alone whether a second-person pronoun refers to one person or to more than one; we have a form for each: *yourself* and *yourselves*.

Our last problem is one we alluded to at the beginning of this subsection: the distinction between *who* and *whom*. So many people have trouble with the latter of this pair that its use has almost come to be a sign of superior education. Most of us are impressed by anyone who uses the word *whom* because we assume that they must be right; after all, who would go out of their way to use the word unless they knew they were correct? In truth, the distinction between the words is lessening; we know this because even quite literate people don't usually use *whom* comfortably in speech.

The best advice we can give is this: since *who* is a subject form, use it wherever a subject-form pronoun (*I, he, she, they*) would be correct:

Who (he, she) is there? Who (they) are the actors?

The people who (they) came were well entertained.

The corollary to this is that since *whom* is an object form, you should use it wherever an object-form pronoun (*me, her, him, them*) would be correct. This part of our advice is not so easy to apply. We suggest that if you're faced with framing a question, you think about whether the answer would be one of these object-form pronouns:

Who/whom did you see? Answer: her, him, or them.

So our choice here would be *whom.* In practice, however, almost all handbooks accept *who* in questions. When the *who/whom* choice comes in the middle of a sentence, handbooks are not flexible:

She was the girl who/whom I saw.

To make the choice here, you need to realize that the pronoun is the object of the verb *saw,* and since you would say "I saw her," *whom* is the correct choice. Keep in mind when you're seeking the correct choice that you should make your decision on the basis of the words following the *who* or *whom.* But, in this case, there's an easier solution since the sentence would be correct without the pronoun:

She was the girl I saw.

You can also use *that* in sentences like these:

She was the girl that I saw.

So what all this comes down to is that if you're shrewd, you almost never need to worry about the *who/whom* choice: there's a way to get around it most of the time.

You can't always get around the *who/whom* issue when you're deciding between *whoever/whomever.*

Give the book to whoever/whomever asks for it.

You can substitute a subject-form pronoun here (like *he*), so "whoever" is the correct form. Again, when making the decision, forget the words in front of *whoever/whomever.* This warning is particularly important in sentences like this because *to* can be misleading.

Give the book to whoever/whomever you see.

Here again you ignore everything before "whoever/whomever" and figure out what the subject-verb-object core of the rest of the words is. In this case it's: "You see X." Only an object form (like *her*) can replace the "X," and so you need *whomever.*

Try the same process with these two:

The choice is available to whoever/whomever wins first prize.

You always seem to be willing to speak to whoever/whomever I send to see you.

Since, in the first of these, you can say: "She wins first prize," "whoever" is the correct form. In the second sentence, we must recognize that the subject-verb-object core is: "I send X to see you." Since only object forms can replace the "X," "whomever" is the correct form.

There's one more construction which doesn't allow you to avoid the *who/whom* choice.

I didn't know who/whom it was.

Following the procedure we outlined above, you should realize that the final part of this sentence is "it was X." Most of you would probably replace the "X" with "her" or "him." This realization would lead you to choose "whom," and you'd be wrong. You can either avoid this construction altogether or recognize that the verb *to be* is different from other verbs: it must be followed by a subject form of the pronoun. *Who* is thus the correct choice in this sentence. If you're having trouble with all this, so do many other people—including those who have almost no trouble with any other feature of the standard language. If you can't make a choice between *who/whom,* just say the sentence aloud to yourself a couple of times and choose the one that sounds best to you. It will probably sound OK to others also.

When we're in a conversation, we don't have much time to consider choices. Obviously, we can't keep people waiting while we go through some process that helps us decide whether to say *who* or *whom.* Some people who recognize the necessity for a choice become victims of "overcorrectness." What probably happens is that they realize the necessity for the choice quite suddenly and, feeling insecure about their language use—as so many of us are—they pick the harder of the two words, the one that sounds less right. As a result, they use *whom* where it's inappropriate in standard usage.

Overcorrectness is not limited to the use of *whom.* The other spot where it causes nonstandard usage is in expressions like "The choice is between you and I," a problem we discussed already. We would guess that most people, during their schooling, were faulted for using *me* in places where standard usage requires *I*. As a result, they have become insecure about *me* even in places where it's correct. This gets us back to the second problem we brought up in the introduction to this subsection: "It's I" or "It's me." Standard usage for years allowed only "It's I." Since this was contrary to most people's normal speech, they became anxious whenever they had to make a choice, supposing that what seemed right to them ("between you and me"), must be wrong. As a result, they overcorrected. The more they used the overcorrection, the more it sounded right to them. The irony in this is that "It's me" is widely accepted today; many of you may not even know you have the option of saying "It's I," but you probably do agonize over "between you and me." Problems of language usage will always be with us; they're inherent in the nature of language. As the language changes, old usage problems fade away and new ones appear.

In concluding our comments on pronouns, we should repeat that pronouns and their use are complex. Native speakers use them with almost no thought, and yet attempts to formulate exact rules describing how they are used have proved frustrating. In fact, linguists who have solved many linguistic problems so computers can "read" and "talk" are still struggling to find ways to program pronoun use into sophisticated language computers.

Practice 14

Read the following excerpts from student pieces, paying particular attention to each pronoun. Discuss with your classmates and teacher each of the pronouns and your decision about its appropriateness.

A

Most people believe anything they read or hear; everyone prefers to believe what others tell them. As Joseph Goebels once said "Repeat a lie often enough and it will be accepted as the truth." People believe if they see it in the paper and hear it on the radio, it must be true. Even if we are skeptical, we probably believe, somewhere in the back of our minds, that it could be true. Take, for example, the 1939 "War of the Worlds" radio story. Although most people were skeptical, some people really believed that the world was being invaded by Martians. The media realizes that people will believe what they read and hear and they use it to their advantage. . . .

Now the media publishes an article on the upper middle of the front page with big headlines saying "Police Kill 3 and Injure 20 in Big Strike Demonstration." They would probably have a picture of a policeman hitting a demonstrator. From what I just told you, the reader is going to think the cops just started hitting people because they were demonstrating. In the article the writer will mention some of the things the demonstrators did but not all of them, because the writer is trying to show that the police use too much force. The writer will probably end the article by saying that he was enraged by the police action. From the article one couldn't tell that the mob was threatening law and order. Also you wouldn't even think that maybe the police did everything they could to restore law and order.

What the writer should have done is to make a headline that is neutral. It could have read "Threatening Mob Is Put Down By Police." Also there should be a picture of an angry mob picketing alongside the police in their riot gear. This will not predispose the reader to be biased in any way unless he already is biased. Then in the article, it should state every fact the the writer is aware of, so one can see who was doing wrong, who was hitting who, and so forth. Then you can make up your own mind.

B

There has, for some time, been a debate over who makes the better pet—dogs or cats. The cat is a popular house pet and one of the smartest animals. They also make faithful, friendly companions. That is why to prove that cats make better pets, there should be a mandatory law requiring that every United States household own and register at least one cat.

Cats have good memories. This is recorded in *The World Book,* on page 1269. They are able to remember people who have treated them kindly and those that were cruel to them. That is why one stipulation of this law will provide for testing of all owners to make sure that they are able to properly care for their cat. By no acceptable means will an owner be able to mistreat their pet.

C

Often in life one creates situations that yield physical pain. Whether it was just a mere scratch, a fall or a real painful experience like a broken limb, the incident is not easily forgotten. Physical pain lasting only for a moment can linger on in memory for your entire life.

It really doesn't matter how one does it, the fact still remains the same that painful physical experiences that happen in just a few seconds can leave an imprint in your mind for the rest of your life. For instance, I could remember when I was nine years old; I thought

I was going to lose one of my fingers. I went to get a container of milk from the Seven-Eleven store. Before getting the container you had to slide open this big, heavy door. I got the milk and without realizing that the door would shut in one second flat after you let go of it, I let the door slam hard on my finger. Never has a person heard someone scream so loud, louder than a little kid getting a shot at the doctor's office.

D (From an essay on kiba-dachi, a karate exercise)

To assume this fighting position, one must place his feet slightly wider than shoulder width apart and bend his knees while maintaining a vertical spine position. It's as if one is sitting on a horse.

The physical pain that comes from remaining in this position for ninety minutes cannot be described. However, this pain is only a small fraction of the entire agony experienced during the kiba-dachi practice. After being nailed to the floor like that for only five minutes, feeling the legs burn like hell and the whole body shake, you would prefer to fall through the ground rather than maintain the stance for another second. This is when the real "fun" begins, and it's not only the burning pain that kills you, it's the war that goes on inside your head.

You can't give up no matter what. One is not allowed to move or rub the aching legs. You can't even close your eyes. The only thing you can do is to scream your lungs out.

WHOM.

Boynton

Chapter Six

Words

Old English was a highly inflected language, which means that the form of many words, especially nouns, verbs, and adjectives, was determined by what they were doing in the sentence. Here's a brief example of what that looked like:

```
And ælc þara þe gehierþ þas min word, and þa
ne wyrcþ, se biþ gelic þæm dysigan menn, þe
getimbrode his hus ofer sand-ceosol.  Þa rinde
hit, and þær comon flod, and bleowon windas,
and ahruron on þæt hus, and þæt hus feoll; and
his hryre wæs micel.
```

Here's a literal translation:

> And each of those who hears these my words, and them does not work, he is like the foolish man, who built his house on sand. It rained, and there came floods, and the winds blew, and fell on the house, and the house fell; and its fall was great.

This portion of the Bible is from the Gospel of Matthew, 7:26–27. You'll notice that in the Old English there's no -s on the end of *word,* but there is an -as on *wind* to indicate the plural. The -on ending on *com* and *bleow* is the third-person-plural-past-tense ending. The þ ending on *gehier* and *wyrc* is the third-person-singular-present tense ending. This strange letter, called a thorn, is pronounced like modern English *th.* The -an ending on *dysig,* an adjective modifying *menn,* is masculine plural to agree with the noun it modifies.

By the time of Shakespeare, most of these variant forms had disappeared. We do have a few left. We add endings to nouns now only to show the plural and the possessive (-s or -es, -'s and -s'). We do not change the form of an adjective at all, no matter what it does in the sentence: that is, no matter whether it modifies a noun used as a subject or a noun used as an object and no matter whether it modifies a single or a plural word. The number of verb endings has also decreased. The -est and -eþ, spelled eth, remained longer than the others, mostly in religious prose and in both religious and secular poetry. *Thou* and *thee,* the subject and object forms of the second-person-singular pronoun, remained even longer, again mostly in religious usages.

> The Lord is my Shepherd: I shall not want, He mak*eth* me to lie down in green pastures: he lead*eth* me beside the still waters. He restor*eth* my soul: he lead*eth* me in the paths of righteousness for his name's sake.
>
> —*Psalm 23, King James Version*

> And another came, saying, Lord, behold, here is thy pound, which I have kept laid up in a napkin: For I feared thee, because thou ar*t* an austere man: thou tak*est* up that thou layed*st* not down, and reap*est* that thou did*st* not sow.
>
> —*Luke, 10:20-21*

And here's the King James Version of the excerpt we took from Old English:

> And everyone who heareth these sayings of mine, and doeth them not, shall be likened unto a foolish man, which built his house upon the sand: And the rain descended, and the floods came, and the winds blew, and beat upon that house; and it fell: and great was the fall of it.

Verbs

The only regular verb endings we have now are the -s or -es ending to mark the third-person singular form in the present tense, the -ed to mark the past tense and the past participle, and the -ing to mark the present participle. In addition, modern English makes no distinction between singular and plural forms of verbs in the past tense with the one exception of *was* and *were.*

Although our verb system is considerably simpler than it was 1000 years ago, some aspects of this system may puzzle you. All dead and living languages, according to linguists, have a way to indicate the time when a particular event occurs (although not all languages divide time into past, present, and future). In modern English, the lack of any ending on a regular verb or the presence of an -s or -es ending usually indicates that the action did not occur in the past.

I jump; they jump; he jumps.

We traditionally call this tense the present tense, although it doesn't always signal present time, or time at all. The addition of an -ed usually indicates that the action of the verb occurred in the past:

I jumped; they jumped.

Many of our most-used verbs have irregular past-tense forms (see pp. 161–65) English has not true future tense; the present tense can acquire a future sense in certain contexts, or we can use the auxiliaries *will* or *going to,* in combination with other verbs.

This is the general pattern of our verb system, but there are important subsidiary rules:

1. In verb phrases which begin with *can, could, may, might, must, do, does, did, will, would, should, shall, won't,* the final verb has no ending, regardless of the time or nature of the action. Note too that these verbs, with the exception of *do,* don't add present-tense or past-tense endings.

   He will leave. She can sing. They did go.
   I may agree. You might fall. He would dance.

2. English has three perfect tenses created by using the auxiliary or helping verb *have.* In such constructions the final verb form is called a past participle. For regular verbs, the past participle form is the same as the past-tense form: "He has *jumped."* The -ed appears even though the auxiliary verb is in the present tense. Unfortunately, there are many irregular past participle forms: "He sang," but "She has sung." Following are examples of the three perfect tenses:

   Present perfect:
   I *have observed* the animals all day.

   Past perfect:
   He *had observed* the animals all day.

   Future perfect:
   By midnight tonight, he *will have observed* the animals all day.

3. We talked about passive verbs earlier. A passive verb is created by using some form of the verb *to be* plus the past participle: "The videos *are displayed* every Friday night." Here again, the -ed

appears even though the auxiliary, or helping, verb is in the present tense. Following are examples of passive verbs:

Present passive:
The animals *are observed* all day.

Past passive:
The animals *were observed* all day.

Future passive:
The animals *will be observed* all day.

Present perfect passive:
The animals *have been observed* all day.

Past perfect passive:
The animals *had been observed* all day.

Future perfect passive:
By midnight tonight, the animals *will have been observed* all day.

Some special circumstances exist for which special rules have developed. The most important of these is that the present (or non-past) tense is used to describe eternally true conditions. For example:

Columbus believed that the world is round.

The teacher said that gravity affects all falling objects.

A similar specialized use of the present tense, called "the literary present," often appears in discussions of literature:

Hamlet speaks to his mother in a threatening tone.

Odysseus' wounded pride keeps him in his tent.

It's also acceptable to discuss literature in the past tense:

Hamlet spoke to his mother in a threatening tone.

Odysseus' wounded pride kept him in his tent.

What's not acceptable is to be inconsistent. If you start discussing *Hamlet* in the present tense, shifting to the past tense may cause considerable confusion for your readers.

The present tense obviously creates a sense of immediacy which the past tense cannot create as easily. As a result, you may have heard people in speech begin retelling an exciting event using the past tense and then, without realizing it, slip into the present. It's as though the person were reliving the experience. And, in fact, this immediacy makes for good story-telling. Here's the beginning of an oral retelling of an event:

> I was standing out in the field last night behind the barn about ten
> o'clock. It was dark, and the moon kept darting in and out behind
> the clouds. Suddenly I see the grass rustling and hear a strange
> grunting sound. I was terrified.

Obviously, this same sort of tense shift can occur when someone is
writing about an exciting event, but unless you're quoting someone's
speech directly, you should avoid this kind of tense shifting in your
writing. When listening to someone, we have her presence as proof
that the actions of which she speaks occurred in the past; while
reading, we don't have such clues and therefore we may become
perplexed about what-happened-when unless the writer makes that
clear to us through the verb forms. We also have to remember that
fictional time (the time during which the events of a novel or story
take place) also has a past, present, and future. If you use the present
tense to describe events in the novel, you're going to have to save the
past tense for the fictional past of the characters in the novel.

Even when we can figure out a particular sequence of actions,
there's something disconcerting about the inconsistency created by
unwarranted tense shifting. Here's an example from a student paper
on *The Mill on the Floss*:

> At this particular point of the novel, Tom has approached his uncle
> Deane for a job. His uncle asks Tom if he knew bookkeeping and
> Tom admits that he doesn't. Maggie comments that if she knew
> bookkeeping, she could teach it to Tom. Instead of taking this
> comment as a sign of love and care, as it was meant, Tom perceived
> it as some kind of blow to his ego, to his manhood and to his
> competency. Why does Tom often misread his sister Maggie who
> loves him so dearly? Tom certainly has "Tulliver pride." Like his
> father, Tom wants no charity or help from anyone; this attitude
> obviously includes even his sister. At this moment and throughout
> the entire book, Tom wants to establish his role as a "man" who can
> take care of himself and his family if necessary. Tom felt, as a child
> and an adult, that he was able to judge when others were to be
> punished. He never let Maggie be his "equal" and he would always
> correct and punish her when he felt it necessary.

There are six shifts in tense here; and, although a reader can probably
work out the sequence of events, the student's inconsistency in tense
use can be irritating.

Another special problem in tense use occurs when we want to
show the time relation between actions:

> I remembered that I had seen him.

The actions expressed by both verbs in this sentence occurred in the
past; the second of the two actions is described in the past perfect

tense to show that it's the earlier of the two actions. In general, what you need to remember about this matter (often called "sequence of tenses" in handbooks) is that when two actions occur at essentially the same time, the verbs expressing these actions should be in the same tense:

Present:
I see him everyday when he comes to school.

Past:
I saw him everyday when he came to school.

If one action is completed before the other starts, the completed action should be in the appropriate perfect tense:

Present:
I think she has gone home.

Past:
I thought she had gone home.

Future:
By the time I arrive she will have gone home.

The general rule about all perfect tenses is that the action which they describe occurs earlier than some other action being talked about. Notice how this works when you use the present participle:

Smiling, he opened the book.

The writer here means that "he" smiled and opened the book at the same time.

Having said goodbye, he opened the book.

Here the writer means that "he" said goodbye before opening the book.

The present-perfect tense is used in two other situations. The first is for action which began in the past and continues into the present:

I have been going to school for fourteen years.

The second is for habitual past action which remains habitual in the present:

I have gone to camp every summer for ten years.

Not all verbs fit neatly into the patterns we've been talking about. Historically, *would* is the past tense of *will*, but its use as a helping verb has superseded that use. "I would do it" and "I will do it" differ in meaning, not in time, in modern English. Still, its history as a past-tense verb affects certain constructions in modern English. As a result, standard English requires the following verb sequences to describe a habitual action:

If it rains, I go.

To describe a particular action which may or may not happen in the future:

If it rains, I will go.

To describe a hypothetical action which could have occurred in the past but didn't:

If it had rained, I would have gone.

The choice between *may* and *can* occasionally presents problems too. Traditionally, *may* includes the sense of what we call "if-ness": "I may go" suggests something iffy. Here's a hypothetical conversation which illustrates our point:

"Are you going?"

"I may go."

"What do you mean, you may go?"

"Well, *if* I've finished writing my paper and *if* I don't fall asleep."

"If you finish your paper and aren't sleepy, will you go?"

"Yes, then I'll go."

Can traditionally means "be able to"; "I can go" means "I'm able to go." Here's another hypothetical conversation:

"Are you going?"

"I can go."

"I didn't ask you that. I know you *can* go, but *are* you going?"

"Well, I can go, but I may decide not to if. . . ."

"If what?"

"If I'm too tired after I finish my paper."

Most of us observe the traditional distinctions between *may* and *can* in contexts like our hypothetical ones. But we don't necessarily observe them when the context shifts slightly. If someone asks an authority figure: "Can I go?" the speaker is usually asking for permission. A snide language conservative might reply to that question with another: "Why, is your leg broken?"

Just because you understand all we've said about verb forms doesn't mean you won't make errors when using them. As you write, it's internalized unconscious or intuitive knowledge that dictates what comes out. So what you need to do is to work toward making your conscious understanding of the verb system functional on the level of intuition. When you're rewriting and copyediting, of course, you can use conscious knowledge directly *once you have identified a potential source of error.* It's usually your intuitions about language which guide you to such identification. One of the ways you can begin to work on sharpening your intuitions is by close analysis of your own writing. Select a paragraph from something you've written recently and use this book to help you justify for yourself the validity of every verb form you use. One of our students used the following paragraph from one of his papers, first reading through it and underlining all the verbs. You can practice identifying verbs by underlining all of them in this excerpt.

> My story starts way back in the summer after sixth grade. My family and I moved to Plainview after I graduated from elementary school. We had been moving in gradually over the weekends. During that time, I had met my soon to be best friend Willy. We became next door neighbors and began growing close. We were very much alike, neither one of us overly aggressive. We were only kids, more worried about playing games and having fun than anything else. This was all fine and good until seventh grade. We weren't hermits, we had friends. We just didn't belong to a crowd. Everyone wants to be in a crowd. You get invited to parties, and always have someone to hang out with.

Following are the reasons he gave for each of the verbs he used. You might want to make your own list before reading his.

starts: third-person singular, present tense, always true
moved: past tense, action finished
graduated: past tense, action finished
had been moving: past-perfect tense, action started before "moved" and lasted a while
had met: past perfect tense, action occurred at same time as "had been moving"
became: past tense, action
began growing: past tense, action finished
were: plural past tense, no longer like this
were: plural past tense, no longer kids
was: singular past tense, no longer that way
weren't: past tense, describes what we were like in the past
had: past tense, describes what we were like in the past
didn't belong: past tense, action finished

wants: third-person singular, present tense, always true
get invited: present tense, always true
have: third-person plural, present tense, always true

One of the pleasant rewards of doing this exercise is the discovery of how much you already do correctly and how little you need to worry about. But if you do have problems doing it or feel unsure of yourself, this is an exercise you may want to check through with your teacher or do with the help of a tutor in your Writing Center. What you'll discover when you do this is that discussions of verb forms quickly become discussions of your intentions and meaning in a piece of writing. As we've said over and over, the chief value of conscious attention to the built-in rules of standard usage is that it forces you to clarify your meaning for yourself and others.

One warning about exercises like this: doing them benefits you because it makes you focus on certain aspects of your personal language and allows you to align them (if you wish) with accepted conventions. The more you do such exercises, the more likely it will be that your intuition will sense deviations from standard usage *as you start to write them*. However, exercises alone can't accomplish this change—it's essential also for you to continue to write a great deal.

Irregular Verbs

We're going to finish verb forms with a list of the most common irregular verbs—we don't know anyone (including us) who doesn't have trouble with at least one or two of these. Where it makes sense, we've grouped verbs which show similar changes. Those which have no affinity to any of the groups are listed alphabetically at the end of the entire list. The forms in the first column fit into sentences beginning: "Today, I. . . ."; forms in the middle column, into sentences beginning: "Yesterday, I. . . ."; and forms in the third column, into sentences beginning: "The day before, I had. . . ."

Present	Past	Past Participle
bear	bore	borne (but Liza was born in 1970)
swear	swore	sworn
tear	tore	torn
wear	wore	worn
begin	began	begun

drink	drank	drunk
ring	rang	rung
shrink	shrank	shrunk
sing	sang	sung
sink	sank	sunk
stink	stank	stunk
swim	swam	swum

These below are almost, but not quite, like those above:

fling	flung	flung
sling	slung	slung
slink	slunk	slunk
spin	spun	spun
sting	stung	stung
string	strung	strung
swing	swung	swung
wring	wrung	wrung

This one is something like the above:

strike	struck	struck (but I was stricken with a disease)

bend	bent	bent
lend	lent	lent
rend	rent	rent
send	sent	sent

blow	blew	blown
flow	flew	flown
grow	grew	grown
know	knew	known
throw	threw	thrown

A near relation of the above:

draw	drew	drawn

And still another near relation:

show	showed	shown

Almost similar:

fly	flew	flown

Don't mix this up with:

flee	fled	fled

Or with:

fly (out)	flied (out)	flied (out) (which is only for baseball)

creep	crept	crept
keep	kept	kept
leap	leaped or leapt	leaped or leapt
sleep	slept	slept
weep	wept	wept

bind	bound	bound
find	Found	found
grind	ground	ground
wind	wound	wound

drive	drove	driven
ride	rode	ridden

Keep this separate from:

rid (which is the word you want when you're talking to the exterminator)	rid or ridded	rid or ridded
write	wrote	written

Two related words are:

give	gave	given
prove	proved	proven

Another word which is a little bit like those above:

bite	bit	bitten

deal	dealt	dealt
feel	felt	felt

Slightly related:

dream	dreamed or dreamt	dreamed or dreamt
take	took	taken

shake	shook	shaken

Just a little different:

wake	waked or woke	waked or woke (but I was awakened)

Some similarity:

choose	chose	chosen
freeze	froze	frozen

We're grouping the following ones together because of the similarity of their past tenses:

bring	brought	brought
buy	bought	bought
catch	caught	caught
fight	fought	fought
seek	sought	sought
teach	taught	taught
think	thought	thought
let (allow)	let	let
set	set	setpay
	paid	paid
say	said	said
break	broke	broken
speak	spoke	spoken

Here are the remainder:

am	was	been
beat	beat	beaten or beat
bid (order)	bade	bidden or bid
bid (offer)	bid	bid
build	built	built
burst	burst	burst
come	came	come
cost	cost	cost
dig	dug	dug
dive	dived (dove)	dived
do	did	done
drown	drowned	drowned
eat	ate	eaten
fall	fell	fallen

fit	fit or fitted	fit or fitted
get	got	got or gotten
go	went	gone
hang (suspend)	hung	hung
hang (execute)	hanged	hanged
have	had	had
hear	heard	heard
hurt	hurt	hurt
lay (put, placed)	laid	laid
lead	led	led
lie	lay	lain
light	lit	lit or lighted
lose	lost	lost
make	made	made
rise	rose	risen
run	ran	run
see	saw	seen
sew	sewed	sewn or sewed
shine (give off light)	shone	shone
shine (polish)	shined	shined
shoot	shot	shot
set	set	set
sit	sat	sat
slay	slew	slain
sow	sowed	sown or sowed
stand	stood	stood
steal	stole	stolen

Nouns

Nouns have far fewer forms in modern English than verbs do: only the plural s ending and the plural and singular apostrophe s endings. The latter we discussed in our punctuation section. In general, pluralizing is simple: you just add an -s or an -es. Which of the two to add is solely a matter of sound. Try to say: "The churchs are beautiful," and you'll understand why an -es is added to certain words rather than an -s.

Native speakers have no problems with irregular plurals: *children, women, geese, feet, mice, wives,* and so forth. One of the most unusual is *oxen;* many more words used to be pluralized this way: more than one *shoe* was *shoen,* and more than one *eye* was *eyen.* And then there are certain words for animals which are the same in the singular and plural: *deer, sheep, fish, moose.* These irregularities have their roots in the history of the language. Occasionally, we've heard and seen the word *deers;* perhaps in twenty years or so it will be an accepted form. *Sheeps* doesn't occur very often, but perhaps that's because of what it sounds like: all those *s*'s! *Fishes,* though, is no longer rare; increasingly, we've seen and heard it and suspect that it's acceptable now to all but the most diehard grammarians. Still, there's often a difference in meaning between the old plural with no ending and the new plural with an -*es* ending:

> There are many fish in the sea.

> There are many fishes in the sea.

To most native speakers, the first sentence is a statement about the number of gilled creatures in the sea, but the second sentence is a statement about the number of *kinds of* gilled creatures in the sea.

Adjectives and Adverbs

Many adjectives in English can become adverbs with the addition of -*ly: easy* to *easily, anxious* to *anxiously, rapid* to *rapidly,* and so forth. That isn't to say that all adverbs end in -*ly* and that all words which end in -*ly* are adverbs. *Fast* and *slow* are both adjectives and adverbs. Yes, we've all seen the adverb *slowly,* but it's just as proper to say "Drive slow" as it is to say "Drive slowly"; in fact, "Drive slow" has more historical precedence than "Drive slowly" (though that's no reason anyone should consider it "more correct"). The differences that do exist between the use of *slow* and *slowly* are not likely to cause a native speaker any anxiety. No native speaker would say: "He slow drove through the crowd" instead of "He slowly drove through the crowd." It's when the adverb follows the verb that choice is possible.

Adverbs and adjectives are used differently: adverbs modify or give additional information about verbs ("She traveled *quickly*"), adjectives ("She made an *extremely* quick trip"), and other adverbs ("She traveled *extremely* quickly"); and adjectives modify nouns ("She made a *quick* trip"). Most problems in differentiating between adverbs and adjectives arise when comparative forms are needed. "He worked *more quickly* with good tools" is probably more acceptable to most teachers than: "He worked *quicker* with good tools," although the latter is common even in the prose of good writers.

Problems also arise in choosing between *bad* and *badly* and *well* and *good.* It's easy to see that *badly* is an adverb; it isn't possible to see that *well* can be an adverb also—you'll just have to remember that. This means that "Leslie plays well, and Jean plays badly" satisfies standard usage, but "Leslie plays good, and Jean plays bad" doesn't.

Before we can finish our discussion of the choices between *bad* and *badly* and *good* and *well,* we need to digress a bit. Back when we were talking about pronouns, we touched briefly on the "It's I" or "It's me" choice. There we said that not long ago only "It's I" was accepted standard usage. The logical reason for this is that in the sentence "It's I," the "It" and the "I" refer to the same person. Also, *me* is an object form, and object forms signal that the persons or things designated by them feel the results of some action ("He hit me"). But *is* is not an active verb and cannot, therefore, have an effect on someone or something else as an active verb does. *Me* is thus inappropriate. This prohibition is weakening, of course, but there are related problems—which brings us back to the choice between certain adverbs and adjectives.

By calling *to be* a linking verb, what we're suggesting is that it links the word(s) before it and the word(s) after it in a special way; what comes after any form of *to be* refers to the same person or thing as what comes before it: "She's a lawyer." By this same reasoning, a modifier which follows some form of *to be* modifies the subject: "He is wise." Since this modifier modifies a noun or pronoun, it must be an adjective (that's the function of adjectives). And since *bad* and *good* are adjective forms, we say: "That is good, and this is bad."

We need to go one step further. *To be* is not the only linking verb in English. The others are mainly verbs which express the act of using one's senses: smelling, feeling, and so forth. The thing to remember is that if you use a linking verb followed by a modifier which describes the subject of the linking verb, that modifier should be an adjective:

The flower smells good.

These vegetables taste delicious.

He feels bad.

They look well in blue.

There's one final word on this complicated subject. We said earlier that *well* can be an adverb as in "He plays well." It can also be an adjective—which means it can modify a noun or pronoun as in "He is not a well person." As an adjective it almost always describes a person's health: "He's well" does not mean the same thing as "He's good." The latter is probably a statement about the subject's skill in some particular activity or about his moral character.

Practice 15

Read the following excerpts from students' papers and discuss with your classmates and teachers whatever errors you see—particularly errors in tense and verb, adjective, and adverb forms.

A

The language that the author uses is very plain and straightforward. As a matter of fact, for such a complicated subject, he comes across very smooth. In fact, the sentence about Princess Lea of *Star Wars* was quite amusing. But, here is the author's flaw. His paper was good reading and quite humorous but he does not get his point across with enough emphasis. Instead of being very witty about the subject, he should have come across a lot tougher. After all this is an immensely important subject. More of a hardline stance would have been appropriate. I feel that if the author would have expanded his ideas a little more and perhaps put more emphasis on where the money would have been better spent, I would have been more receptive to his ideas. He offers no alternatives, and did not offer enough facts to back his claims. Even though I was receptive to his thinking, he just does not create enough of an emotional impact to alter my position on this subject.

B

There is a stillness in the air. The football field is empty, except for a few seagulls and myself. The bleachers are completely desolate. As I look around I noticed that the field seems to be much larger than I remembered it. Maybe it's because of its loneliness, maybe because of time.

Memories crowd my thoughts as I look over to the school; it was once my high school. For the first few moments only the good times that I had spent there passed through my eyes. I never thought that the images would remain so clear after four years. I never thought that I should miss those memories so much. Then without warning all those wonderful memories turned quick to a much more tormented past.

I had been here a few times since the day I graduated on this very same field. Each time I fought with myself to forget the part of my past which was still haunting me. But it wouldn't let go and each time I could only leave here with bitterness and anguish. What was it about this place that drew me to itself? Why am I here, torn between wonderful thoughts of the past and the bitterness that it brought me? There's only questions without any answers.

The stands are lifeless. It looks as if no one had been here in years. The wooden ramp creaks as I walked its length. A new barrage of images puts tears in my eyes. I sit at the very spot where I had spent every autumn Saturday not so long ago. From here I would watch the football games and at the same time keep one eye on the group who always end up behind me.

Slang

In contrast to the other choices we've discussed in this section so far, the choice we discussed in the last paragraph is not based on making a distinction between two forms of the same word. Although it has connections to the problem of adverb/adjective distinction, it really comes down to making a choice between words which have different meanings. As such, it serves as a link to this section in which we're going to discuss the problem of choosing between or among different words which mean almost the same thing. Such choices make it necessary for us to think about levels of formality, about slang, colloquialisms, and regionalisms, and about other problems of word choice.

Definition: "highly informal language that is outside of conventional or standard usage and consists of both coined words and phrases and of new or extended meanings attached to established terms" (*Webster's New World Dictionary,* Second College Ed.). As you can see from this quotation, slang is defined as nonstandard language—language which is *by its own nature* out of place in a formal, academic context. In its most general sense, slang is a form of language which identifies its user as belonging to a particular group of people. Almost any identifiably separate group in a society develops a language of its own; psychologically this special language—the ability to produce and understand it—makes its users feel a part of the group, helps them establish their own identity to themselves and to the rest of the world. The special language of professional groups is usually called jargon instead of slang; the special language of a particular ethnic group or geographic region is called a dialect. The term *slang*, in everyday use, is generally reserved for the special language of adolescents, although in today's world with its heavy reliance on spoken language and rapid communication, slang tends to spread beyond teenage culture and even across oceans and ethnic groups.

Slang is a positive force in language. The dictionary entry we quoted earlier goes on to say: "Slang develops from the attempt to find fresh and vigorous, colorful, pungent, or humorous expression." A language without slang is a language which has lost its imaginative strength and its playfulness, characteristics which insure continued health. But we must recognize too the limitations of slang, which are inseparable from its basic nature: it's short-lived and confined to certain groups. As the dictionary notes, slang "either passes into disuse or comes to have a more formal status": in either case what was once slang no longer is.

The traditional academic disapproval of slang is based on the reality that young people need to learn to write for a wider society than their own immediate peers. They need to become a part of the conversation of many groups in order to make an impact as adults. That wider society may well not know what slang words mean. Another reason for the academic disapproval is that teachers realize the power inherent in a large vocabulary. The mental struggle to discover the words which most exactly convey meaning to a reader outside one's immediate social group is, in reality, a struggle not only to make meaning clearer to one's audience, but to make it clearer to oneself. Adding to your vocabulary words which are likely to be serviceable for many years is just good common sense.

The problem of slang for most users of it is that they don't recognize it as slang, since it's just a part of their vocabulary—no different from the other words they use. Those who make heavy use of slang in their everyday speech need someone outside their speech community—an older brother or sister, a parent, a teacher—to point out to them which words are slang. Reading a wide range of written material is another way to become sensitive to what is and is not slang.

Writing which contains many slang words has a strong informal tone, a tone close to everyday speech. In general, it's probably true that the fewer slang words a written piece contains, the less likely it is to sound like something you might say to your friends at a Saturday-night party. So if your essay does sound like Saturday-night party talk, you had better examine it closely for slang.

Another way to identify slang is by using a dictionary. Some dictionaries label certain words as slang. The problem with this is that current slang words haven't existed long enough to get into a dictionary, and by the time they do, their slang meanings are likely to be obsolete. And then, of course, there's the perennial problem: if you don't know a word is slang, you'll feel no need to check it in a dictionary. Very few slang words are new to the language; what's new about them is what they mean. "Cool," for example, has been a word in the language for centuries; it's the meaning given to it in its slang use that's new. At first, as a slang term, it meant "not emotionally responsive, not showing any warmth or commitment, sophisticated enough never to be amazed, enthusiastic, frightened, or emotional in any way, or at least in any visible way." From this meaning developed the expression: "Cool it," which means "calm down, don't get excited, stop doing what you're doing." Perhaps because these traits were admired, "cool" began to develop a secondary slang sense, equivalent to another slang term, "far-out." Perhaps this meaning owed something to a drug culture in which a "cool," emotionally unresponsive person might be far removed from involvement as a result of taking drugs: he was "far-out." So, cool came to mean "different," not like dull, ordinary things or people. And since this too was admirable, "cool" developed another slang sense: "likeable, acceptable, more than just OK, not to be feared." Of course, by the time you read this book, "cool" may have taken on other meanings.

A slang word many of us have been hearing for a while now is *dis* meaning to show disrespect to someone. Our dictionary only lists *dis* as a preface derived from Latin and meaning "away, apart," "deprive of, expel from, cause to be the opposite of," or "fail, cease, refuse to or do the opposite of." This prefix is apparently the source of the word which results from erasing *respect* in the noun *disrespect*. Thus, instead of saying that someone is not respecting you, you can say "You're *dissing* me." We hear it mainly in the expression "Don't *dis* me." We have not yet seen the word in a dictionary, but we did come across it in an article on teenage clothing on page 74 of *The New York Times* of December 8, 1991:

> Practical clothing that is warm, comfortable, safe and easy to replace has caught on. But the main reason for dressing in hype gear is to be with it, to avoid "getting dissed." Michael Jong of Murray Bergtraum High School in downtown Manhattan has been dissed.

The slang word we discussed in our first edition was *rag,* used as a verb. Our dictionary lists the word as a slang term meaning "tease" or "scold," and posits a possible origin in nineteenth-century British university slang. As a nonslang term in Britain, it means "to play a practical joke or jokes on." Any of these may have served as the basis for a slang term, but experts (adolescents who used it) defined it as "finding fault with, picking on, complaining about," as in: "Stop ragging on me." We admitted in our first edition that we were taking a risk even including the word because slang words tend to be so shortlived. We were right about that; we almost never hear the word any more. Perhaps by the time the second edition appears in print, *dis* will also have become linguistic history.

All of you are shrewd social users of language. You can switch from the language appropriate for your parents to that appropriate for your friends in seconds. You probably even speak differently to your friends in the presence of your parents than you would if they weren't there. And we know that your conversation can be conditioned by physical environment too: you won't talk the same way in a funeral parlor as you do in a locker room. We suspect too that your intimate conversations make little use of slang. Our point in saying this is that you already have the tools that can help you differentiate slang from standard usage—you need to refine the skills you already have. After all, language is always learned within a social setting, so an awareness of the relationship between language and social situations is inevitable, even though we may have difficulty articulating exactly what this relationship is.

Our advice is this: you need to become sensitive to which words are slang and which are not. Perhaps you could write a paper on slang or work collaboratively with a group to compile a slang dictionary. You might want to start with "cool," the example we used, and ask each of your classmates to write the definition of it and several sentences or phrases in which he would use it. Using all these definitions, you and your group, acting as editors, can write an entry for your dictionary. Your classmates can undoubtedly suggest other words for you to include. Once you've finished, you and your class-mates can discuss all the words with your teacher and come to an agreement about which to avoid in the papers you write for her. On the other hand, these slang words may be just the words you should use if your purpose is to convince your peers of something important to you. Any group is more likely to be persuaded by those who speak as they do than by those who sound like outsiders. You might try writing the same argument two ways: once for your teacher and once for your friends.

Colloquialisms

Colloquial expressions are much harder to identify than slang because they're used by many more people and are appropriate in many more contexts. They're not as informal in style as slang, but they may still not be formal enough for some teachers. All this makes it extremely difficult for us to give you any guidance about them. What we do believe is that context is crucial, that colloquialisms are identifiable mainly against a formal background—the equivalent of rhinestone earrings worn by someone in a grey flannel suit. It's the grey flannel suit that makes us label the earrings inappropriate; it's the formal language that makes some teachers label certain words as colloquialisms.

What all this suggests is that colloquial language is quite appropriate for many academic tasks if the overall style of the writing is colloquial or informal. Not all academic writing needs to be formal. This book is written in colloquial language; Joan Didion, Russell Baker, Loren Eiseley, William Safire, and Lewis Thomas usually write in a colloquial style. This brings us back to our previous point: we think that most teachers object to colloquialisms only when they appear in contexts too formal for them, contexts which are not colloquial in style. As you become more aware of slang terms, you'll become more sensitive to which words might be considered colloquialisms. *Kids* is not a slang term; it's too widespread and too ingrained in our vocabulary to be called slang; but it's a colloquialism that most college professors don't want to see in papers they assign. Still, we've met teachers who find no fault with *kids.*

We have quite mixed feelings about too much frowning on colloquial expressions. Unfortunately, students begin to plug in more formal words where the colloquial word would be natural for them. They often end up with a piece of writing that is neither formal nor colloquial, but a hybrid monster of some sort which no one can read without being bewildered. Colloquial language is appropriate in some contexts; formal language is appropriate in other contexts.

If you need or want to master formal writing, you'll first need to become comfortable with contexts which require formal language. To some extent, that knowledge will come to you naturally as you read materials written in a formal style about the subjects you want to use a formal style for. It won't be enough just to change a few words here and there in your writing. You'll need to see your whole task and its context differently. That takes time. And it doesn't mean you'll abandon your colloquial style, since you'll still use it for most of the writing you do.

Maybe you have a teacher who sees all this differently than we do, one who demands or rewards only formal style. If this is your situation, we recommend the following:

1. Ask the teacher if she can show you a paper, preferably a student paper, which achieves the level of formality she wants.

2. Compare this paper to one of your own (maybe with the help of a tutor in your Writing Center) and see if you can pinpoint the differences. Are the sentences longer? Is the sentence structure more varied and complex? Is the vocabulary different from yours, that is, are there words in the other student's paper which are not a part of your usual vocabulary? What sort of introduction and

conclusion does the other paper have? How does its organization compare to yours?

3. Try writing a paper which imitates the characteristics of the other paper. This is risky, and before you submit such a paper to your teacher, you should get some help with it. Any writer who tinkers with her natural style is going to have trouble at first.

4. When you do submit your paper to the teacher, ask her if she'll identify for you several sentences or segments which she likes and several which she still considers too informal.

We think most of you won't have to do anything as drastic to your natural style as what we've just outlined. What you may have to do is simply eliminate certain expressions from your paper which your teacher marks as colloquialisms. You can use a dictionary or thesaurus to find synonyms for the offending words. But remember that what we said earlier still holds. If you replace words you may create some sort of monster. Try to rewrite whole sentences which contain colloquialisms; in this way, you can begin to sense the interaction between words and their contexts. Keep a list of the colloquialisms your teacher points out (different teachers often point out different ones) and create a matching list of possible synonyms. Whenever you find one of these colloquialisms in your writing, look at your list of synonyms and see if there's one which matches the level of formality you're striving for. One of our students made the following list for himself:

washed out	tired, energyless, finished, no longer able to succeed
pull off	succeed
guy	man, person, human being
take (as in "Take your average ballplayer. . . .")	think about, consider
gives it his best	does his best, does as well as he can, tries as hard as he can
doesn't register	has no effect

Two other language features which some teachers condemn as too colloquial or informal are use of the second person (*you*) and use of contractions. Both of these features make writing sound less formal. You'll notice that we've opted to use both in this book; we like the tone. But we recognize that it's a tone that's not appropriate for certain purposes: formal academic papers, scholarly research studies, official statements, and so forth. Again, you'll have to find out your particular teacher's tolerance for these features. We suggest that you ask her directly. (For more on the problems of *you*, see the pronoun section.)

Some of you may have been criticized for using *I* in papers also. This is another thing to ask your teacher about. We're willing to recognize some justification for the arguments against *you* and contractions in certain contexts, but we see little justification in those against *I*. The justification given by those who disapprove is that "I" statements tend to be less authoritative sounding, too subjective. Perhaps. But the truth is that all ways of looking at the world, of deriving knowledge from viewing the world, are subjective. Today, even scientists are beginning to recognize that suppression of the "I" is consciously or unconsciously misleading.

Students' efforts to avoid the first person in their writing often lead them into writing around ideas, and this can create a muddle. And even if the meaning doesn't get muddled, the language often becomes stilted, losing all sense of any connection to a human, individual voice. Ken Macrorie has given this kind of language a name: *Engfish. Engfish* can be defined as the language some students think some teachers like: depersonalized, highly abstract, multisyllabled, and syntactically complex—in his words, "phony, pretentious language."

Dialects and Regionalisms

Some teachers object to dialectical expressions and regionalisms as well as to slang and colloquialisms. Dialects tend to be associated with groups of people, whereas regionalisms are associated with geography. In practice, dialect expressions and regionalisms often overlap. Both usually disappear from a student's used vocabulary quickly when necessary—that is, when she moves away from a particular dialect group or region—since her peers will find them as puzzling as her teachers do. It isn't likely that you'll ask for a "grinder" and "pop" more than once in New York City; you'll quickly learn to say "hero" and "soda". If young people stay within a particular region or dialect area when they go to college, they'll have no trouble with regionalisms either, since it usually takes an outsider to recognize them. Midwesterners will have no problem with: "This is all the farther I can go" until they move East where they'll be expected to say: "This is as far as I can go." Easterners may garner puzzled looks in the Midwest when they say "Bring this with you when you stand on line," since most Midwesterners would say: "Take this with you when you stand in line." Staunch upholders of standard speech are likely to favor Easterners in the first of these two examples and Midwesterners in the second. Reasons for these preferences can probably be cited, but we don't know what they are. In a way, it's a shame that regionalisms are in a decline in our country—perhaps as a result of nationwide radio and television—because they have the potential to enliven the standard vocabulary. We usually find it refreshing to run across someone who has consciously decided to value his regionalisms and use them.

Repetition

Up to this point, we've been talking about replacing words which are synonyms in terms of meaning but which operate on varying levels of formality and academic acceptance. Now we're going to talk about synonyms on the same level of formality. Perhaps you've had English teachers who criticized you for repeating the same word or words in your writing. Repetition can be annoying to the ear and, since most of us have a sense of hearing the words we read, repetition in writing can be annoying too. Repetition, however, can't be mindlessly condemned. Back in the sentence-structure section, we spoke briefly of the repetition of little words (like *to* and *of*) as a means to improve parallel structure. These repeated words are valuable as markers or indicators of sentence structure, as units of syntax which aid meaning. There's also potential value in the repetition of words that carry substantial meaning: verbs, nouns, adverbs, and adjectives.

All speech and writing is redundant for the same reason most computer languages are redundant: the redundancy lessens the chance of miscommunication. In addition, repetition of words or phrases in a piece of writing often helps provide a sense of unity and coherence, or a poetic quality. Witness these paragraphs from the beginning of a novel:

> Where shall the weary rest? When shall the lonely of heart come home? What doors are open for the wanderer? And which of us shall find his father, know his face, and in what place, and in what time, and in what land? Where? Where the weary of heart can abide forever, where the weary of wandering can find peace, where the tumult, the fever, and the fret shall be forever stilled.

> Who owns the earth? Did we want the earth that we should wander on it? Did we need the earth that we were never still upon it? Whoever needs the earth shall have the earth: he shall be still upon it, he shall rest within a little place, he shall dwell in one small room forever.

> — *Thomas Wolfe,* Of Time and the River

The repetition creates an incantatory, poetic tone as well as thematic unity. In the following paragraphs, from an essay on Samuel Johnson, the repetition is effective mainly as it creates a unifying thread:

> Thirdly, one cannot hope to escape humbug of either kind—the humbug of deception or the humbug of self-deception—without courage—the courage to ignore, when necessary, hostile opinion, and the courage to face unpleasant facts. That courage is another of Johnson's greatest qualities.
>
> Fourthly, helped by his honesty and courage, Johnson was one of the great champions of reason. Our rather seedy century has often lost faith in reason, as in individual liberty. . . .
>
> No doubt some eighteenth-century characters trusted too exclusively in reason; but that was because they failed to reason enough. It was Freud, not Bergson or neo-Thomists, who, by reasoning and observation, discovered the irrational Unconscious, with its terrible powers of distorting and misleading the rational part of the mind. And the only hope I can see for the future depends on a wiser and braver use of the reason, not a panic flight from it.
>
> —F.L. Lucas,
> "The Search for Good Sense"

There's quite a lot of repetition here, particularly of "humbug," "courage," and "reason." These words keep a reader's attention focused on the author's key ideas.

Just how much repetition is too much repetition, we can't say absolutely. Each written piece is unique. Here's an excerpt from a student paper on the evils of television. What do you think about the repetition here?

> The reasons for the worthlessness of television are not only in the day time. At night there are shows like Dallas and Dynasty that keep people up all night. These shows come on CBS and ABC respectively. They come on once a week so people have to anticipate what is going to happen. It is hard to believe that a grown person worries about what is going to happen on a television show week after week. People actually give up their sleep in order to see these shows. These shows deal with incest, divorce, sex, and infidelity. Is staying up late hours, watching divorce, sex, infidelity, and incest a good way to use your time? What is the purpose? What do you get out of watching these shows? These are the questions for the people who keep the ratings for these shows very high. People might reply that they are only losing a few hours of sleep. They should ask themselves if they are losing their sleep for something that is constructive. When people will give up something as important as sleep, this is reason to call television an addiction.

Some of the repetition is effective, particularly the repetition of "divorce, sex, infidelity, and incest" and of the word "week." Some of it is annoying: the repetition of "shows" in the second and third sentences adds little to the text; the repetition of "come on" in the third and fourth sentences is annoying, as is the presence of "what is going to happen" in the fourth and fifth sentences. The overuse of "shows" and "people" throughout creates a monotonous thud. Probably what this all comes down to is that readers accept repetition for which they can see a purpose and reject that which seems to demonstrate only an unwillingness or an inability on the part of the author to seek other words or tighten sentences.

We suggest that you read your writing aloud; your ear may be more aware of repetition than your eye. When you hear repetition, make a decision: is it helpful or annoying? Do the repeated words reenforce your meaning or are they relatively insignificant? You can ask others these questions also. If you decide you should use a synonym, remember to keep in mind the level of formality of your essay; you don't want to choose a word that's either too formal or informal.

Many students use a thesaurus to help them select words. We don't want to discourage anyone from doing this; an increase in vocabulary can only strengthen your language. But—no one's vocabulary improves by mindless acceptance of words as absolute synonyms of one another; we need to know how words are used. Say, for example, that a student writes: "He was a bad boy." Thinking this sentence too immature in tone, the student checks her thesaurus and rewrites the sentence: "He was an inclement stripling." *Inclement* does mean *bad,* but the word can't be used to describe people. A *stripling* is a *boy,* but the word *stripling* connotes "mere boy" and highlights youthfulness and lack of mature development. "He was an inclement stripling" will be meaningless to those who do not know the words and humorous to those who do. If neither of these outcomes matches your intentions, you had better write: "He was a bad boy." When you're attempting to eliminate repetition by replacing a word with an apparent synonym, test the substitution out on a few people. It's usually better to repeat yourself than to use a word which will be as out of place as a top hat with jogging clothes.

We're not suggesting that you should be satisfied with your current vocabulary; you should try using new words, since this is the only way you're going to add them to your vocabulary. Experiment with words during your early drafts of a piece of writing; this will help develop that intuitive sense of context which you need to have in order to use words properly. However, if the word or words you choose to experiment with are not a part of your vocabulary, you'd be wise to ask your teacher about them before using them in a paper you're planning to submit for grading.

A specific kind of repetition, overuse of forms of the verb *to be* (*am, is, are, was, were, been, being,*) can have a particularly deadening effect. It's easy to understand why, since *to be* is a verb which simply links what goes before it to what goes after it. It expresses only a mental or physical stasis: "She *is* happy"; "He *was* alone." But, we hear you asking, why is this verb around? It's around because no other verb can do what it does, no other verb can suggest so powerfully the sense of what *is*. It does this *because* it's devoid of movement and development:

> God who was, is, and ever shall be.

The power of this statement grows from the verbs and from the repetition of them in the sequence given: past, present, future. We all need to be aware, though, that the verb *to be* cannot retain its inherent strength when weakened by overuse; it must be used sparingly. Using it too much can deaden a piece of writing; trying to find ways of eliminating it will force you to be more specific.

Select a paragraph or two from your own writing. Underline all forms of the verb *to be* and ask yourself if your intentions are served by the verb in each case. If so, your original choice will be confirmed. If not, try variant rewordings. Here's the beginning of a student's essay on homogeneous vs. heterogeneous grouping of children:

> There *are* two educational philosophies found in the western world. In the United States, the concept *is* that all students deserve an equal education through high school. In the rest of the western world, a standardized test *is* given about the age of twelve. The results of this test *are* used to define specific limitations to the education available to individual students.
>
> The latter educational philosophy *is* the better of the two. It *is* more realistic in that there *is* a distinction in the level that individuals *are* able to learn on. Not everyone can learn at the same rate, and to develop a system around the belief that everyone *is* intellectually equal *is* a wasteful process.

Try rewriting this before you look at what the writer herself did. Then compare what you did to what she did:

> Two educational philosophies coexist in the western world. In the United States, the concept that all students deserve an equal education through high school prevails. In the rest of the western world, all students take a standardized test at the age of twelve. The results of this test determine the specific limitations to the education available to individual students.

The latter educational philosophy works better. It reflects reality more fully in that it acknowledges distinctions in the levels that individuals learn on. Not everyone can learn at the same rate, and to develop a system around the belief that everyone is intellectually equal creates wasted effort.

This student didn't change all forms of *to be* in her writing; she simply considered alternatives. You'll want to do the same. The other thing to remember to do is to read aloud your rewritten piece to hear how it sounds with the changes. In that way, you'll find out whether changes you've made in one place suit larger contexts than just sentences. Changing a word is similar to dropping a pebble in a pond; you can never quite tell how far its influence will go.

Only through experience will you gradually learn how much repetition is enough and how much is too much—just as you might learn exactly how loud to talk to a hard-of-hearing relative. And just as you can't make absolute statements about the latter (obviously you need to talk louder if the stereo is on), so you cannot judge the effect of repetition except in context.

Practice 16

Read through the following excerpts from student papers and consider the level of formality of the language; are there words and expressions you could call slangy, colloquial, or too formal? Discuss these with your classmates and teacher and decide which are appropriate and which are inappropriate.

A

Probably one of the biggest thrills of my high school senior year was partying. I suppose this happens because you are in the homestretch. I don't think I did whole lots of partying, that is, to the extent of going out every night and getting delirious; however, I did my share.

The kind of partying I did could best be described as "hanging out." There was something awesome about senior year, some kind of soaring feeling that came over me I just can't describe. In previous years I was tremendously shy and did not know that many people. I'm still shy, but this past year in high school was a turning point in my social life.

The Class of '90 had a lot of party-type people. I mean the kind of people that go out every night and just do not care about school one tiny bit. I knew one guy who I once asked: "What about school this year—have you just been hanging out?" He said, "Are you kidding me man; I don't even know how to spell my own name." I knew a lot of guys who would skip school every Friday, just about, after third period. These guys would go to someone's house and drink beer. When everyone got wasted, they would come back to school and hang out in a place called THE COMMONS.

The Commons is a place in between the hallway and cafeteria at my school. It was actually an area just outside the cafeteria stretching approximately 50 yards in length and 40 feet in width. There were benches and bleachers spread out through the area where everybody could sit. There was a television screen and once in a blue moon a movie would be shown. But it was mostly a meeting place for a lot of kids. The Commons was a place where most of your "cool" people hung out, such as your athletes and party people. You would always see a lot of good looking girls and guys as well.

On a typical Friday afternoon, most "common-people" would ask, "Hey, what's goin' on tonight? Is anybody going to have a party?" If there was a party, the word went out and we'd all get directions to the place. Some of the parties were really outrageous. One in particular was set up by a guy who was supposed to move the very next day.

He told everybody to tell everybody. That was exactly what they did—about 250 to 300 people showed up. There was so many people crammed into that house, it was incredible. The house was very small and you could barely move around. Everyone said it was a wowaroo of a party, of course; however, when his dad showed up around midnight, he could not believe his eyes. He just walked around with his mouth hanging open. I really felt sorry for my friend because his father was shocked out of his skull and upset at what happened. Miraculously, they were able to move the next day.

There are some parties, however, that are great stuff without being totally out of control. These parties are generally better, because you do not have nearly as many people and you do not have an abnormal amount of people getting squished.

Twelfth grade is something I will never forget. It will remain in my memory as one of the most fantastic years in my life. I cannot describe the feeling when you get to be a senior in high school and I hope it will only be topped by being a senior in college.

B

Our mean transportation was a 1990 Nissan 240SX. We had the music pumping at extremely high decible levels while Jake, emulating the driving skills of Mario Andretti, darted between traffic with great celerity, like a professional Nascar driver, as the cars we passed seemed to be motionless. The view of the mountains was ineffable: the trees were sprouting elegantly their spring leaves, bushes were becoming fuller each moment and streams were flowing as the water moved in a somewhat undulating motion downstream. . . .

We decided to begin our escapade by driving along the beach. As we strolled slowly up and down the sea-shore a few times, we saw many interesting sites. Needless to say, we tried our blandishments in a suave manner by affronting each and every female of reasonable charisma. Unfortunately, it didn't work as well as in Miami Vice. . . .

As we cautiously approached the hotel, looking ever so suspicious, this behemoth of a policeman stopped us and asked, "What do you two boys have in the cooler?" I had a coup! "There are just a few beers," I said. "Oh yeah," he questioned, "let me see." The plan failed. As the lid opened I pictured my whole life in front of me; and the latter part of it was behind bars with a huge mongrel named Butch. As our pitiful efforts to temporize contined to fail, we were trying to presage what imminent punishment could be forced upon us. All sectitude had left us. We were forcefully taken up to an eerie room in the hotel where this carping figure questioned us rather rudely. . . .

They then took all of the beer without questioning anyone. We were then told what could be done to us and what actually would be done to us. A silly question was asked by one of my friends. "Can we have our beer back?" This pejorative statement contained no propriety and was followed by a stern "no" coming from the officer who was not mutable in the least bit. Everyone left as Jake and I lay still on the beds in total astonishment, now becoming pariahs.

Common Errors

"There's glory for you!"

"I don't know what you mean by 'glory,'" Alice said.

Humpty Dumpty smiled contemptuously. "Of course you don't— till I tell you. I meant "there's a nice knock-down argument for you!'"

"But 'glory' doesn't mean 'a nice knock-down argument,' " Alice objected.

"When *I* use a word," Humpty Dumpty said, in a rather scornful tone, "it means just what I choose it to mean—neither more nor less."

"The question is," said Alice, "Whether you *can* make words mean so many different things."

—Lewis Carroll,
Through the Looking-Glass

In this final section on words, we're going to list words that are commonly confused and make some suggestions about how you can pick the right one. For the most part, you have no choice: we live in Alice's world, not in Humpty Dumpty's.

We'll begin with words and expressions which current usage considers unacceptable. Directly under the unacceptable term (marked by an *) we've listed the accepted term.

*alright all right	*Alright* probably isn't all right ("satisfactory") to most English teachers. The *alright* spelling probably developed by analogy to *already*. But since *alright* is listed in many dictionaries and defined as though it were a single word, we suggest that *alright* will become accepted usage soon. For many people, it already is.
*could of *would of *should of *might of could have would have should have might have	The "of" in all these expressions is evidence of the impact of speech. In oral language, "could have" (pronounced "could've") sounds like "could of." Your teachers are going to want "have" in all these verb phrases.
*use to *suppose to used to supposed to	This is more evidence of the impact of spoken language. When we say "I used to go" or "I'm supposed to go," we don't pronounce the *d*'s on the verbs because of the following *t* sounds. We do put the *d* sound on in other contexts: "I used the hammer"; "I supposed he would go." You'll notice that in "I used to go" and "I'm supposed to go" the *s*'s before the -*ed* endings are pronounced like *s*'s, not *z*'s. In the other sentences, the *s*'s are pronounced like *z*'s, just as they are in most common English words when an *s* comes between two vowels.

*try and *be sure and try to be sure to	We don't know why "try to" in speech usually sounds like "try 'n" but it does. Certainly "I'm going to try and do it" is different in meaning from "I'm going to try to do it." But the first of these two is a rare expression, and anyone who said it would probably stress the word *and*. "Be sure and go" is also expressive of two actions. If a speaker intended two directives, he would probably pause briefly after "sure."
*alot a lot	We can't say much about this except that "alot" is probably the second most omnipresent usage error in students' papers. (For number one on the list, keep reading.)
*different than different from	The prohibition against "different than" seems to be disappearing, but, of course, you may have a teacher who still frowns on it. Often you can just change the "than" to "from," but sometimes you can't, and so to satisfy purists you need to reword entirely. In the sentence, "This situation is different than that one," you can make the change easily. But in the sentence, "This situation is different than I thought it would be," you can't just substitute "from" for "than"; you have to reword: "This situation is different from what I thought it would be." When we write a sentence that would become quite involved if we rewrote it, we don't; we just let the "than" stay. But then we really don't object to "different than" in any structure.

This second list is made up of pairs of words which often cause trouble for unwary users for a variety of reasons.

a/an	"A" and "an" are used in exactly the same ways, but they are not interchangeable. "An" appears before words whose first

sound is a vowel. Usually that means the first letter is a vowel; the exceptions are words beginning with a silent *h.* "A" is used before all other words.

A habitual liar, and an easy liver, he's a historian not to be trusted; but he'll be here in an hour.

accept/except   "Accept" means to receive; "except" means "excluding."

I will accept all your gifts except the fish tank.

adapt/adopt   "Adapt" means to modify or adjust; "adopt" mean to take as one's own.

I will adopt your cat if you think she can adapt to living in an apartment.

advice/advise   "Advice" is what you give someone when you "advise" them; in other words, the noun "advice" can be a subject or an object in a sentence, and "advise" is a verb.

I would advise you to accept his advice.

affect/effect   As a verb, choose "affect" when you mean "influence" and "effect" when you mean "cause, bring about." You're probably going to use "affect" far more often than "effect." As a noun, you'll probably need "effect" more often; it means "result." "Affect" as a noun fell out of use for many years, but has made a comeback recently; it means "emotion, feeling."

If he effects a solution, the effect on his salary will be noticeable.

The psychologist wanted to study the affect in the classroom; but he didn't want his work to affect the classroom environment.

all ready/already   One who is "all ready" is fully prepared; something which has happened "already" has happened before now.

Peggy already asked him if he was all ready.

allusion/illusion   An "allusion" to *Hamlet* is a reference to it; an illusion of Hamlet is a ghost, or some other purely imaginary creation.

Her allusions to danger dispelled our illusions of a safe trip home.

beside/besides   When you sit beside someone, you're next to him; if you're doing something besides that, you're doing something additional.

Besides sitting down herself, she asked me to sit beside her.

complement/   Something that "complements" some-
compliment   thing else enhances it, brings out its best qualities, or makes it seem complete. A "compliment" is something nice you say about your teacher.

She complimented him because his tie complemented his outfit.

continual/   Things that are continuous never stop, but
continuous   something that is continual doesn't need to be happening all the time, only habitually.

Continuous breathing leads to a long life; continual drinking doesn't.

credible/   "Credible" is probably not as common a
credulous/creditable   word as its opposite: "incredible," which means unbelievable. The credulous person is gullible; he believes anything you tell him. A creditable person is one who has done something worthy of credit or praise.

The jury, in its deliberations, dismissed the evidence of the credulous witnesses and focused on that of the credible ones; the creditable performance of the defense lawyer also influenced the jury.

disinterested/   Judges are supposed to be disinterested, or
uninterested   not partial, but they shouldn't be uninterested (not interested), or they won't be able to make a decision.

We're uninterested in anything a disinterested arbitration panel decides; we're only interested in the opinions of those who believe as we do.

dispassionate/ impassionate   Basically, these words are opposites in meaning. The dispassionate person is not emotionally involved; the impassionate person is strongly emotional.

Impassionate pleas to dispassionate people are not often effective.

emigrate/immigrate   "Emigrate" is something one does *from* somewhere; "immigrate" is something one does *to* somewhere.

His ancestors emigrated from Poland to Germany; later they immigrated to the United States.

eminent/imminent   An "eminent" person is famous. "Imminent" isn't used to describe people; it's used of something that's about to happen.

Many eminent writers fear that nuclear disaster is imminent.

exalt/exult   To "exalt" someone means to put him in a position of honor or praise him. You can't "exult" someone; "exult" means to be very happy or joyous about something, even to gloat about it.

He exalted his friends to positions of power and exulted over the defeat of his enemies.

famous/notorious   These words are synonymous in meaning well-known, but antonyms in terms of the kind of activity or character they describe. The notorious person is well-known because she has done something wrong or evil.

The deeds of the famous glorify our nation; the deeds of the notorious shame us.

flaunt/flout   Boasters "flaunt" what they're proud of; criminals "flout" the law when they commit crimes in front of a crowd.

The hoodlums flaunted their new clothes as they flouted the law by vandalizing the cars sitting in front of the police station.

imply/infer   Human minds can "infer" something from what someone or something, like a newspaper article or a television show, "implies." What you need to keep in mind is that only the human mind can "infer"; it's a close synonym of "deduce." A good synonym of "imply" is "suggest" or "hint at." "Infer" is often followed by "from." The nouns have related meanings: an "implication" is a "hint" or "suggestion"; an "inference" is a "logical deduction," the sort of thing syllogisms lend to.

Bryan inferred correctly from what the letter implied that he had little chance to win the law suit. The implications were clear; the inference he drew was that he should go ahead and pay the parking ticket.

ingenuous/ ingenious

The "ingenuous" person is naive and unsophisticated, innocent and unaware. The "ingenious" person is clever and inventive.

The ingenious science scheme misled a number of ingenuous investors.

in/into

"In" describes where someone or something is; "into" describes movement, tells where someone is going.

After you walk into a room, you are in it.

it/it's

You've now read far enough to find the most omnipresent usage error in student papers. "Its" is a possessive pronoun like "your" or "his"; "it's" is a contraction of "it is." The distinction is an easy one to make; if you proofread carefully, you'll find that you have no difficulty making your choice.

It's unlikely that the supervisor, who's quite attached to her old desk, will give permission for its removal.

lay/lie

We're going to describe to you the hard line on these two, while recognizing that very few people adhere to it and that our own intuitions don't work too well either, especially when we have to make a quick decision in speech. "Lay" means "put down," as in "Please lay the book on the table." "Lie" means to recline, as in "They lie on the beach in the sun." The problem usually occurs when we want the past tense since the past tense of "lie" is the same as the present tense of "lay"; "Yesterday they lay on the beach." The past participles of these two verbs, "laid" and "lain," cause just as much confusion. "He has laid the book on the table"; "they have lain on the beach for hours."

Critter, my sick cat, lay for hours where I laid him; perhaps he should have lain on a different bed because now I want to lie down and the bed is covered with cat hair.

likely/liable   "Likely" means "probably"; "liable" can mean something similar with the added suggestion of harm: "He's liable to get attacked by mosquitoes in that swamp." You can see from these definitions why the confusion arises. What we see and hear most often is the use of "liable" where "likely" would be the more appropriate choice, as in "He's liable not to go." "Liable" can also mean "responsible" or "answerable for," as in "The company is liable for all damage."

After the accident, he realized that it was likely he would be held liable for what had happened and that he was liable to be sued by everyone involved.

nauseated/nauseous   When you're "nauseated" you don't feel very well; something that's "nauseous" is something—like the smell of a garbage dump—that makes you not feel well. Almost without exception, when you hear the word "nauseous," it's being misused for "nauseated." In fact, dictionaries are already listing them as synonyms, so we predict that the distinction has been almost lost.

I'm nauseous from looking at those nauseating pictures of the aftermath of a nuclear explosion.

principle/principal	A "principle" is something to live by, something to believe in, or a standard or rule of some sort as in "the principle of gravity." A "principal" is in charge of a school. "Principal" can also be an adjective meaning "main" or "first in importance."

The principal reason why the principal resigned was that he believed the principle of fairness had been violated.

quote/quotation	Probably only purists insist on the distinction between these two, but if you're writing for one, you'll need to know the difference. It's quite simple: "quote" is a verb and "quotation" is a noun. The customary "error" is to use "quote" in place of "quotation," as in "I need a quote to substantiate my argument."

The quotation she quoted was not appropriate.

raise/rise	There are similarities here to the lay/lie problem, although fewer people mix these two up. "Raise" means to "lift up"; "rise" means to "go up."

The air will rise more quickly if you raise the window.

respectively/ respectfully	"Respectively" means "in the same order"; "respectfully" means "with respect."

I respectfully request that you ask Karen, Janet, Peggy and Bryan to write to Phil, Vincenzo, Oscar and Andrea respectively.

sit/set	When you sit down, you create a lap; when you set something down, you put it down.

If you sit over there, I'll set the cat on your lap.

stationary/ stationery	You write on "stationery"; "stationary" means not moving or fixed.

The stationery you're looking for is on the stationary rack in the corner.

their/there/they're   "Their" is a possessive pronoun, like "her"; "there" specifies a place, as in "The book is there on the table," or serves as a sentence starter, as in "There are stars in the sky"; "they're" is a contraction of "they are."

There's no reason for their reluctance; they're going to be safe.

toward/towards   Although "toward" may be the preferred term to some people, the two words are interchangeable.

You can either walk toward the house or towards the house.

your/you're   "Your" is a possessive pronoun, like "our"; "you're is a contraction of "you are."

You're not likely to find your keys in this room.

Practice 17

Read through the following dialogue which we've written especially to highlight words commonly confused. See if you can pick out those that are not used properly according to current usage.

Humpty: You should of seen the fall I took.

Alice: Where did you take it? Am I suppose to know what happened?

Humpty: Let me give you some advise. Do you think you can except advise from an egg?

Alice: You're no different than any egg I've ever talked to.

Humpty: You make a practice of talking to eggs? Beside that, what do you do in your spare time?

Alice: Your the one who started this conversation. Besides that, beside you sits another egg.

Humpty: What! There's another egg on my wall! Hey, egg, you had better remain perfectly stationary if you don't want to fry.

Humpty, Jr.: Don't you recognize me? I'm the egg you adopted as your number one son.

Humpty: What do you take me for, an incredulous yokel?

Alice: Hey, Humpty, I didn't know you already have children.

Humpty: Ha! So much for what you know! I once had alot of children. I kept showing them how to fall off the wall and they all continually did it wrong. You know what that means?

Humpty, Jr.: I think its time for me to emigrate to a new land where I'm more likely to live a long, happy life.

Alice: Humpty, are you telling me that you know how to have a great fall off that wall and live to tell it?

Humpty: Yes, since that first time I laid on the ground and watched those inept horses and men the king sent trying to put me back together again. I hired my own horses and men after that. Their well trained.

Alice: It seems to me I've heard allusions to those horses and men before.

Humpty: Not from me you haven't—though, of course, my words are always credible.

Humpty, Jr.: I've set here long enough listening to your ingenuous babbling. I'm not sure I like the inferences I'm hearing. I respectfully ask your permission to leave.

Humpty: How are you planning to effect that? It's a established principal of mine that anyone who sits on my wall has to leave by falling.

Alice: What a nauseating thought!

Humpty: You nauseate easily, don't you? Don't flaunt it.

Alice: Well, here's a verse I once heard. Perhaps you've heard it also: "Humpty Dumpty sat on a wall. Humpty Dumpty had. . . ."

Humpty: Please, those words always affect me adversely.

Alice: I really must be going; I was walking towards that notorious chess game down the road when I saw you. I'm liable to miss it if I don't get going.

Humpty: Bye, bye. Now, come here, sonny boy, I'm going to teach you some great tricks. First you lean like this. . . .

Chapter Seven

Mechanics

This chapter includes some quite arbitrary, but nonetheless rigid, rules about the typographical features of written and printed English. All of the topics in this chapter are relevant only to the written forms of the language; we can, fortunately, speak for hours with no concern at all for these topics.

You may be wondering why we included punctuation in the chapter on sentences instead of this one, since punctuation is traditionally considered to be a mechanical aspect of the written form of the language. We'd like to present a new definition of mechanics here, one that raises punctuation to a higher level of importance. Compare it to capitalization, for instance. Miscapitalization doesn't detract from meaning as much as mispunctuation does. In fact, it's difficult to think of examples where incorrect capitalization would cause misunderstandings, yet there are many misunderstandings caused by incorrect punctuation. Another point we'd like to make about mechanics is that these aspects of the written language really are mechanical; that is, an appropriately programmed computer can watch for and correct 99% of errors in capitalization, spelling, and abbreviations. (There are already several computer programs that check for spelling, and they do find misspelled words. But if one of your misspellings creates another perfectly good word—*will* instead of *well*, for instance—the spelling program won't find it. You have to find those errors yourself.) Also, you can find answers in a dictionary to most questions you have about mechanics; that isn't true of usage problems.

Writers are, unfortunately, often judged more by the mechanical errors they make than by the accuracies in their thoughts or the depth of their analyses. But too many mechanical errors distract readers and make it easy for them to ignore ideas. So, if you're going to work hard on making sure your ideas are clear and complete, you should work just as hard to make sure the mechanics are correct.

Capitalization

There's one sure rule about capitalization in English: sentences beginning a piece of writing and all sentences following a period start with a capital letter.

In addition, certain noun uses require capitalizing in English. In German, all nouns are capitalized.

> Liebesgluck, gluckliches Erinnern, Heimkehr und Wiedersehen in nur wenig Fallen; es herrschen die dunklen und schweren Tone: Abschied und Trennungsschmerz, sehnsuchtiges Harren, Sehnsucht und Klage, Treue in Schwierigkeiten, Sorge um die Treue des Geliebten, um den Bestand der Liebe, Schmerz um den Verlust des Geliebten, Verlassenheit, Eifersucht, Triumph uber die Gegnerin.
>
> —Theodor Frings,
> *Minnesinger und Troubadors*

English, in fact, once adhered to a variation of the Germanic style. Notice the following, written in 1712.

> Beside the Grammar-part, wherein we are allowed to be very defective, they will observe many gross Improprieties, which however authorised by Practice, and grown familiar, ought to be discarded. They will find many Words that deserve to be utterly thrown out of our Language, many more to be corrected; and perhaps not a few, long since antiquated, which ought to be restored, on account of their Energy and Sound.
>
> —Jonathan Swift,
> "A Proposal for Correcting, Improving,
> and Ascertaining the English Tongue"

Not surprisingly, conventions have changed over the years, and English uses capital letters less frequently than it did nearly 300 years ago.

Most dictionaries have sections which present the accepted conventions for capitalization; the variety of words to capitalize is extensive, much more so than we can outline here. Below we discuss some of these conventions, but remember that our list is not complete. You should use a dictionary whenever you have questions about capitalization in your own writing.

In current usage, the accepted practice is that all names of specific things, places, or people should be capitalized. For example:

> Eastside High School boasts the best tennis team in the city.

but

> A high school on the eastern side of town boasts the best tennis team in the city.

Since, in the second example, "a high school" is not the name of the school being discussed, those words are not capitalized, whereas in the first example, "Eastside High School" is the name of the school and is thus capitalized. This same rule applies to such pairs as Mother/my mother, Governor Nigh/the governor, the Mississippi River/the river between Louisiana and Mississippi, the South/south of Tennessee, History 1200/my history class, and other similar pairings.

Certain words are always capitalized: Venus, Mars, Neptune (vs. the earth, the sun, the planets); January, February, March (vs. spring, fall); Easter, Hanukkah, Ramadan (vs. weekend, holiday, vacation). Other words are sometimes capitalized and sometimes not (you could continue our list from the previous paragraph for several more lines), and in some instances the rules for when to capitalize seem arbitrary. For instance, English is always capitalized; other subject disciplines are not:

> My English class meets in the same room as my physics class.

The same rule applies to other languages also: you study German and French and Chinese along with your mathematics and computer science and home economics.

As always, there are exceptions. E. E. Cummings decided not to use conventional capitalization in his poems. Other writers try to make political, social, or personal statements in their decisions about whether to capitalize; e.g., not capitalizing "president" when referring to the leader of the United States or another country might have political or personal connotations—the writer may not respect the position or may not like the person holding the position. Very rarely do we consciously choose to omit capitalization where it's required or add it where it isn't required, but we may often find ourselves omitting it because of ignorance or inattention. Again, if you have doubts about whether a word should be capitalized, use a dictionary.

Underlining (Italics) and Quotation Marks

We discuss both of these punctuation marks here as well as in the section on punctuation, since some of their uses are rule-governed (mechanics), while other depend on context (usage). As with the other typographical features discussed in this section, the conventions for italicizing (underlining in typing) and using quotation marks are more thoroughly described in handbooks and dictionaries.

Italicizing (underlining) is guided by fairly simple rules. You should italicize titles of complete works: *Carmen* (opera), *One Hundred Years of Solitude* (novel), *The Mona Lisa* (painting), *Newsweek* (magazine), *Harold and Maude* (film), *Songs from the Big Chair* (album). Subdivisions of such works should appear between quotation marks. In practice, this includes the titles of poems, short stories, essays, articles, chapters in books, and songs. Underlining in typing is a signal to a typesetter to use italic type. Yet, within their typographical resources, most newspapers have neither underlining nor italic letters; as a result, you'll see all titles in quotation marks in most newspapers as well as in some magazines.

Italicizing is also used for the names of ships and trains, for foreign-language expressions that have not become a part of English ("The *ubi sunt* motif shows up quite often in poetry"), and for words, letters and numbers under discussion ("*Pulchritude* looks and sounds the opposite of what it means," "*C* has two sounds in English," "The number *1* looks like what it represents"). Italicizing can also be used for emphasis, a use that we discuss more completely in our section on punctuation.

Quotation marks are used for other than indicating titles. Their most common use is to show where an exact quotation begins and ends. Quotation marks in combination with punctuation marks are governed by quite arbitrary rules. (We discuss this in the punctuation section, so here we'll give just a quick summary.) American style-books recommend that periods appear inside quotation marks. Question marks and exclamation prints go inside quotation marks only if they are a part of what is being quoted; otherwise they belong outside. If the structure of your sentence as you write it calls for a comma at the end of a quotation—even of one word—it goes inside the quotation marks even though it might not be a part of the quoted material. If the structure of your sentence requires a semicolon or a colon which is not part of the quoted material, it belongs outside quotation marks. For more on integrating quoted words into your writing word examples of what this looks like, see Chapter 9, "Research." So check the punctuation section for a discussion of using quotation marks around specific words.

Spelling

Before the invention of printing presses, when manuscripts were handwritten, scribes apparently tried to capture the sounds of the spoken language. In fact, scholars of Old and Middle English draw conclusions about changes in the spoken language by studying scribal variations in these old manuscripts. Even when printing presses began providing a great abundance of written products, spelling tended toward the idiosyncratic; variant pronunciation by native speakers of a language is not an invention of the modern world! But because print fixes form, discrepancies between the oral and written forms of English eventually began to develop. That is, pronunciation changed over the years, but spelling didn't. This is why *ough* has different pronunciations in *though, rough,* and *through.*

Undoubtedly, it was the development of dictionaries which led to the acceptance of "right" and "wrong" spellings. According to Albert Baugh, in *A History of the English Language* (New York: Appleton-Century-Crafts, 1957), "Spelling was one of the problems which the English language began consciously to face in the sixteenth century. During the period from 1500 to 1650 it was fairly settled." Baugh's statement is perhaps too absolute, but for the most part he's right; idiosyncratic spelling has declined in the past 300 years (although changes in accepted spellings still occur).

And, like it or not (we don't at all), our intelligence and knowledge are often judged by how we spell. Because of this, writers often find themselves getting frustrated about this seemingly minor problem. John Irving tells a story about Andrew Jackson who, while trying to write an official paper in the Oval Office, once yelled in frustration, "It's a damn poor mind that can think of only one way to spell a word!" If you're a poor speller, you probably feel as Jackson did, but consistent spelling aids communication (and it's even reassuring to know that there are some things which several hundred million people can actually agree on). If you're a poor speller, you probably don't want to know that there's a system to English spelling (which there is); what you do want to know are some strategies to help you become a better speller.

First of all, read more. Seeing words spelled correctly will help your spelling improve. (The converse is true as well; some English teachers report that they have problems with certain words that their students frequently misspell. This shows how much we can be unconsciously affected by print.) If you write a lot, you probably know which words you're likely to misspell and which ones you have to look up every time you use them. You may even want to keep a list of words that you always have to look up, to save time thumbing through a dictionary. If you have a computer, get a program that checks spelling and use it.

As you write, remember that spelling is the last thing you should worry about. Certainly in the beginning stages, as your ideas are just emerging, worries about spelling will block those ideas, force you to use an inadequate word, or perhaps move you in directions you don't want to go in. In most writing situations you'll have a chance to check your spelling thoroughly before submitting your work. Most professional writers have tricks for dealing with words they can't spell. While writing, some mark the words they're unsure of and then at a later time look them up in a dictionary or ask someone else how they're spelled. John Irving, in an article he wrote for the International Paper Company ("How to Spell," 1983), describes an exercise that helps him: "Beside every word I look up in my dictionary, I make a mark. Beside every word I look up more than once, I write a note to myself—about WHY I looked it up." The notes don't help him learn how to spell the words, but they do help him remember which words he must look up. Most bad spellers simply give their texts to friends who are good spellers and who can find most of their mistakes' or they use word processors with programs that check spelling.

Second, there are some spelling rules with only a few exceptions. Some of these are easy to remember, like "*i* before *e* except after *c*," but you must also be able to remember the exceptions. This rule covers *receive, friend,* and *grief,* but not *neighbor, neither, seize,* or *species.* Another relatively easy-to-remember rule is "change *y* to *i* before adding a suffix," but this one doesn't apply when adding *-ing* or when the root word has a vowel before the final *-y* (except for *pay/paid, say/said*).

Other spelling rules are quite complicated, and thus a bit cumbersome to carry around in your head. These rules cover prefixes, suffixes, unaccented vowels, and doubled consonants, which cause the most trouble for writers. In "How to Spell," Irving gives a complicated rule governing the suffixes *-ible/-able:*

> You add *-able* to a full word: adapt, adaptable; work, workable. You add *-able* to words that end in *e*—just remember to drop the final *e:* love, lovable. But if the word ends in two *e*'s, like agree, you keep them both: agreeable.
> You add *-ible* if the base is not a full word that can stand on its own: credible, tangible, horrible, terrible. You add *-ible* if the root word ends in *-ns:* responsible. You add *-ible* if the root word ends in a soft *c* (but remember to drop the final *e!*): force, forcible.

Another of these complicated rules tells you how to add suffixes like *-ing* to words like *refer* to get results like *referring.*

> For monosyllables or words accented on the last syllable and ending in a single consonant preceded by a single vowel, double the final consonant before adding a suffix beginning with a vowel.

The accent in *refer* is on *fer,* and the final vowel-consonant combination fits the rule, so to add *-ing* you must double the final *r.* Thus, also *referred, preferred, concurred.* Look at *reference, preference; concurrence.*

Right now, you're probably wondering, "Why bother?" We agree if you mean, "Why bother with all these rules?" They don't help all writers, and usually it's easier to look the word up in a dictionary than to try to remember the rule. But if you mean "why bother" with spelling correctly, we'd have to argue with you. There are few occasions when you would consciously decide to misspell words (brand names are an obvious example: Brite for a cleanser; or Quik-Trip, for a store). Out of respect for your reader—to make it easier for him to read what you've written—you should make every effort to check your work and correct misspelled words. You should also make this effort out of respect for yourself: some readers attribute misspelling to ignorance. Richard Rodriguez, in his book *Hunger of Memory,* tells the story of his mother's halted advancement in her career because of a spelling error. Her spoken English was not excellent, but she had terrific typing and spelling skills and had been able to get a job as a bilingual secretary on the California governor's staff. "One morning there was a letter to be sent to a Washington cabinet officer. On the dictating tape, a voice referred to urban guerrillas. My mother typed (the wrong word, correctly): 'gorillas.' The mistake horrified the antipoverty bureaucrats who shortly after arranged to have her returned to her previous position." The results of Mrs. Rodriguez's misspelling were disastrous, but they do emphasize the importance of correct spelling to many people. And academics are as rigid about spelling as are business executives or government bureaucrats.

As always, some contexts justify misspelling. One time you might decide to misspell words is when you take on the voice of a nonliterate narrator. Below are two examples of how authors have dealt with the problem of how a nonliterate writer would spell.

Huck Finn ends his narration with:

> . . . and so there ain't nothing more to write about, and I am rotten glad of it, because if I'd 'a' knowed what a trouble it was to make a book I wouldn't 'a' tackled it, and ain't a-going to no more. But I reckon I got to light out for the Territory ahead of the rest, because Aunt Sally she's going to adopt me and sivilize me, and I can't stand it. I been there before.
>
> —Mark Twain,
> *The Adventures of Huckleberry Finn*

There are plenty of usage "errors" but only one misspelled word. Mark Twain evidently decided that he didn't want to strain his reader, and thus Huck Finn rarely misspells.

Russell Hoban's Riddley Walker, though, writes an almost indecipherable text:

> Wel I cant say for cern no mor if I had any of them things in my mynd befor she tol me but ever since then it seams like they all ways ben there. Seams like I ben all ways thinking on that thing in us what thinks us but it dont think like us. Our woal life is a idear we dint think of nor we dont know what it is. What a way to live.
>
> Thats why I finely come to writing all this down. Thinking on what the idear of us myt be. Thinking on that thing whats in us lorn and loan and oansome.
>
> —Riddley Walker

We suspect Hoban allowed Riddley to misspell words in order to partially represent the chaos the world went through after a nuclear holocaust that destroyed practically everything, including all printed materials. Yet even with this (to us) chaotic language there is pattern.

The only other time you'd misspell words in what you're writing is when you're quoting someone else's error and you want to quote that person's exact written text. Researchers studying the writing of children and of people learning foreign languages often reproduce the errors the people make as they write. Also, misprints occur in texts, and to be as honest as possible, you would have to quote those errors as they occur. At times like these, if there could be any doubt about who made the error (you or the person you're quoting), you can add *sic* in brackets ([sic]) to show that the other person misspelled the word, not you. (*Sic* can be used to attribute any kind of error to the original writer—grammar, vocabulary, punctuation, even incorrect information; see the next section on abbreviations for an example of how it is used.)

One final note: the hardest thing about spelling is knowing when you've misspelled a word, and developing a sense that helps you recognize misspellings takes time. If you're a poor speller, don't get discouraged. Just find someone who can help you proofread and don't let concerns about spelling distract you while you're writing.

Abbreviations

We've listed below the most common abbreviations you'll find in scholarly texts. Most dictionaries define these, as well as any others you may find that aren't on this list; handbooks also list the most frequently used abbreviations. You'll probably use some of these abbreviations in any writing that has drawn information from outside sources (see the section on documentation for research for more on this). As always, the context of your writing and consultation with your instructor will help you decide which abbreviations are appropriate and which aren't. For example, in informal writing, "etc." is perfectly acceptable, though "q.v." might seem out of place; but in formal writing, most instructors would object to your using "etc." yet would have no problem with "q.v." Occasionally, you may have to base your decision simply on how the abbreviation looks: In addresses, for instance, for most readers "NY NY" on an envelope causes no problems, but some might be bothered if "NY NY" appeared in the actual letter, especially if the letter is typed on fancy letterhead stationery. ("New York, NY," however, might be acceptable. Using the Postal Service state abbreviations is becoming standard practice.)

A.D.: *anno Domini.* Latin for "in the year of the Lord." Precedes numerals; no space between *A.* and *D.* Not used in references to centuries, e.g., A.D. 150; eighteenth century.

anon.: anonymous. Usually appears after quotes, but not in the text, e.g., "The anonymous writer. . . ."; " . . . going home" (anon.).

art., arts.: article(s). Usually appears in footnotes.

B.C.: Before Christ. Follows numerals; no space between B. and C. Jewish writers sometimes use B.C.E. (before Christian era). 200 B.C.

bibliog.: bibliography, -er, -ical. Usually appears in footnotes.

bk., bks.: book(s). Usually appears in footnotes.

ca. (c.): *circa.* Latin for "about." Used with approximate dates, e.g., "The antique chair dates from ca. 1650."

cf.: *confer.* Latin for "compare." Used to refer reader to differing or opposing opinions.

ch., chs. (chap., chaps.): chapter(s). Usually appears in footnotes.

col., cols.: column(s). Usually appears in footnotes.

ed., eds.: editor(s), -ion(s), -ed. Usually appears in footnotes.

e.g.: *exempli gratia.* Latin for "for example." Rarely capitalized; no space between *e.* and *g.*; set off by commas.

esp.: especially. Usually appears in footnotes.

et al. (never et als. or et. al.): *et alii.* Latin for "and others." Only used for people, as in lists of authors.

etc.: *et cetera.* Latin for "and so forth."

f., ff.: "and the following page(s) or line(s)." Exact references are preferable, e.g., pp. 53-54 instead of pp. 53 f.; pp. 53-58 instead of pp. 53 ff.

fig., figs.: figure(s). Usually appears in footnotes and in captions for illustrations.

i.e.: *id est.* Latin for "that is." Rarely capitalized; no space between *i.* and *e.*; set off by commas.

illus.: illustrated,-or,-ion(s). Usually appears in footnotes.

l., ll.: line(s). Usually appears in footnotes.

MS(s)., ms(s)., ms(s): manuscripts(s).

N.B. (or n.b.): *nota bene.* Latin for "take notice, mark well." Usually used in footnotes.

n.: footnote (occasionally fn. is used, but n. is preferred). Usually used in footnotes when referring to other footnotes.

p., pp.: page(s). Usually appears in footnotes.

passim: Latin for "here and there." Usually appears in footnotes to indicate several references throughout a work, as in "pp. 16, 22, 25 and passim."

q.v.: *quod vide.* Latin for "which see." Used most often in encyclopedia entries to refer to other entries.

sic: "thus, so." Between square brackets when used as an editorial comment, i.e., to assure the reader you have quoted someone else's error and not made one of your own.

s.v.: *sub verbo* or *voce.* Latin for "under the word or heading." Used most often when referring to encyclopedia entries.

viz.: (with or without a period) *videlicet.* Latin for "namely." Set off by commas; sometimes this is interchangeable with i.e.

vs.: *versus.* Latin for "against."

Most of these abbreviations appear most frequently in footnotes, and few of us read footnotes unless they contain further explanation of something brought up in the text. Checking footnotes for this kind of information is a good habit to develop; some writers now make attempts to avoid discursive footnotes, but in older texts the notes can contain quite interesting information. Another benefit of reading notes is that you'll become more familiar with how some abbreviations are used. The footnote below is an example of the kind you might find in academic prose.

[21]Chs. 17 and 33 above, passim, refer to this problem; see pp. 107 f. and 225 ff., esp. pp. 226-227. Groutte, et al. (1978) question the efficacy of the dating process and argue that even ca. 4,000,000-2,000,000 B.C. is too specific a date; cf. Podner and Hras (1979) for arguments against Groutte. The *Encyclopedia Galatea* (s.v. *archeological dating processes*) states that "none of the processes is infallible." It would seem then that the arguments have proven only to muddle the issue and make finding any definite answer somewhat like chasing a chimera. The *Encyclopedia Galatea* entry brings into question almost all prehistoric dates, e.g., the beginning of the universe, the beginning of life on earth, and the birth of upright-walking humanoids. The entry also states, "Vroth (q.v.) frequently questioned the point of trying to date events so exactly. He flustered many conference presenters by posing embrassing [sic] and difficult-to-answer philosophical questions on scientific methods. It's possible that in Vroth we find an example of a scientist *manqué,* a sort of dog-in-the-manger, 'if I can't have her nobody will' villian

who could relieve his frustrations only in this manner." It is important to note, however, that the *Encylopedia's* writers missed an important point in Vroth's tactics, viz, that his questions challenged many of the more worthy researchers to re-examine their methods. I.e., scientists like Arx, Manne and Feldton felt obliged by Vroth's attacks to look at their data more carefully and revise findings. [N.B.: None of the dates first proposed by Arx, Manne and Feldton changed more than 0.7% after being revised (editor's note).]

Typed Manuscript Form

At the risk of telling you the obvious, we've added this final section to cover questions we've often gotten from our students about how their papers should be typed. Whether you type a paper for a course or for publication, there are typographical conventions which make your writing easy to read. Stylebooks usually reproduce manuscript pages to give you an idea of what they should look like, and you can find descriptions of styles requirements in most journals.

Unless your instructor gives different directions, your typed papers should be double-spaced with 1" to 1½" margins on all four sides. Double-spacing will allow you room to make last minute additions or corrections before you submit the paper; the margins will allow your reader room for comments. (Triple-spacing and leaving extra-wide margins will tip any reader off to the fact that you're trying to help your paper meet some kind of minimum requirement for length. Few teachers mind your doing this, but also few are fooled into thinking you've written more than what's there.) Other conventions of typed MS. form are indenting the first line of each paragraph (five to seven spaces), numbering each page, and using a title page for lengthy papers. Not many style manuals or teachers require footnotes now; most accept endnotes, notes that appear in a list at the end of the paper rather than at the bottom of each page. Yet, if your paper is going to be microfilmed, or if your teacher requires it, you'll need to put your notes at the bottom of each page. This means you'll have to remember to leave space for the notes and still have the 1½" margin at the bottom of the page.

One thing stylebooks rarely discuss is correct word division at the ends of lines. It may seem like a minor consideration, another arbitrary rule invented to make producing a perfect text a difficult task. True, some rules are arbitrary, such as "Don't divide between two-letter suffixes or prefixes and the base word." You've probably noticed that newspapers and journals violate this "rule" all the time. There is, however, a good reason behind dividing words correctly between syllables. As people read, they subconsciously predict what's going to come next. If you misdivide a word at the end of a line, you may force your reader into an incorrect prediction. Consider the following passage:

> But the song that followed, "M.A.S.S."(Music Against Second Slavery) was in proportion; it lasted more than an hour as members of the 30-person troupe, Egypt 80, took instrumental and dance solos. And the inspired music was as confident, eccentric and earthy as the speech. It was a leisurely concert, with Mr. Anikulapo Kuti leading the band for three hours, following a half-hour of war-
>
> — *The New York Times,* 7/17/91, C:13

What do you expect will be the completion of "war-"? Within the context of this paragraph, about the militant Nigerian musician Fela, it's possible that there was a half-hour of something concerning war before the music began. But look at how the paragraph ends:

> mup, including a tune sung by the bandleader's young son, Olawe-seun.

What probably happened is that the newspaper's computer, which set the type, divided "warmup" between the two consonants—a rule that usually works, but not in this case. This mistake, though humorous, probably momentarily confused the article's readers—it's not a serious mistake, but it shows how much readers rely on a text to help them make predictions about what is to come. You need to make sure you don't mislead your reader through improper hyphenation; for much the same reason, no line of type begins with a hyphen, comma, semicolon, or any of the endmarks (period, question mark, exclamation point). Some writers occasionally begin a line of type with a dash if they've run out of room on the previous line.

This has been a lengthy explanation, but it's difficult to defend readable word division in fewer words. Misdividing words is no crime, just as misspelling them is no crime. But if you persist in misdividing (and misspelling), you'll give your reader the impression that you don't really care about what you've written or about whether it can be read without needless disruption.

It's important to realize also that even just the look of a paper can turn a reader off. If there are too many pencilled-in corrections, too many crossed-out or whited-out words, a reader's first response could be "What a mess!" You should make a point to find out how many handwritten corrections your teacher will tolerate, and if you find yourself making too many, you should consider retyping the page. Other options, of course, include hiring a typist, using a cut-and-paste method and a xerox machine, and working on a word processor. But if your paper is being printed on a word processor, remember that dot-matrix print is sometimes difficult to read and often doesn't reproduce well. If possible, you should have your papers printed on a letter-quality printer.

Documentation (Footnotes and Bibliography)

Documentation is not a way to show your instructor that you've read the required number of books and articles; instead it serves two vital functions, especially for academic communities. First, very few ideas develop in a vacuum, and acknowledging the sources of your ideas is a courteous and honest way of giving credit where it's due. In addition, careful documentation will provide your readers with a list of sources they can explore for further information on the problem you're discussing as well as on related problems. You probably know this yourself if you've checked a bibliography for further reading, or looked up a footnoted quote to better understand the context it appears in.

Though documentation may seem only secondary to your paper, and though you'll probably wait to complete this part until the final step before editing and submitting your paper, it deserves some thought and careful attention to make it useful for the reader. The most important criteria are that footnotes and the bibliography be consistent and easy to read. Traditional footnotes, whether they appear at the bottom of a page or at the end of the paper, restate information listed in the bibliography and refer to specific page numbers as well. Traditional bibliographies may include not only the sources that contributed ideas and information to a paper, but also related sources the writer wishes to recommend for further reading. But, because some fields have adopted a simpler documentation style in recent years, they no longer advocate traditional footnotes and bibliographies. It's therefore important to find out from your instructor which documentation style to follow before preparing the final draft of your paper. Below we've described three methods suggested by various style manuals (MLA, APA, Turabian). Since we can't give complete explanations, with appropriate examples, of these three methods, you should check the manuals for fuller descriptions.

MLA Handbook for Writers of Research Papers. 3rd ed. (New York: Modern Language Association, 1988) and *MLA Style Manual (New York: Modern Language Association, 1985).* The documentation style recommended by these handbooks is used most widely by people writing for the humanities (for example, literature, art and art history, music and music theory). According to the *MLA Handbook,* the backbone of documentation for a paper is the list of works cited, formerly known as the bibliography. Like a bibliography, the "Works Cited" page comes at the end of the paper. But, as the title of the list suggests, only those sources which are specifically mentioned in the paper should be included. (If you call the list "Works Consulted," you can include readings that aren't cited in the paper. To suggest related readings, compile a separate list and call it "A Selected Bibliography"). The *MLA Handbook* says that because the list of works cited provides complete publication information, there's no need to replicate it in footnotes. Instead, it urges the writer to make brief parenthetical references to sources in the body of the paper itself. In the following excerpt form a paper entitled "The Female Figure in Georg Büchner's Work," you'll see an example of a parenthetical reference:

> At the time of his son's escape, Ernst Büchner became upset, primarily because the departure was abrupt; he had little idea of the seriousness of the situation. But when *Danton's Death* was published, the father grew angry. If it was not the excessive political stance that offended him, it was more than likely the obscene language and lewd manner of the play. Whatever the exact cause, Herr Büchner cut off aid to his son and severed communications for two years (Beacham 53).

The parenthetical reference at the end of this portion of text lets the reader know that it was derived from a specific source—page 53 of a work by Beacham. The reader can now flip to the "Works Cited" page where he will find complete information about the source:

> Beacham, R. "Büchner's Use of Sources in *Danton's Death.*" *Yale/Theatre* 3 (1972): 45-55.

The reader will understand this information to mean that Beacham's article, "Büchner's Use of Sources in *Danton's Death,*" may be found of pages 45–55 in volume three of a journal called *Yale/ Theatre.* Abbreviations such as vol. and pp. do not appear.

The information that must be included in a parenthetical reference depends on whether the author's name appears in the text. In the excerpt above, the name Beacham isn't included in the text, so it must be cited in parentheses. In the following excerpt from the same paper, the author's name is part of the text, so it doesn't have to be repeated in parentheses. Note that the quotation is indented because it's more than four lines long:

> Herbert Lindenberger's work with speech styles is of interest, for he talks about one we've looked at already: Marion's.

> In striking contrast to Robespierre's inflated arguments and abstractions, Marion's story consists largely of a series of sense impressions, made without comment on her part. Her sentences are built out of simple clauses, usually connected by "and," and without causal connections. When she describes her emotions, she states them directly, as though they were simple facts. (28)

Here only a page number is in parentheses. Again, since we know the author's name we can easily find it in the list of works cited, where it's listed alphabetically:

> Kayser, Wolfgang. *The Grotesque in Art and Literature.* New York: McGraw, 1966.
> Lindenberger, Herbert. *Georg Büchner.* Carbondale: Southern Illinois UP, 1964.
> Majut, Rudolf. "Some Literary Affiliations of Georg Büchner with England." *Modern Language Review* 50 (1955): 30-43.

Note that the second and subsequent lines of each entry on the "Works Cited" page are indented. On a typewriter, use five spaces, and double-space the entries and the block quotations.

Basic documentation, then, according to the *MLA Handbook,* requires parenthetical references and a list of works cited. The handbook gives instructions for how to document radio and TV programs, lectures, films, works of art, performances, interviews, and recordings, as well as the more usual printed materials: journals and periodicals, encyclopedias and dictionaries, dissertations, pamphlets, etc.

APA handbook, or *Publication Manual of the American Psychological Association,* 3rd ed. (Washington, DC: APA, 1983). As this handbook's title implies, the style recommended here is most often used by people writing in the social sciences such as psychology and linguistics, as well as the natural sciences (biology, physics, chemistry, etc.). Like the *MLA Handbook,* the APA handbook advocates parenthetical references, but its bibliography is called "References." You'd notice other differences if you compared the two documentation styles. For example, in a paper about fever, you may want to cite Elisha Atkin's recent article in *The New England Journal of Medicine.* Here's how your citation might look, using APA style (there are three options):

> A recent discussion on fever (Atkins, 1983) states . . .

or

> Atkins (1983) reports that fever . . .

or

> Atkins's 1983 article suggests that . . .

In all three instances the only information given is the author's last name and the date of the reference, but no page numbers. MLA recommends providing the author's name and page numbers, but no date. (Note, too, that in the first option, Atkins and the year are separated by a comma.) A reader looking in the bibliography for Atkins's article would find:

Atkins, E. Fever—New perspectives on an old phenomenon. *The New England Journal of Medicine,* 1983, 308, 958-960.

The reader would know that "Fever . . . phenomenon" is the article's title, and that "308" is the journal's volume number.

There's a slight variation in the text reference if your source is a direct quotation. The date is still given after the author's name, but quotations need exact page references in parentheses (p. or pp. precedes the number or numbers). For example, in a paper on psycholinguistics:

Cairns and Cairns (1976) discuss in great length "linguistic creativity." They write that there are "three aspects of the creative use of language . . . any human being can say things that have never been said before . . . humans can hold discourse about . . . abstractions . . . [and] human utterances are usually appropriate either to the external context or at least to the thought going through the mind of the speaker . . ." (pp. 5-7).

And the entry on the "References" page would be:

Cairns, H.S., & Cairns, C.E. *Psycholinguistics: a cognitive view of language.* New York: Holt, Rinehart and Winston, 1976.

As with the MLA style, in a typed manuscript, bibliographical references are double-spaced. Also note that only the first word of a title (except for journal titles) is capitalized. Abbreviations like *vol.* and *no.* do not appear.

The APA handbook describes how to reference articles, books, monographs, abstracts, dissertations, government publications, and films. In addition, it includes useful guidelines for nonsexist language.

Student's Guide for Writing College Papers, 3rd ed. (Chicago: Univ. of Chicago Press, 1976) and *A Manual for Writers,* 5th ed. (Chicago: Univ. of Chicago Press, 1987), both by Kate L. Turabian. Turabian's style recommendations include instructions for making parenthetical references, very similar to the *MLA Handbook*'s recommendations, but she also gives instructions for using traditional footnotes, single-spaced, at the bottom of the page. Here are a few footnotes, using Turabian's style, that might occur in a paper on Persian manuscript illuminations:

[3] G.M. Meredith-Owens, *Persian Illustrated Manuscripts* (London: The Trustees of the British Museum, 1973), pp. 18-19.

[6] Ibid., p. 23.

[7] Marie Lukens Swietochowski, "Persian Painting," BMMA 36 (Autumn 1978:12). [BMMA is an accepted abbreviation for the Bulletin of the Metropolitan Museum of Art.]

[8] Meredith-Owens, p. 27.

[9] Martin Bernard Dickson and Stuart Cary Welch, *The Houghton Shahnameh* (Cambridge, Mass.: Harvard Univ. Press, 1980), pp. 5-7.

[10] Haim's *Shorter Persian-English Dictionary* translates this word as "narrow, slender; delicate, subtle."

The works would appear in the bibliography (also-single spaced) as:

Dickson, Martin Bernard, and Welch, Stuart Cary. *The Houghton Shahnameh.* Cambridge, Mass.: Harvard Univ. Press, 1980.

Haim, S. *The Shorter Persian-English Dictionary.* 3rd ed. Tehran: V. Beroukhim and Sons, 1976.

Meredith-Owens, G.M. *Persian Illustrated Manuscripts.* London: The Trustees of the British Museum, 1973.

Swietochowski, Marie Lukens. "Persian Painting." *BMMA* 36 (Autumn 1978): 12-33.

Like the MLA and APA handbooks, this one lists sample footnote and bibliographic entries for most possible sources.

These handbooks also recommend formats for abstracts, charts, diagrams, tables of contents, margins, pagination—answers to practically every question you might have about how to type your paper once you've written it. These books are valuable only as guides for editing and typing your texts—they can't tell you how to do research or how to write a research paper. For more about doing research and writing research papers, see Chapter 9.

hHApp y helo heLLee
hap pyha olloee oops
HALooEe hallw ha lllowin
hoLLOine hapPY hu
hOllowen hal

HA~~LooEe hallw ha lllowin~~
~~holLOine hapPY hu~~
~~xhOllowen xhalx~~

boo.

Chapter Eight

If English Is Not Your First Language

If you've left your country to come to school in the United States, particularly if you have come here to attend college, you were probably confronted with a shocking realization: The English courses you took back home did not prepare you for the writing (and perhaps reading) assigned to you at college here. After taking a timed placement exam, you may have found yourself in a special writing course for students whose first language isn't English (ESL students). Or you may have ended up in a freshman writing course with peers who are all native English speakers but who can't write in English as well as you can write in your first language.

There are many foreign students in similar predicaments across the country. Researchers estimate that by the year 2000, ESL students will make up more than 25% of the college student population; colleges in some large cities have already reached this percentage. Teacher education programs are beginning to realize the importance of understanding how to address the needs of students like you, and special ESL courses are being developed to meet these needs.

But this is small consolation to you, as you try to understand just what it is that you're doing wrong when you write. Some of your teachers will correct all your grammatical errors before returning a paper to you; others will fill the margins with question marks implying your language was too confusing for them to understand at all; still others will just write a note at the top of the first page: "See me after class. You need help!"

Try not to be discouraged by the responses you get from your teachers (and from your peers). Read between the lines to get to the basic message, which is: You're intelligent, you just need to learn more English so that your readers can understand what you're trying to say.

Actually, you may need to learn more than just the language to be an effective writer. The writing style you developed in your first language may not be appropriate for college writing in the U. S., so you may have to adjust it to satisfy your readers. (For example, French speakers generally have a more formal, flowery style than American readers are used to.) The range of approved topics may be broader in the U. S., so you may have to be open to new possibilities. (Students from the People's Republic of China, for instance, have probably never been asked to write their opinions about their government's actions.) Even minor things like sentence length could be affecting how your readers evaluate your writing. (Spanish speakers, for example, typically write long sentences that Americans readers lose patience with.)

What to do? After all the chapters you've read so far, our advice should come as no surprise to you.

1. Read as much American English as you have time for—college texts, newspapers and magazines, novels, even advertisements. This reading will give you a sense of the appropriate levels of formality for various contexts of American English (and you'll pick up a lot of vocabulary and grammar in the process).

2. Talk to your peers and ask to see samples of papers they've written. Then ask them to explain decisions they made about topic, organization, vocabulary, and anything else that strikes you as important. Other students' papers can be helpful models of the type of writing that's acceptable in American colleges.

3. Talk to your teachers to get a specific idea of what criteria they use when evaluating students' papers. Ask if they have samples of good papers that you could read. And if they've returned a paper to you, ask for an appointment to discuss their evaluation of it. Don't be defensive—don't try to change the teacher's mind about your paper—just try to understand his evaluation of it.

The only part of writing that will cause you long-term frustration is the language itself. We have some advice to give you about improving your grammar and vocabulary, but first we want to tell you a few facts about language acquisition. These are Very Important Facts (VIFs).

VIF **#1:** Once a person has passed puberty, he needs on average a *minimum* of five years to achieve academic fluency (the ability to read and write for academic purposes) in a second language.

VIF **#2:** The last grammatical items an ESL student will master in English are articles and prepositions. Idioms are the last vocabulary items mastered.

VIF **#3:** A person's passive vocabulary (words he can understand when heard/read) is always larger than his active vocabulary (word he can call to mind for speaking/writing). Words move from the passive to the active list only through constant *real* use.

VIF **#4:** Language (vocabulary, grammar, etc.) acquired through real use stays with the learner longer than language learned through memorization and study.

And now, here's what you should do to improve your English. Again, read as much as you can. And talk to others who don't speak your first language. Reading will add words to your passive and active vocabulary lists, and it will give you a better sense of English grammar. Talking will force you to use new vocabulary, and your listener can help you out if you get stuck.

When you write, focus first on developing your ideas; save editing for the end of the process. It's difficult to concentrate on your ideas if you are also concerned about not making mistakes, so let those mistakes happen. Write as much as you can, organize it, revise it, and read it to a native English speaker. Then use that person's comments to help you revise again. Just before handing it in to the teacher is the time to edit carefully (of course leaving yourself time to retype if necessary).

When editing, you may have to use a sequence of steps to make sure you find all the errors. Look first just at the punctuation, checking each sentence. Then check the verbs—are they all in the right tense? do they all agree with their subjects? Then read the whole paper aloud, listening for places that don't sound right. It may even help you to read the paper aloud to a friend—sometimes the presence of a listener can make you aware of errors you wouldn't find while reading silently to yourself.

After a teacher has returned a paper to you, study his comments. Look for errors you make frequently. If you're a Spanish speaker, for instance, you may have had a lot of run-on sentences, or you may have omitted the initial subject in some of your sentences. After studying your teacher's comments, make a list in your journal of Most Frequent Errors, with samples of the mistake, how to correct it, and why you made that error. Here's a sample entry from a Chinese student's journal:

Incorrect	Correct
Although I was hungry, but	Although I was hungry,
I didn't eat anything.	I didn't eat anything.

> I make this mistake because in Chinese we say "although . . . but"
> but in English we don't. I must remember this.

Then, each time you prepare to edit a paper, review the list to remind yourself of the kinds of errors you tend to make. Once you have mastered a problem, you can draw a line through the appropriate entry, marking the date you took it off the list; this will help you keep track of your progress.

When you are editing another student's paper, don't be afraid to ask about any correction you're unsure of. Before marking his paper, make sure he understands why you're making that correction. And when you've finished, take the time to discuss the corrections with him. This discussion will help him categorize his errors, and it will help you sharpen your knowledge of correct English.

A final word. It's difficult to not become discouraged, especially if your readers don't understand what writing in a second language entails: the search for the best word, the wrestling with syntax, the agonizing over verb tense. If encouragement doesn't come from your readers, you have to provide it yourself. Congratulate yourself for every assignment you complete. Reward yourself for every grammatical point mastered. And continually remind yourself that you are doing what most Americans can't: learning complex material in a second language; and you understand something many of them don't: the value of knowing more than one language.

It's like the old joke. One American says to another, "Those European children are so intelligent!"

"Yeah?" says the other. "How's that?"

The first answers, "They all speak a foreign language!"

Chapter Nine

Research

Imagine that you're part of a culture that has its members participate in elaborate rituals marking valued life-events. Such rituals might include processions to a sacred place, the donning of fancy costumes, and the incantation of magic words. As a member in good standing of this culture, you faithfully discharge your duties even though you often don't comprehend the meaning or value of the rituals. Rituals don't, in fact, have to be understood or approved of; they simply must be done.

The rituals of this hypothetical culture may or may not resemble those of our Western culture, but they're strangely reminiscent of the way some teachers and students treat schoolwork. They see it as a series of rituals to be performed without question and, often, without understanding. At no time is this view more prevalent than when a research project or paper has been assigned. To some, a research project is little more than a ritual to be endured, a rite of passage for students that marks entry into the academic world.

Test your own first reactions to the following assignment: write a research paper on Alaska. What comes to mind? A trip to the library with a stack of 3 × 5 index cards? Pulling together quotes from a bunch of dusty books? Writing an outline using Roman numerals and letters of the alphabet? Footnotes? Associations such as these aren't uncommon. In fact, they're the rituals of research paper writing that most students and teachers observe. At best, however, these rituals represent only the most superficial operations that the writer of a research paper performs. Our intentions here are to challenge such

215

superficial thinking about research and provide you with alternative and, perhaps, exciting ways of handling your research assignments.

But before we discuss the processes that go into researching and reporting research results, we'd like to share portions of a conversation about research that we had with a professional researcher, Judy F., a cultural anthropologist who has had a great deal of experience doing fieldwork. For example, she recently completed a two-year ethnographic study on Hispanics living in East Harlem in New York City, which entailed practically living with her research subjects in order to gain a thorough understanding of their daily lives.

We offer this somewhat philosophical conversation in the hope that it will help loosen the grip of any rigid, preconceived notions about research you may have. We will then take you step by step through the experiences of two students who tackled their research assignments in different ways. We will also give practical advice on avoiding plagiarism, choosing a topic, looking for information, taking notes, quoting, paraphrasing, and summarizing.

Conversation with a Researcher

US: When you hear the word "research," what do you think of?

JF: No matter what "science" one practices, we all start with the assumption, conscious or unconscious, that there is order and predictability in the universe. For example, in social science you start with the assumption that human behavior is understandable. So when you do research you assume that what you'll find will be understandable—there will be patterns, not utter chaos. I like to use the word research because, in a sense, when you search for something, you search for something new. But to get to something new, you usually have to go over old territory. Sometimes what you discover may not be new, but it is new for *you* in the sense that you reformulate it in your own way. That's why it's called *re*-search—searching again or searching anew.

US: When you do research, how do you know where to look for the answers to your questions?

JF: Once you're out there and your objective is to understand whatever you have isolated as your interest area or an important question to answer, you have to see the question as a puzzle. You try to understand it from as many different perspectives as you possibly can. Even though I'm an anthropologist, I borrow from whomever or whatever has something to offer. The way the issue I'm looking at presents itself to me—the questions it makes me ask— leads me to try any relevant perspective to attempt to explain what I'm observing.

US: How do ideas for research come to you?

JF: When I started as a researcher, I thought that my research interests were a function of my whims. But in time, I realized that my research choices were also somewhat dependent on other conditions. For example, if funding sources are not interested in the topic you're crazy about, you probably won't have the luxury of following through with your research idea. So it's actually a compromise between what you want to pursue and opportunities that exist out there.

US: So, in other words, your research ideas arise from the need to gain new knowledge in an area you're interested in as well as pragmatic concerns.

JF: Yes. Another thing that's important is that often in the process of looking for an answer to a research question, you may surreptitiously discover something else that grabs your attention, and then before you know it, you're traveling along that less-traveled road rather than that of the first inquiry. That's why I don't approach a research subject with a very structured research instrument. Sometimes I sort of stumble onto my subject for research, and then one thing leads to another.

US: Your approach to research sounds a lot looser than the way people usually learn to do research in school.

JF: In fact, I didn't do this kind of research until *after* I got my degree. If I were involved in curriculum building (and I did this when I taught college courses in cultural anthropology), I would get students, for example, to interview their immigrant grandmother, if they had one, and derive lessons from that interview. The physicians that take my social science course now have to do a research project, and I recommend that they do it on something they already do anyway, such as documenting and analyzing their clinical encounters with patients. Or they can go out into the community to observe the way their patients live. They end up learning a lot about themselves and what they do as doctors.

US: It sounds like you have students start out with their own experience.

JF: Yes, that's right. I even picked my own dissertation topic in the same way. I was taking my kids to Central Park, and when I got to Fifth Avenue I noticed the Puerto Rican Day parade in progress. I realized that through this parade, the Puerto Ricans were expressing their need to feel equal in mainstream U. S. society, as well as their need to be distinct and separate. This was an example of the contrasting ideologies of assimilation and pluralism that are so much a part of U. S. society, and that's what I wrote about in my dissertation.

US: Most people think of research as something outside themselves, and not part of their personal experience.

JF: That's true. But I think research should be a process of making sense of reality for *yourself.*

As our anthropologist points out, ideas for research should reflect both your interests and the constraints within which you must work. For example, if you're dying to understand the history of women's rights in the U. S., but have only two weeks to do the research and write the paper, it would make sense to limit the scope of the project so that it is doable in that timeframe.

Researchers often choose their line of inquiry and even build their careers on personal interests and experiences. A microbiologist may have embarked on a career in cancer research because his father died of the disease. Such a personal choice doesn't stay personal for long, however, since others can learn and benefit from this re-searcher's work.

A research topic, suggests Judy, is a puzzle to solve, and the way you formulate that topic or puzzle will suggest ways of finding the information you need. While researching, be flexible because, as Judy explains, sometimes an unexpected discovery can lead you in unpre-dictable directions that may be more fruitful in the end. The danger to avoid here, however, is becoming so distracted by a new path of inquiry that you lose sight of your original purpose. In other words, researchers must be somewhat open to the unforseen twists and turns of the research process while remaining focused on a goal. We occa-sionally have students who can't settle on a research topic because they keep getting carried away with seemingly better and more interesting ideas. These students are usually among the brightest and most capable in the class, but their failure to focus often results in their not being able to complete their research project on time.

As we continue to discuss the goals of research and how to achieve them in the rest of this chapter, you will see further practical implications of the research principles we just discussed.

What is Research?

All research begins with a need to know something; it often ends with a need to know more. Researchers sometimes express their need to know in questions ("What has caused the current drought in Af-rica?"), sometimes in hypotheses ("The African drought is due to population growth"). These questions and hypotheses actually state the researcher's goals. They also help the researcher with his data collection. The person who decides to find out how scientists are explaining the causes of the African drought, for example, has set his research goal, and this, in turn, will help him locate relevant infor-mation. If he expressed his research goal in less precise terms ("I want to know something about the drought in Africa"), he would be less discriminating in his collection of information. In other words, just about every bit of information on the drought—from scientific studies to economic analyses to human interest stories—would seem useful. He would soon be overwhelmed by the quantity of available information and feel unable to organize it all into a coherent paper. This is the point at which many students get stuck. The way to get unstuck, or the way to avoid getting stuck in the first place, is to make your research goals clear by asking precise questions or making clear hypotheses. In fact, in the real world of research, no one ever begins a project without questions or hypotheses; no one goes deliberately into the world looking for . . . well, anything he might stumble upon, and then calls it research.

An esteemed philosopher once said, "The genuine researcher is motivated by a desire for knowledge and by nothing else," which is another way of saying that genuine research always begins with a need to know something. At this point you may be wondering: is searching for something you need to know always "research"? Does looking up a word in the dictionary because you need to know its meaning constitute research? Is asking for directions to the nearest gas station in a strange town an example of doing research? In a very general sense, the answer to all three questions is yes. However, as we all know, neither looking in the dictionary for the definition of a word, nor asking directions to a gas station would qualify as research in the academic community. This is because the community doesn't consider such projects to be significant undertakings. Besides, it's doubtful that the researcher would contribute very much to the body of knowledge that already exists on those subjects.

But, let's say, for example, that the first thing you decide to do after you are given an assignment for a research paper is to look up "research" in the dictionary simply because you want to verify your own understanding of this word. Furthermore, let's say that you look it up in three different dictionaries. One dictionary says this about the word "research": "careful, systematic study and investigation in some field of knowledge." The second dictionary says "discovery of facts," and the third says "collecting of information about a particular subject." You are struck by the fact that dictionaries define words differently. Research as "study and investigation," you suspect, gives quite a different impression than research as "discovery of facts." So, you decide to pursue this investigation by asking the question: What are the possible effects of the different dictionary definitions of the word "research" on a reader?

You decide that the best way to answer your question is to test the effects of the definitions on yourself and, then, to make sure your interpretations of the definitions are not totally idiosyncratic, you prepare a questionnaire for your classmates that asks them to explain their understanding of the three dictionary definitions. As you read through the responses to the questionnaire, you begin to notice some patterns of agreement and disagreement. Then, because you don't want to take this inquiry any further, you decide to write up the process and results of your research—your "research paper."

This hypothetical research project is an example of research using "primary" sources, that is, sources that have not been interpreted by someone other than the researcher. The primary sources in this research project were the dictionary and the questionnaires. In this example, all interpretation was done by the researcher ("you") who studied the definitions in the dictionary and the responses to the questionnaires. Other examples of research using primary sources include studying the collected works of an author, experimenting in the laboratory, observing just about anything, and interviewing people.

A simple activity, like looking up words in dictionaries, can, under certain circumstances, become a valuable research project. Let's return to our second situation—asking directions—and examine how it might evolve into an interesting topic for research. Suppose you've noticed that men and women seem to respond differently when asked directions by a stranger. You hypothesize, "Women are more reluctant than men to give strangers directions, but when they do, they're more thorough than men." You decide that the best way to test your hypothesis is to go out and ask a lot of men and women for directions, and keep copious notes on their responses. Your research paper will tell the story of how you tested your hypothesis and came to your conclusions.

People are a wonderful source of information, but students often don't realize this. Probably because our school system encourages it, students believe that "secondary" sources (i.e., library books and journal articles that interpret primary sources) are the only legitimate place to look for information. But, there are times when using primary sources is not only more desirable but also quite necessary. Our two hypothetical research studies above could not be done without primary sources of information. The studies could, however, be expanded with the inclusion of information from secondary sources. For example, the student who hypothesized about men's and women's responses to a request for information might want to compare the results of her own experiment with what theorists say about the subject. The student could consult psychology and sociology texts, reports of similar studies (if they exist), and even articles from popular magazines. By referring to other sources, the student would show that she is aware of other work done in this area and how her own research efforts support, refute, refine, or complement it.

Here is how Cy Knoblauch and Lil Brannon, authors of *Rhetorical Traditions and the Teaching of Writing* (Portsmouth, NH: Boynton/

Cook, 1984), explain their use of references to other authors who have written on the same subject:

> The writing of our book . . . acknowledges the scientific convention of appealing to "sources" as a demonstration of our reliability. We are obliged to make use of other texts pertinent to our subject and to borrow the conceptions of other writers as part of the process of making meaning in our own text. Doing so insures a continuity of understanding (even for our statements of disagreement) that is desirable in academic discourse. Ignoring or rejecting without cause the information of major historians of rhetoric . . . would not be regarded as a sign of creative independence by our anticipated readers; it would simply be thought ignorant and foolish. We certainly also conceive our own information relevant to the subject through our own intellectual analysis or imaginative intuition. But that information must be such that interested readers could retrace our steps, read what we have read, confirm the judgements we have made: our authority in readers' eyes for declaring our information to be true and significant depends on this possibility of independent verification.

There are very good reasons why reseachers/writers refer to the work of others in their papers. According to Knoblauch and Brannon, borrowing from others is necessary to maintain "continuity of understanding" in a field. A researcher's need to know something leads him to search for information. When he writes the paper which reports on this search for information he must acknowledge those sources which helped him answer his questions or test his hypotheses. This researcher/writer borrows from others in order to create a new work of his own. Students who think that writing a research paper means putting together other people's ideas in a clever way do not comprehend how, why, and when to borrow from others. We hope that the ideas, examples, and suggestions in this chapter will make it easier to understand the different ways in which writers of research papers (or any other papers, for that matter) can use and refer to their sources.

Plagiarism

While you may borrow other people's ideas and words in order to contextualize and lend validity to your own, borrowing from others *without acknowledging them* is one form of plagiarism. Plagiarism, in general, refers to the practice of "stealing" someone else's ideas or words or other work and passing it off as one's own, and it is a serious offense in our culture. Accusations of plagiarism have hauled many a famous and successful personality off to court, and in some cases, ruined careers.

Some of the most notorious cases of plagiarism in recent years have occurred in the music industry. The singer Huey Lewis, for example, accused the writer of the song "Ghostbusters" of plagiarizing the melody and bass line of Lewis's song "I Want a New Drug." With the rise of electronic music, plagiarism has also become an issue in connection with a technique known as "sampling," whereby just a few notes programmed into an electronic instrument can generate a whole song or other piece of music. In a case of "sampling" plagiarism, the singer Vanilla Ice was accused of stealing a four-note phrase from "Under Pressure," a song by David Bowie and Freddy Mercury, and generating it into his own song "Ice Ice Baby."

Sometimes plagiarizing is a deliberate act, such as when one intentionally lifts a passage from a book and inserts it in one's own writing without footnoting or otherwise acknowledging the fact that the passage was written by someone else. Frequently, however, plagiarism is inadvertent: A writer may not know when or how to document sources, for example. Or a writer who has read vast amounts of source material for his research project may lose track of who said what, when, and where, and, without realizing it, use someone else's original material but not credit it properly. Unfortunately, intentional or inadvertent, plagiarism is plagiarism; nobody cares if you have a good excuse for the transgression. Some years ago, a famous and reputable Harvard psychiatrist, former director of the National Institute of Mental Health, was accused publicly of plagiarism by a graduate student, who, while doing some research of his own, discovered that the psychiatrist had plagiarized another writer in one of his articles. Most of the Harvard professor's colleagues and others in the field were of the opinion that the lapse was accidental, that the well-known and respected psychiatrist had not intentionally purloined the passages in question. This was not accepted as a defense, however, and the psychiatrist was fired from his job.

This incident illustrates one other point: If you think that your act of plagiarism will not be found out ("No one will ever notice"), think again. One of your readers may be familiar with the plagiarized material—ideas or actual words "borrowed" from another without acknowledgment. Or the reader may notice a sudden and significant change in the writing style. In the absence of quotation marks or footnotes, such a gross change in style is almost always a red flag for writing teachers.

It is really not so difficult to avoid plagiarism—properly crediting your sources should do the trick. However, knowing when and how to "borrow" from others is not as easy. For more on this, turn to the section on quoting, paraphrasing, and summarizing toward the end of this chapter.

Researching and Writing

Most handbooks that have a chapter on research usually give a lot of practical advice on such things as using the library, taking notes from books, preparing footnotes and bibliographies, etc. While we agree that practical advice is in order, we won't give any until the end of this chapter. We think it would be more useful right now to describe how two students went about doing their research papers. The excerpts from their drafts that you'll read, and the students' explanations of how they came to write them, illustrate some of the points we made above. You'll see, for example, that one of the students started her research with a question; the other began with a problem in mind. One of the students learned most of what she needed to know from interviews; the other used secondary sources. And, both students were very careful not to let the information they collected from their sources overshadow their own ideas. As you read their stories, try to make connections between the theories about research expressed earlier in this chapter and the actual practice of these students.

Alka Sarwal

When Alka's teacher gave the class an assignment to do a research paper, and left the choice of topic up to the students, Alka's first thought was to research something that had to do with the feelings immigrants to the U. S. have about their new country. Specifically, Alka wondered why some adults she knew (her parents included) complained so much about the American way of life but decided to remain in the U. S. anyway, instead of returning to their home countries where they would presumably be happier. To help Alka get started, her teacher suggested she formulate a question that she would answer through her research. Alka's question became, "Why do immigrants who are unhappy with American values and ideas stay in the U. S.?"

Alka began her research by asking people this question and studying their answers. It soon became clear, however, that the responses she got were not particularly enlightening. In fact, they were rather obvious and, hence, not so interesting. "The question of why people stay in America when they are unhappy with American values and ideas led to a complete dead end. Everyone told me that it would be economically disadvantageous if they uprooted and left again."

Alka needed a more interesting question, for her own sake as well as for the sake of her readers. Her teacher suggested she ask a question that would be more immediately relevant to her own situation. She agreed, and came up with the following question, which was to become the title of her research paper, too: "To what extent have Indian teenagers assimilated into the American culture?" Alka's first paragraph will show you just how important the issue of assimilation is to her:

> The loss of one's native culture and the acquisition of another culture is a major decision faced by all immigrants. Throughout my 13 years in America I have been told by various history and social studies teachers that America is a "melting pot," that it is the immigrants who have made the American culture. I, however, never included myself as one of those immigrants. Although I am an American citizen I have never been able to identify myself as an "American." Is my reluctance to give up my Indian identity common among other Indian young people? Are others comfortable with the assimilation process they went through?

Changing her research question in this way gave Alka several advantages. First, it allowed her to investigate further a subject she already knew a lot about. In other words, she didn't have to start at ground zero. Second, it helped her to identify her most important source of information right away, i.e., other young Indians. Third, it allowed her to touch upon her original question, which still interested her—Why do people stay in America when they are unhappy with American values?—without having to make it the central focus of her paper.

Even though Alka knew she had to interview other Indian teenagers to find out how much they have assimilated into American culture, like most students, she headed straight to the library to look for books on the subject. Unfortunately, there were none on Indian assimilation. "I was afraid this might happen when I decided on my question for the paper. There were many books on European assimilation but there was only one book that dealt with India. S. Chandrasekhar's book, *From India to America,* dealt mainly with statistical information about the number of Indians who had come to America during different time periods. There was very little about the active assimilation process. Chandrasekhar says in the preface of his book that he was motivated to write a book about Indians in America when he could not find a single book on the subject himself. I think I know how he feels."

It was clear to Alka that she'd have to rely more on interviews with other teenagers than on books in order to shed light on the "active assimilation process." Of course, she had herself as a source as well. The more Alka thought about the fact that she cannot consider herself an American, the more she wanted to find the origin of this feeling. A hypothesis did come to mind which led her to another important source. She tells of this process in the second paragraph of her paper:

> I have had a strong belief that my religion, Hinduism, plays a major role in my reluctance to fully assimilate. I asked my mother why did it seem as if other ethnic groups such as Italians, Irish and Spanish assimilated into the American culture easily? Why do Indians take longer in assimilating? She said that in her opinion these other cultures were very similar to American culture. Their way of dressing, social attitudes and religion did not need any drastic conformation. This made sense to me, since the only major change I could see in their move to America was the language change. To find out more about the religious aspects of assimilation I spoke to a professor who teaches religion at my school. I first asked what assimilation meant to him. In his opinion it was the taking on of a new culture. He believes a person is fully assimilated when he/she can say, "I am an American." Once a person can say this and "really feels that from deep down inside then he's assimilated." I wanted to know if it was necessary to lose one's native culture while assimilating. He replied that it was not necessary, but it always was a strong possibility. He then said that the struggle against assimilation is very hard and rarely successful. "It's much easier to assimilate than to fight it." I understand this to mean that those who consciously try to remain unassimilated in every sense rarely succeed and that some time in their life they have to accept to some extent the values and ideas of the society which they are now a part of.

Alka's interviews with other students, her conversations with the religion professor, and two books from which she quoted in her paper led her to make some conclusions and hypotheses that could lead to more research:

> Harry H. Bash in his book, *Sociology, Race and Ethnicity,* describes assimilation as a type of conformation. The people whom I spoke to saw it as a total change. I believe this is due to the fact that when one is actively involved in the process one tends to feel more emotional with each step. What may be a slight conformation to an American is usually thought out very carefully and judged by the person who is assimilating.

And, later:

One other similarity which all the people I talked to experienced was the obstacle of discrimination. Most of the discrimination occurs in school during the first year or so when one does not know how to speak English properly. It is perhaps the most difficult time. At times children in school can be extremely insensitive and cruel. It is very humiliating when he/she is put down in front of others for his/her lack of knowledge about schoolwork, social activities and English. However, these obstacles can be overcome with time and I believe it is necessary that they are overcome for the assimilation process to continue.

Among new hypotheses Alka formulated as a result of her research and that could be studied further is this one:

I noticed that as there was an increase in age one moved closer to the non-assimilated mark.

Reflecting back on the process of researching her topic and writing her paper, Alka had this to say, "Researching for this paper was not the chore I thought it would be. The people I interviewed sometimes surprised me with their remarks and often relieved me by telling me they had many of the same difficulties I did. Writing this paper has provided me with an insight into my culture and traditions. I have begun to question what I accepted before."

Stewart Morales

When Stewart Morales decided to research the problem of drinking age legislation, he was 19, the minimum drinking age in his state at that time. Most people were certain, however, that the age would eventually be increased to 21. Stewart, who was finally "legal," felt angry at the prospect of having to spend two more years unable to buy liquor in stores or bars (or having to drink on the sly). He heavily favored the anti-21 position, but he still wanted to understand the other side's—the pro-21—point of view, so that he could argue with it intelligently. The goal for his research, then, was to find out which arguments the pro-21 groups used to support their bias and why.

Stewart's position in the drinking-age debate, so firm when he began his research, soon began to waver. The more he read, the more he realized that the issue was far more complex than he'd imagined. He was also shocked by the number of alcohol-related automobile accidents involving teenagers that occur each year, and he began to believe that there really was a connection between the high number of accidents and a minimum drinking age of 18 or 19. "Along with the problems of actually writing the research paper," he said "there were also problems going on within myself—namely, my opinion on the issue was shifting away from the anti-21 view I started the paper with to a view that was beginning to see beyond my identification with being a victim of this law."

Stewart had to face the fact that his research was taking him away from the simple task of finding and summarizing the other side's arguments. Suddenly, there was more at stake: his sense of confidence in his own opinions about the drinking age issue. He really needed to find the answer to the question: Should the drinking age be raised to 21? And so, this question became his new research topic.

In asking himself the question, Stewart managed to pinpoint and personalize his topic at the same time. In fact, it was the precision of this question which helped him choose the information to include in his paper. Unlike Alka Sarwal, Stewart had found a lot of material in the library about his research topic—perhaps too much—and began wondering about how to cope with it all: "When I started writing my research paper, 'Should the Drinking Age be Raised to 21?' I felt quite confident about what I was going to do and roughly how I was going to do it. Getting started seemed simple enough, with a trip to the library to fish through the card catalogue, through which I found two great books—*Minimum Drinking Age Laws* and *Alcohol and Public Policy.* Things seemed to be taking shape better than I expected. This was until I got into reading the books and articles, finding myself overwhelmed with information. The big problem was how to make sense of all this information—putting it into some kind of coherent paper." But then Stewart remembered the purpose of his paper—to answer the question: Should the drinking age be raised to 21? for his own satisfaction. This question steered him toward the information that would help him answer it, and away from the information that wouldn't.

Stewart's paper reflects the development of his own thoughts. He begins by telling the reader why the research was undertaken and specifies his goals:

> This particular issue has gotten a lot of attention lately due to the fact that the nation is considering establishing a uniform drinking age of 21. It has a particular significance to me, being a 19-year-old college student in a state where the drinking age is currently 19.
>
> My goal is to come to my own conclusion on this controversial question that has been the subject of fierce debate. I will do my best to be as objective as possible to properly obtain both views and arrive at an intelligent, informed decision. While trying to maintain objectivity, I must take into account that my direct involvement might result in an unconsciously biased attitude. As one reads this paper, they should keep in mind the author responsible for it—a 19-year-old who has been breaking the law for the past two years.

The next part of the paper reflects Stewart's own process of learning about drinking age legislation. First, he provides some background historical information. Then, he summarizes the two opposing points of view from which he will have to choose the one that convinces him:

> The issue of whether to raise the drinking age back to 21 is a highly volatile two-sided issue.
>
> On one side are those who believe it should be restored to 21. They are led by groups like MADD (Mothers Against Drunk Drivers), SOS (Save Our Students), and SADD (Students Against Driving Drunk). The chief argument by such groups is that statistics show that a higher drinking age would save lives lost in teenage automobile accidents involving intoxication. . . .
>
> On the other side of the issue are college students, the liquor industry, civil liberties advocates and tavern owners. Their main assertion is that raising the drinking age to 21, foreclosing the privileges of 18 to 20 years old, would contradict volumes of legislation that classified 18 as the age at which a person may exercise their full civil and personal rights.

The final part of Stewart's paper shows the process of his weighing the merits and drawbacks of both points of view and coming to his own conclusions:

> Based upon my research and interviews, I have come to the conclusion that this is a very emotional moral and ethical issue. . . .
>
> The main problem is that any age chosen to separate those who can and cannot drink will be arbitrary because such legislation is based on generalizations. There is no perfect way to separate the mature from the immature, so some of the mature will have to be penalized to protect society from some of the immature.
>
> While I'm convinced that a drinking age of 21 would save lives at the price of my right to drink, I feel that this goal could also be accomplished through strict drunk driving punishment for all drivers of all ages.
>
> If drunk driving is a societal problem, as I have found it is, then the only effective way of combatting it would be to punish all drunk drivers. Teenage drunk driving is the reflection of an adult problem. Since adults are responsible for setting the patterns of behavior that teenagers follow, it's only logical that if they were severely punished for drunk driving, they would set a better example for their children, saving more lives in the long run. Others, however, might argue that both strict punishment and a drinking age of 21 would best accomplish the goal of reducing drunken driving. Perhaps they are right.

When Stewart first formulated his research question, he realized right away that he had chosen a topic that is pretty common—

especially in the eyes of an English teacher who each year might have to read more papers about teenage drinking than she cares to. It's not that the common topic can't be interesting. It's just that a reader who feels as if she's already read everything that could possibly be said about a subject will not feel very sympathetic toward yet another paper on that subject. If the writer of such a paper is aware in advance of the reader's possibly negative frame of mind, he can make an effort to avoid rehashing the old and try, instead, to approach the subject in a fresh way. In personalizing his topic and sharing with the reader his process of thinking it through, Stewart managed to elevate his paper from a mere restatement of the same old stuff to a unique close-up of a 19-year-old trying to make sense of a part of his world.

Now for the practical advice we promised earlier. Read over these suggestions carefully. They'll help you save time and energy in the long run.

Choosing a Topic

When your teacher assigns a research paper, make sure you choose a topic that you'll be able to research and write up within the time and page length allotted to you. Make sure, too, that you find a topic that interests *you*. Ideally, your topic will come from a need to know something you didn't know before, or a need to know more about something you're already familiar with. Writing teachers typically assign research papers toward the end of a semester, and, more often than not, students don't give research much thought before the assignment is given. Suddenly, there's a mad scramble to find a suitable topic. Some students are lucky because one easily comes to mind; others end up using their limited time thinking of a topic rather than reading and writing.

The way to avoid that last minute rush to find a research topic is to keep a journal throughout the semester. In this journal, jot down any questions that come to mind. Since questions are an unavoidable part of experience, you shouldn't have much trouble coming up with some. Try, too, to speculate about answers to your questions. When a research paper is assigned, you'll be able to choose from a storehouse of topics for which you've already done some preliminary writing. A student who had trouble getting up in the morning, even though he had had eight hours sleep, wrote in his journal, "Why can't I get up in the morning? Do other people have the same problem?" He then conducted a mini-research project by recording in his journal how he felt every morning for a week. He began to connect his feelings to the events of each morning, wrote about some patterns of behavior he was beginning to notice, and then moved on to other questions. When his teacher assigned the research paper he looked through all the questions he had recorded in his journal during the semester and found his writing about this topic. He realized that his question about not being able to wake up in the morning still interested him, and he decided to pursue it for his research project.

One more example. Another student couldn't stop wondering why the students in her classes remained silent during class time. She wrote in her journal, "Why don't students speak out in class?" She jotted down some hypotheses as well: "They don't talk because they haven't read the material the prof. is talking about. They don't want to talk in front of the class because they're shy. They're afraid other students will think they're trying to impress the teacher." She then informally interviewed some of her classmates, got their opinions on the subject, and took notes in her journal. Her questions, hypotheses, and interviews eventually led to an interesting research paper.

So far, of course, we've been assuming that you have a teacher who will let you choose your own topic. But, what happens if you have a teacher who *gives* you a topic? We'll invent a worst-case scenario and discuss possible options. Remember the beginning of this chapter on research when we asked you to react to the following, "Write a research paper on Alaska"? When we wrote that, we were exaggerating for the sake of dramatic effect. But, what if you really did get that assignment? What would you do? What *could* you do?

The first thing you do is make two lists. Call one list, "Things I Know about Alaska." Call the second list, "Things I would like to know about Alaska." The very adventurous might want to make a third list and call it, "Guesses about Alaska." We recommend concentrating on the second list, or the third. What if, for the sake of argument, one of the items on your second list read, "How has the U.S. government dealt with the native population of Alaska?" This question would lead you to research the Inuit tribe and governmental agencies that are responsible for maintaining the well-being of native American peoples. You might even want to compare how governmental agencies treat American Indians and how they treat the Inuit. Are there similarities? Differences? Or, if you've made some guesses about Alaska on your third list, you might want to find out if you've guessed right. Everyone knows that there's lots of oil in Alaska—or is there? Through your research you could find out if this common belief is true or false. If you've got imagination, time, and commitment, you'll be able to turn just about any assigned topic into an interesting subject for research.

Looking for Information

Once they've chosen their research topics, many students run to the library without first stopping to consider whether the library is their best source of information. Alka Sarwal, you'll remember, discovered that interviews provided more valuable information for her research project than the books she could find in the library. Another student, who had a theory that Miles Davis's album "Bitches Brew" was the precursor to and inspiration for the music known as fusion, got the information he needed to support his theory not in the library, but at home, listening to music and taking notes. (Incidentally, this student's research paper ended with a 10-page discography—not a bibliography—and won a prize for the best research paper of the year at his college.) The trick is to choose the most appropriate source of information for the topic at hand. If you're unsure about what kind of information you need, or where to go to find the sources you've decided upon, ask your classmates, your teacher, your family, a librarian—everybody you can think of. Maybe because writing teachers often put so much emphasis on avoiding plagiarism, students think that they're breaking the rules when they ask someone for help. Or maybe it's because our society seems to value individual accomplishment more than collaboration. In any case, most honest researchers will tell you that genuine research is rarely done in a vacuum by the solitary scholar. So, don't ever be afraid to seek help.

If, after weighing your options, you decide that library sources are right for your topic, don't go to the card catalog, or the "online catalog" that you can call up on the library's computer terminals, without first considering other possibilities. Card and online catalogs are good for finding books, but they do not list the articles that have appeared in periodicals—newspapers, magazines, and journals—and other important information such as government publications and special collections. So, if you wanted to write about a current topic, like the dissolution of the Soviet Union or the 1992 presidential election, you probably wouldn't find very much about it in the card or online catalog. A better place to look for information about a current topic of international importance is a major newspaper like *The New York Times* or *The Washington Post*. Your library has indexes that list published articles under subject headings for these and other newspapers.

If newspapers don't give you all the information you need, you can expand your search to magazine articles. The Reference Room of your library has an indispensable book for people who want to locate magazine articles on their topic: *Readers' Guide to Periodical Literature*. *Readers' Guide* indexes over 100 popular magazines and lists, under subject headings, all the articles that these magazines have published since 1890. The general Reference Room of your library has other resources too, such as abstracts, which provide brief summaries of the articles cited, and indexes that cover large subject areas, such as the *Humanities Index* and the *Social Sciences Index*. Most college libraries also publish their own research guides for general subject areas, such as sociology, psychology, literary criticism, and so on, that list useful reference sources and their call numbers.

These are only a handful of resources you can find in the library. There just isn't enough space in this book to mention all the others, so you'll have to do some exploring on your own, or, if the library provides it, take an organized tour. The more you know about your library's holdings and how they're distributed in the building, the easier it will be to find information when you need it. And, don't hesitate to ask the librarians for help.

Taking Notes

Note-taking is an integral part of the research process. The notes you take while interviewing, reading, observing, and listening are the raw materials with which you'll construct your product, the research paper. When the raw materials are good, chances are greater that a better product will emerge. Good notes for a research paper include quotations, paraphrases, summaries, and, perhaps most important, your responses to your sources of information. Since the primary purpose of a research paper is not simply to repeat what others said about a topic, but to present *your* research findings and interpretations of sources, it's vital to keep track of your ideas and questions about the information you have found. Writing these ideas and questions down allows you to actually see what you think. When your ideas are on paper, you can begin the process of working them out: you can reread them as many times as you want, reject them, revise them, and determine what additional information you'll need to make a stronger paper.

Below are samples of three note-taking techniques that meet the requirements we've just outlined. Try using one or all of these techniques the next time you take notes.

The student who wrote the following notes after having read a chapter called "The Uses of Grammar" in *Grammar for Teachers* by Constance Weaver (Urbana, Ill.: NCTE, 1979) summarized it in the first paragraph, then jotted down some of her reactions in the second.

The Uses of Grammar

The article stated that the long standing rule that grammar must be formally taught no longer applies. That, in fact, the way to learn grammar is by using it – the way to learn to read is by reading – to write by writing. The article implies that the best way a teacher can teach grammar is by using students' own knowledge of grammar in helping them understand & use language more effectively.

One can't argue with an article that is so clear cut and states its facts so plainly – at least this 'one' can't (me). However, I'm sure – it's obvious that there are opponents to this 'new school' but after such a convincing case I can't imagine what their argument can be.

Before she began reading *Pedagogy of the Oppressed* by Paulo Freire (New York: Continuum, 1970), another student folded some pages in her notebook in half lengthwise. As she read, she copied in the left-hand columns those parts of the text for which she had responses. In the right-hand columns she wrote her responses. (See figure p. 234.)

The third set of notes were written by a student during a lecture/discussion. These notes combine summary, direct quotation, and the student's own comments and questions. (See figure p. 235.)

When taking notes while reading, it's a good idea to jot down page numbers after you record direct quotations or paraphrase parts of the text. This will save you the trouble of searching for page numbers later on, when it's time to document sources in your final draft. Also, record all publication information, as well as the title and author's name on index cards or separate pieces of paper. When it comes time to write the bibliography, all you'll have to do is put the cards or pieces of paper in alphabetical order and copy the information according to the method prescribed by the style manual you use. For more on style manuals, documenting sources, and writing bibliographies, see "Documentation," pp.205–210.

"talks about reality... motionless, static, compartmentalized + predictable"

this I don't comprehend- reality is (pretty much) all those things. It would be unfair for a teacher to thrust his/her views on a student.

"contents of his narration... detached from reality... words... become hollow, alienated + alienating verbosity"

this is far from my experience (as a student). Asking questions, pertinent ones, cures this. Thinking a little too.

"student records + memorizes, repeats these phrases w/o realizing true significance"

"four times four"'s significance is obliterated in the terminology. 4, 4 times. To apply common sense and reason to other subjects would be as effective.

"memorize mechanically... filled by the teacher... more completely he fills, the better teacher is."

That's the author's opinion. I respect the teacher who expects his/her students to deduce things for themselves + teacher asks appropriate questions.

"they have the opportunity to become collectors + catalogers of the things they store"

they also have the option to go to school or not. The desire to learn and to think comes from curiosity. Most bright people get curious about concepts that they don't quite grasp, but understand somewhat.

Quoting, Paraphrasing, and Summarizing

One of the most challenging parts of writing a research paper is deciding when to quote and when not to. Even when your source of information is an interview, you still have to determine when direct quotation is necessary and when paraphrase or summary is preferable. While there's no formula that would help you decide in every

CJ said "the editor is wrong—I know that" (This is the confidence we're trying to teach.)

Grades can never satisfy students because they judge from the outside. The satisfaction must come out of the student to "inform" the grade received—D- to A. Somehow something as slippery to understand as integrity is at the heart of this issue. To teach/learn format only for socio-political goals produces "A Nation At Risk" integrity would/can use as well as the Gettysburg address forms but enliven them and create. There is at issue here time constraints and evaluation that comes from outside of the class, administration. I'm not sure how, yet.

possible case, there is something you can do that will help you judge whether to quote. Each time you're tempted to quote a source ask yourself the question, Why am I quoting here? If you shrug your shoulders in response, or answer, "Because I have to make the paper longer," or "I have to show my teacher that I have read the material," then you know that your reasons for quoting have nothing to do with wanting to strengthen the points you make in your paper. The consequence of quoting a lot in your paper, and for no good reason, is that your readers will find it difficult to follow your train of thought. If they can't they'll lose interest in your ideas—even if you've quoted some of the most brilliant minds of our time. On the other hand, if you answer, "I'm quoting because I need an authority to back me up on this point," or "The exact words of my source make an impact I couldn't make in any other way," then you have some good reasons to quote.

If quoting your source doesn't seem appropriate, try paraphrasing. Paraphrasing involves putting someone else's text into your own words. The advantage of writing your own words instead of someone else's is that it helps keep the paper uniform in style and tone. Readers won't have to shift gears every time they move from the main body of the paper to quotes, and back again. In the process of paraphrasing, unnecessary material that might distract the reader from the main points can be eliminated, making the paper more focused and crisp.

Take a look at the following section of Alka Sarwal's research paper in which she paraphrases and quotes:

> To find out more about the religious aspects of assimilation I spoke to a professor who teaches religion at my school. I first asked what assimilation meant to him. In his opinion it was the taking on of a new culture. He believes a person is fully assimilated when he/she can say, "I am an American." Once a person can say this and "really feels that from deep down inside then he's assimilated." I wanted to know if it was necessary to lose one's native culture while assimilating. He replied that it was not necessary, but it always was a strong possibility. He then said that the struggle against assimilation is very hard and rarely successful. "It is much easier to assimilate than to fight it."

Alka decided to paraphrase most of this interview because she thought that reading a series of questions and answers would become tedious for the reader. Alka also had important points to make, and paraphrasing allowed her to delete material that didn't help make those points. The two quotations she did include backed up the paraphrases. They "prove" that Alka's interpretations of what the religion professor said are accurate.

Summarizing, like paraphrasing, requires rewriting source material in your own words, but summaries condense material more than paraphrases do. Strategic summarizing lets the writer present important ideas without having to get bogged down in details that might be interesting, but aren't essential for the paper. In the following excerpt from Stewart Morales's paper you'll see that a large amount of material—all the information he'd found about people who advocate a higher drinking age—was reduced to two sentences. This summary allowed Stewart to communicate some basic facts and quickly move on to his next point:

> On one side are those who believe it should be restored to 21. They are led by groups like MADD (Mothers Against Drunk Drivers), SOS (Save Our Students), and SADD (Students Against Driving Drunk). The chief argument by such groups is that statistics show that a higher drinking age would save lives lost in teenage automobile accidents involving intoxication.

Whenever you integrate other people's ideas or words into your own writing you must give those people credit. Remember, failure to do so is plagiarism. It's easy enough to avoid plagiarism by documenting your sources, but it's hard to know exactly what to document and when. Most practiced writers depend on their experience and common sense. If you want to get to the point where you too can depend on common sense, start paying attention to the way the writers you read document their sources. The style manuals we describe in the section on documentation, pp. 205–10 will give some help, but not much about when and how to document. They also provide all the information you'll need about formatting the final draft of your research paper.

Chapter Ten

A Writer's Tools

As disparate as their work may seem at first, carpenters, sculptors, and writers do have something in common. They all begin with raw materials, whether they be wood, clay, or words, and, through a process of careful crafting, create a product—a cabinet, a sculpture, an essay. Writers, like carpenters and sculptors, use tools to help them reach their goal. Of course, their tools don't resemble those of carpenters and sculptors, and here is where our analogy has to end.

The tools writers use include pens or pencils and paper, typewriters, computers, word processors, tape recorders, dictionaries, thesauruses, spelling aids, and usage and style handbooks like this one. In this chapter there's some advice on buying and using all of these. But, before moving on, we feel compelled to plug the most useful, and most often neglected, of all writers' tools—feedback.

Feedback, i.e., responses to writing, lets writers know the effects their writing has on readers. Readers' responses help writers decide whether to revise their writing, and, at times, give them ideas for how to revise. If readers tell you, for example, that they're confused about the meaning you're trying to convey in a paragraph, then you may want to revise your writing so that they do understand. If your readers can tell you what *exactly* is confusing about that paragraph, you'll get an even better idea of what needs to be changed, and perhaps, how to change it. No other tools can give you this kind of information.

While responses from all kinds of readers can be useful to a writer, there are times when only feedback from experienced readers will do. If your classmates do a lot of reading and responding to each other's work in class, then they may have enough experience to give you the kind of feedback you need. Your teacher is, of course, another experienced reader to consult. And you'll find many experienced readers whose job it is to give writers feedback at your school's writing center.

Incidentally, it's just as important to practice *giving* feedback as it is to get feedback from readers. In practicing responding to other writers' work, you'll develop your critical reading abilities, and eventually, be able to apply them to your own writing. Really good writers are always good readers of their own writing as well as other writers' work. If your teacher has you read and respond to your classmates' writing in class, then you'll have plenty of opportunity to practice giving feedback. If this isn't part of the curriculum, you might consider starting a writing group that meets outside of class to which members can bring their writing and receive feedback. In this case, you might want to consult an excellent introduction to starting and maintaining a writing group entitled *Writing Without Teachers,* by Peter Elbow (Oxford University Press).

Computers and Word Processors

When personal computers (PCs) and word-processing programs first appeared on the market, heated debates developed between writers who believed that computers were a boon to their trade and others who denounced the new technology as impractical, superfluous, cold, unfeeling, and generally detrimental to the art of writing. Nowadays, with PCs becoming so common in homes and schools, the argument between writers has lost most of its energy and hardly seems worth pursuing. Nonetheless, it's important for writers who plan to purchase a personal computer and word-processing program to understand what the computer can and can't do for them.

First of all, a PC needs to be loaded with a word-processing program before it will be of any use to a writer. Alternatively, some writers use "word processors." Word processors are computers that are pre-loaded with a word-processing program. Computers have the capacity to run a variety of software programs (e.g., word processing, financial spreadsheets, games, music, etc.) which are either already stored in the computer or loaded manually each time they are needed. Word processors, on the other hand, are capable only of running their pre-loaded word processing program.

A word-processing program allows you to write, revise, and correct (all known as "editing" in computer lingo), save your document on a hard drive or a floppy disk, format the document for printing, and recall it at a later date. There are many different kinds of word-processing programs on the market today. Some of the most frequently used are WordPerfect, Microsoft Word, MacWrite, Word-star, and Multimate. The companies that make these and other word-processing programs are continually upgrading them, so more powerful programs that are easier to use keep appearing on the market.

A personal computer with a good word-processing program can take a lot of the drudgery out of writing: the mechanical aspects—inserting or deleting, "cutting and pasting," correcting errors, to name just a few—are made less tedious by word processing. Some writers say that they're more likely to experiment with words and ideas when writing on a computer because they're not afraid of making mistakes (since "erasing" them is only a matter of hitting the "delete" key), and they're not worried about having to retype a clean copy each time they change their text. If you're a good typist and thoroughly learn all the commands of your software program, word processing will save you time and energy. If you write a lot, a computer will make a world of difference in your life.

You should know, though, that while computers make writing less like menial labor, they don't really make writing, in the sense of "composing," any easier. People who believe that they will miraculously become excellent writers just because they use a computer will be disappointed. The same mental effort that goes into writing with a pen must go into writing with a computer. The only way we know of to improve as a writer is to write and revise a lot—on paper or on a computer—and get as much feedback as possible.

Buying a PC

If you go to a school where the purchase of a particular PC is mandatory, then you will be spared the necessity of comparative shopping. However, if the choice is left up to you, it's a good idea to educate yourself about PCs and word-processing programs before buying. This doesn't mean you have to learn all the technical details—most personal computer users successfully operate their machines without knowing very much about how they work. It simply means talking to dealers, perusing catalogs, trying out the computers and programs in your school's computer labs, and, if possible, seeking advice from people who use PCs for their work. Your final decision may be influenced by the potential for compatability (e.g., the programs you will use are designed for a MacIntosh, not an IBM, PC), the feel of the keyboard, monitor quality, and the size and look of the system, as much as by the cost. For example, if you don't have much space for a computer in your room, or if you like the option of taking your computer along to the library, you might prefer a laptop computer to a desktop model. You'll also want to take into account such things as memory capacity, number and type of disk drives, printer interfacing, and other aspects of the personal computer that we can't get into here but that you can easily learn more about from catalogs, books, and dealers.

Choosing the right word-processing software can be as challenging as choosing the hardware. Unless you can spend a considerable amount of time trying out a program, you really won't know if it's what you want and need until you've used it for a while. So, to an extent, picking out a program that has the features you need for your particular application is a matter of good luck. You can remove something of the risk factor, however, by familiarizing yourself with the word-processing programs currently available on the market, such as the ones mentioned earlier in this section, and comparing their features. Again, dealers, catalogs, computer labs, computer magazines, and people who write a lot with a computer are sources for this information.

Finally, some special features such as "spelling-checking" capability may be included with your word-processing program, but other features may only be available as add-on software. Programs have been developed that let you check your grammar and syntax, tell you how much passive voice you've used, give word frequency counts, and perform other mechanical functions. Some users are skeptical about the efficacy of much of this add-on software; others swear by it. As with all other purchases, only you can decide whether the job it'll perform for you is worth the cost.

Computer Labs

A good place to try out computers and word-processing programs is your school's computer lab(s). If the facilities are large and accessible enough, you may be able to do all your writing there, so the purchase of your own computer may not be necessary (assuming, of course, your school doesn't require its students to own computers).

Computer lab facilities vary from school to school. Therefore, it's not possible for us to describe every possible kind of lab design here. You should, however, familiarize yourself with the computer labs in your own school and find out how they can be of use to you. In some schools, writing classes are taught in word-processing labs with networking capabilities. In other words, students write using the computers in the lab, call up each other's work on their monitors, and respond to the writing directly on the screen—no paper need change hands. In this system, the teacher can monitor the students' progress and comment on the students' writing as well.

In other schools, the computer lab component of writing courses is limited to exercises on grammar, punctuation, etc., which students must complete on their own time as a course requirement. Sometimes, the exercises are meant to prepare students for a particular writing proficiency exam. Computer labs for English-as-a-second-language students are frequently of this type; they are usually not set up for word processing, in the sense of composing.

How and when you use your school's computer labs depend on space availability, course requirements, and other factors. Whatever your particlar case is, it must be abundantly clear by now that to survive college writing courses it's essential, at the very least, to know how to type and be somewhat computer literate.

Cat got your word processor?

Dictionaries

Dictionaries (like cars and computers) come in different sizes, from the Lilliputian version you can hold in the palm of your hand to the Gargantuan multi-volume model for which you need to build a new bookcase. As you might have guessed already, for everyday use, we recommend something in between, namely the softcover "pocket" dictionary or the hardcover "desktop" model, or both. We say both because these two varieties of dictionaries aren't equally good for all purposes. A pocket dictionary just doesn't have the space for all the words, definitions, and other information you'll find in a desktop dictionary, but it's great for checking spelling and quickly looking up words, while reading. Although it won't fit into your pocket, unless your pocket's the size of a kangeroo pouch, you can carry it to class in a briefcase or book bag if you want to. A desktop dictionary may be a bit unwieldly for quick reference, and you can't take it with you to school, but it's indispensable for more complete word definitions, etymologies, and usage examples. It also provides other useful information such as a brief history of the English language, foreign words and phrases, biographical and geographical names, and notes about grammar and style.

For a long time, dictionaries were thought of as *the* authorities on the proper use of language. Many people still regard dictionaries in this manner, but the editorial policy of most, if not all, dictionaries of the English or American language has changed over the years. Recently published dictionaries strive to *describe* as accurately as possible the language as it has been and is actually used, rather than *prescribe* good usage and condemn the use of words and expressions that don't live up to their standards. This change in orientation has undoubtedly disappointed some scholars, linguists, and grammarians who believe that the dictionary's function is to make the language uniform by clearly stating what is acceptable and what is not.

The *Random House Webster's College Dictionary* caused an uproar when it appeared in 1991. In a venomous article from *Time* magazine (June 24, 1991, p.51), the author writes:

> At its core, the *Random House Webster's* is a laudable achievement, the work of many excellent minds. It is in the core's wrapping that trouble lies and English suffers erosion, mainly because the editors choose to be "descriptive, not prescriptive." As a result, numerous entries and usage notes, wafting in the sociological winds and whims of the day, are inconsistent and gratuitous, undermining any pretense of rigor, let alone authority. Most notable in these pages is the influence of special-interest groups, prominently feminists and minorities.

The author then indicts the editors of the dictionary for including such words as "herstory" (in addition to history), "womyn" (as well as women), "heightism" and "weightism" (which recognize discrimination against short and fat people), as well as other words and expressions. According to the author, "such permissiveness can only invite a further tattering of the language—and already has."

At the other end of the spectrum are critics who don't believe that publishing houses have gone far enough in the "democratization" of dictionaries. They have often cited. . . . the *American Heritage Dictionary of the English Language* as an example of the descriptive method gone wrong. In their effort to present readers with attitudes towards usage, the publishers established a "usage panel" of 120 "experts" who were asked to respond to questions about the acceptability of certain words and expressions. The results of this survey sometimes accompany word definitions in the following way:

"gift . . . tr.v. gifted, gifting, gifts. 1. *Informal* To present with a gift. See Usage note. *Usage:* The recent use of *gift* as a transitive verb, though not incorrect, has not established itself on a formal level. The following representative example involving the active voice is termed unacceptable by 94 per cent of the Usage Panel: *He gifted each of his nephews.*" The problem with the "usage panel," say critics, is that it only represents the viewpoints of a minority and encourages members to respond conservatively, since they know their responses will be printed in a book that is still considered the final authority on language use.

American Heritage's "stuffiness" doesn't bother one of the writers of *The Right Handbook,* even though she's aware of the criticism leveled against it. She uses and likes the desktop *American Heritage* for its illustrations: "All dictionaries should have lots of drawings and pictures," she says. The second writer uses the *Webster's Ninth New Collegiate Dictionary:* "It includes really good illustrations of usage, and I like the fact that they tell you when a word first appeared in print. I think it's interesting that "earthling' was first used in the 16th century." And the third writer's dictionary is the *Random House College Dictionary:* "It has a great historical sketch of the English language at the beginning, and the essay on dialects and functional varieties of usage is good too." Our editor uses *Webster's New World Dictionary* because it's "enlightened." He won't explain why he thinks so. Are there substantial differences among these dictionaries? Perhaps. But if we have reasons for using different dictionaries, they aren't particularly scholarly. Somehow, we've each become accustomed to one. We feel satisfied with our choices, and we gladly recommend them to others.

In addition to English language dictionaries, writers sometimes use specialized dictionaries, which define terms and concepts commonly used in particular disciplines. There's a dictionary of literary terms for literary critics, a dictionary of psychological terms for psychologists, a dictionary of physics terms for physicists, and so on. If you read and write a lot about a particular field, a specialized dictionary will come in handy.

Thesauruses

A thesaurus, which sounds like a prehistoric animal but, alas, is very much alive today, is supposed to help increase your vocabulary, vary your writing, and make you sound educated. That's why some teachers prescribe it for their students, and students like to use it. But, there's a world of difference between what it's supposed to do and what it often does, namely, ruin perfectly acceptable writing. Although publishers would claim otherwise, thesauruses are really written for people who already know a lot of vocabulary and are, therefore, very sensitive to the sometimes subtle differences in the meanings and uses of synonyms. Novices, to whom the books are usually marketed, should use them with extreme caution. In fact, affixing a label onto thesauruses that reads, "WARNING: Uninformed use of this book can be detrimental to your writing," seems like a pretty good idea.

By "uninformed use," we mean looking up a word in the thesaurus, choosing one of its synonyms at random, and using it to replace a word that's already acceptable for your purpose and context. In a previous chapter we showed you how "He's a bad boy," a simple but good sentence, was turned into a monstrosity through indiscriminate use of synonyms. Instead of sounding sophisticated, the alternative, "He's an inclement stripling," is funny, like a parody of high-brow discourse.

Instead of considering the thesaurus a book to use whenever you need a better, longer, or more unusual word, try looking at it as a book to consult when your memory needs jarring. Imagine, for example, that you're writing a sentence and use a word that's similar to the one you really want, but can't think of at the moment. You look up in the thesaurus the word you've written, check its synonyms, and find the one you originally wanted. You try it out in your sentence and decide that it works. Using the thesaurus in this way is very different from using it in the haphazard way we described above. Because you're consulting it to remember something you already have an inkling about, you can better avoid selecting an unsuitable word for your purpose and the context you've created. The same holds true for dictionaries, which some people use instead of thesauruses to find synonyms.

All major dictionary publishers produce hardcover and softcover thesauruses, but the classic still remains *Roget's Thesaurus,* written by Dr. Peter Mark Roget, an English physician. It was first published in 1852 and has been revised and enlarged several times since then. Now that we've warned you against using the thesaurus in a certain way, we feel we can recommend *Roget's II The New Thesaurus, Expanded Edition* (Berkley Books, 1988). One of the good features of this thesaurus is that words are often put in a sentence first, showing how the word is used, and then followed by synonyms which can be used in the same *context.* In *Roget's II,* for example, the verb "to call" is first defined: "1. To demand to appear, come, or assemble: calling the doctor; called a meeting." This is followed by appropriate synonyms: "convene, convoke, muster, send for, summon." A second use of the word "call" is listed next: "To describe with a word or term: called me a liar." Again synonyms follow: "characterize, designate, label, style, tag, term." We like this approach because it helps the user discriminate among the many possible alternatives offered.

Spelling Aids

Bad spellers who use a personal computer to write may get some relief from a "spelling checker" program. There are drawbacks to spelling-checking software, however. If your misspelled word is a legitimate word in its own right, the computer won't pick it up because the computer can't recognize context. For example, if you wrote, "I'm going to the *stare,*" instead of *store,* the error would not be identified because "stare" is a correctly spelled word.

There are some good spelling guides that you can find at the bookstore, such as *Instant Spelling Dictionary,* 3rd edition, by M. M. Dougherty, J. H. Fitzgerald, and D. O. Bolander (Warner Books, 1990). It is an easy-to-read paperback listing 25,000 words. Like most spelling guides, it also helps with word division and pronunciation. Short of consulting a spelling dictionary or using a spell-checking program to highlight misspelled words in your writing, asking a good speller for help is an equally good solution for bad spelling problems.

P.IGG   PYGGE   PEEG   Ph.G.

Usage and Style Handbooks

The Right Handbook can't answer all your questions about English usage and style. In fact, *all* handbooks on the market today provide only a partial view of the whole language picture. It's therefore necessary sometimes to consult more than one source. The problem is, given the fact that there are so many usage and style handbooks on bookstore shelves, how do you know which one(s) to buy? To make choosing a little easier, we're going to recommend and briefly describe the books that represent the most common types published today. While these books may cover some of the same material, each has its own focus and biases. They don't always make for easy reading, but the effort is usually well worth it.

Harper's Dictionary of Contemporary Usage, 2nd ed., by William and Mary Morris (Harper Perennial, 1985), is a highly entertaining as well as practical usage guide. The authors collated the opinions of 166 "consultants on usage" (who are, as a group, all over the political map) on often-disputed usage problems. Generally speaking, the consultants respond to the question, "Would you use this word either in speech or writing?", and their edited comments are presented as if they were part of an actual conversation among the consultants. These comments are usually quite interesting and often very funny. What is most striking about this approach to questions of usage is that there is frequently extreme disagreement among the consultants about what is "acceptable" and what is not. This illustrates, once again, that language is not a fixed, immutable entity, and that people have widely differing and often very strong opinions about how to use it.

The *Merriam Webster Concise Handbook for Writers* (Merriam Webster, 1991) is an affordable, easy-to-use paperback that provides practical advice on such issues of style as punctuation, capitals, italics, plurals, possessives, abbreviations, grammar, quoting, copyediting, and proofreading.

A Dictionary of Modern English Usage by H. W. Fowler (Second Edition, revised by Sir Ernest Gowers, Oxford University Press 1965) is wider in scope than the preceding books and also a delight to read. Fowler has been criticized for his conservatism, but even though he proudly admitted to being a "prescriptive grammarian," he spent much of his time debunking language myths. Some of his cautions will strike readers as outdated and petty, such as this one about the phrase, "Don't blame it on me," which, says Fowler, "is a colloquialism not yet recognized by the dictionaries, a needless variant of 'don't blame me for it,' and not to be encouraged." In contrast, the reader will also find wonderful invectives against grammatical know-it-alls, as in the case of *aggravate, aggravation,* about which he writes, "For many years grammarians have been dinning into us that to *aggravate* has properly only one meaning—to make (an evil) worse or more serious—and that to use it in the sense of *annoy* or *exasperate* is a vulgarism that should be left to the uneducated. But writers have shown no less persistence in refusing to be trammelled by this admonition. . . . It is time to recognize that usage has beaten the grammarians, as it so often does, and that the condemnation of this use of *aggravate* has become a FETISH." It's hard not to like a man who could write that! *Modern English Usage* is a book for people who enjoy reading details about where words and expressions came from, how they developed through history, how they are now used, and which ones should be avoided. Although Fowler's book is mainly about British practice and sometimes uses examples that only the most knowledgeable readers will understand, reading it can be a treat for all lovers of language and good writing.

The Chicago Manual of Style 13th ed. (The University of Chicago Press 1982) a far more technical book than the other two, is really designed for professional authors, editors, and copywriters, all of whom need to know specifics about manuscript preparation. Although some of the book is too detailed for most writers' needs, its sections on punctuation, spelling, reference lists, and bibliographies are useful for anyone who writes papers. This manual will also be of interest to people who write in disciplines that use special terminology and symbols. For example, if you were writing about computer software and wanted to know whether or not to capitalize the software names, you would find this information in a chapter called *Names and Terms:* "Software (languages, programs, systems, packages, routines, sub-routines, statements, commands) terms indicating specific units are generally in full capitals, with a few exceptions given with initial capitals only: APL, BASIC . . . SCRIPT, SAIL, Assembler, Pascal." Or, if you were typing a mathematical paper in which you had a series with the variable x, and needed to know the standard punctuation for such a series, you would find the following information in the chapter called "Mathematics in Type": "In elisions, if commas or operational signs are required, they should come after each term and after the three ellipsis dots if a final term follows them. For example: $x_1, x_2, \ldots, x_n$ NOT $x_1, x_2, \ldots x_n$." *The Chicago Manual* is more expensive than the other books, but for the serious writer it can't be surpassed for thoroughness. In the publishing world it's regarded as the bible of style.

As you shop for style and usage handbooks consider the ones we've mentioned here, browse through others, and pick the one that feels most comfortable for you. Keep in mind, however, that handbooks alone can't solve every style and usage problem that might creep into your writing; rely on your own knowledge of the language as well, and don't hesitate to ask others for help!

Chapter Eleven

Writing Outside the English Class
In-School and Out-of-School

In-School: Writing in Other Classes

Although within the past five years or so, some teachers and professionals in schools at all levels have become increasingly aware of the role of writing in all fields. Most students and teachers continue to see writing as relevant only in English courses. And, in truth, almost all writing instruction does occur within English or literature classes. Too often we hear students majoring in engineering, mathematics, physics, chemistry, economics, and so forth say that they just want to get their writing requirement out of the way so that they can concentrate on what's important in their major field. Encouraging this attitude in their students, teachers in other fields often assume that all writing instruction should be done by English teachers, and that once a student has learned to write well in an English class, he can write well in any and all classes he takes. We don't believe this.

In order to write well within any subject area, a writer has to know certain things about that field: he has to understand that field's approach to the world; he has to know what that field considers important and basic and what that field considers good evidence to be. Often experts within a field who are insecure about their writing skills will hire a "ghost" writer if they are planning to write for an audience outside their field, but the "ghost" writer could not do the writing without the knowledge of the expert. This same expert might not use a "ghost" writer when he is writing to his peers because he already knows how to talk to them—if he didn't he would never have become an expert. As you can see, awareness of audience is crucial in all fields.

What we're saying is that you cannot assume that because you've written successfully in a class whose primary focus is the improvement of writing, you'll automatically be able to write effectively in an economics or chemistry class. Before you can do that, you need to learn the language of that field; you can do this by reading and by listening to your professor and others in the field lecture and talk to one another and to you.

It might sound like we're saying you should not write anything in other classes until you become well versed in the subject. But we don't believe that at all. What we *do* believe is that you must begin writing as soon as you enter these specific discipline areas. Only in this way can you begin to make its language your own, to make its language say what you want it to say. Actually, at first, the quality of your writing may deteriorate a bit because you aren't quite sure about the new knowledge you're being exposed to. It's difficult to write well about things you don't understand. But as you read more, listen more, speak more, and write more, you'll slowly begin to use the language of the field. You'll also begin to develop a sense of how to write for those outside that field in contrast to how to write for those within the field. Clarity is always a function of audience and context. What is clear to a nuclear physicist will not usually be clear even to an educated layperson. And the nuclear physicist doesn't want to have to wade through reading what is obvious to him in order to learn something new. The nuclear physicist wants an author to assume what is true: that he knows a great deal already.

Having said all this about the differences between writing in various subject areas, we now want to say the opposite: that there are certain similarities to all writing tasks. Chief among these is the process of writing. Process is inherent in all writing—it's the way you go about getting it done. Some writers say that their processes never change, that they go about writing in the same way whether they're working on a short story, a business report, or a scientific description. Other writers say they have developed different ways of getting different pieces of writing done. Nonetheless, being conscious of process is valuable to any developing writer, and learning whether you function best using the same or different processes for different sorts of writing is an important bit of learning.

Often, teachers in subject areas assign only one paper per term and ask for it to be handed in during the final week. We encourage teachers not to do this, but it does have the advantage of allowing you to profit from what you've learned during the whole semester. The disadvantages, of course, are that you have to write it during the busiest part of the term and that you are not being encouraged to use writing throughout the semester. You can get around some of this disadvantage by writing from the very beginning as we advise in this chapter and by starting the assignment as soon as you have it. Nonetheless, you may not want to finish it until the end of the term for fear that some material will be covered then that's important for your paper. The final disadvantage of the one-paper-at-the-end is that it's difficult to get a sense of your teacher as an audience, a sense of what he values most in a piece of writing. But you can make that a part of your challenge.

Suggestions and Advice: Beginning to Write

Based on the above philosophy, we make the following suggestions to you when you begin writing in a new subject area:

1. Begin writing immediately. If your teacher lectures, take notes. As soon as possible, after class is over, rewrite those notes in language you can understand. Sometimes students take notes by recording almost verbatim what the lecturer says. This might be okay if you understand him, but not at all helpful if you don't. If you don't understand your own notes, try to phrase questions which get at your difficulty. We suggest that you reserve the left page of your notebook for notes taken in class and the right page for your own writing after class is over. If you write out questions, you'll be prepared if the teacher starts out the next class by asking for questions. And even if you do understand the language of your teacher as you have recorded it, it is useful to rewrite it in language of your own.

   Two things will be happening as you do this. First, you'll be developing skill in writing and speaking and thinking within the given subject area and secondly you'll be learning the material. Writing facilitates learning. We can almost guarantee you that if you write out class notes in your own language after every class, your grades will improve. Apparently, as your brain works to make sense of new knowledge by finding language for it, it at the same time stores that new knowledge in retrievable ways, i.e., by linking it to what you already know.

   Many teachers in subject areas are beginning to harness the learning power of writing by incorporating directly into the classroom what we're suggesting here. Consequently, you may run across a teacher who gives you five minutes or so during the class and/or at the end of the class to write down what seems most important or most confusing in the day's lecture. The teacher may or may not collect these papers, but usually does so only to get some feedback for himself about how information is coming across to students. Teachers do not usually grade such writing, although they may check off that it has been done. Teachers who have used these techniques have gotten very positive responses from students who believe that they've learned more and gotten better grades as a result.

2. Attend carefully to writing assignments. When the teacher asks you to write something to hand in, make certain you understand what he is asking for. If you have any doubts, we suggest you rewrite the assignment as you understand it and then ask the teacher if that's what he's looking for.

3. Do some exploratory writing on your subject before you begin the paper itself—preferably on a word processor where there's a better chance that your writing can keep pace with your thoughts (see Chapter 10). It's good to do this sort of writing without thinking of the final product because you can allow yourself freedom in thinking. You don't need to be thinking about structure or logic or appropriateness or audience. This exploratory writing will do several things for you: it will stimulate your thinking; it will focus your interests; it will uncover areas of doubt; it will serve as a basis for outside research (what subjects you need to read up on and such before you can complete the paper), it will preserve ideas, and it will give you ungraded practice in using the language of the subject area. If possible (and we *do* know how busy college students can be with classes and work), do this exploratory writing at least a day before you begin writing a more formal draft. Good thoughts need time to develop; exploratory writing will get them started; time will build them into something stronger. Of course, you can do all this exploratory thinking without writing—perhaps by setting aside some private thinking time when and where you won't be interrupted. The problem we have with this is that we don't always remember what we've come up with but have some lingering sense that the most fruitful ideas (like the biggest fish) got away!

4. Ask the teacher if you can submit a draft of your paper and get some feedback from him to help you with revision. Even if the teacher says no, he'll probably be impressed by your asking. If the class is large, the teacher may simply be unable to grant your request, but may be able to refer you to a graduate student assistant

to the class as a reader for your draft. If none of this happens, you can take your draft to your school's writing center. And if your school doesn't have a writing center, find someone else who will at least listen to your draft before you begin final revision. This can be valuable even if the person who listens or reads it is not the designated audience for the piece. Again, if your draft is on the word processor, you'll be in a better position to take full advantage of advice for revision. Having to retype papers considerably dampens anyone's enthusiasm for revision!

5. Even if the teacher agrees to read your draft, you may also want to ask him whom he sees as the audience of the paper: himself (an expert in the field) or an educated layperson.

6. Again, even if the teacher agrees to read your draft and specifies a particular audience, you may also want to ask him if he has on file copies of successful papers from previous years—even if they aren't from the same class.

7. Form a writing-study group with other members of your class. Research done on the results of such groups demonstrates fairly conclusively that peer groups are an aid to learning. You can share and discuss class notes and homework in such groups, but you can also share drafts of papers with one another. One rule you should always keep in mind is never never to turn in a paper which someone else has not read. Even if your teacher regularly reads drafts, you'll want to show the draft to someone before the teacher reads its. Study groups are good places for trading drafts.

8. We assume that your teacher will specify in the assignment whether or not you are to use outside sources and what form of documentation to use for footnotes and such. But if he doesn't supply this information, you'll need to ask. You will find the section on documentation (in Chapter 7) useful even if you are not working on a full-scale research paper.

Suggestions and Advice: Finishing

9. Once you've gotten feedback on a piece of writing you're preparing for a grade, you're ready to do a final revision. Depending upon how confident you feel on the basis of this feedback, you may want to ask someone to look at your revision also before putting it into final form. This only points up more strongly the advantages of writing on the computer.

10. If your assignment is designated by the generic name "research paper," we suggest that you read Chapter 9 in this book before

completing it. We urge you particularly to read the sections on paraphrasing, quoting, and citing authorities. Many students have been accused of plagiarizing when the problem was that they just didn't fully understand how to use source material. If you have questions, it would be smart to bring them to your teacher. If that's not possible, we suggest that you attach a photocopy of your source with an explanation of what your problem with it is. Teachers face the same issues in their own writing.

11. Once you have a final version of your paper, you can use this handbook just as you would for any paper—beginning by checking paragraph division and sequence and ending with checking spelling and other small details.

12. When your teacher returns your paper, read his comments carefully. If you do not understand them, ask for an appointment so he can explain them to you more fully. Ask him, too, what would have made the paper better. You can store these ideas for future use, for better grades—but, in a more lasting sense, you will be developing your abilities as a writer in the field.

Conclusion

It's tempting to believe that once you've learned how to write for one teacher in a particular subject area, you've learned to write for all of them. But that's simply not true. Teachers in, say, economics, vary as much in their expectations of a piece of writing as teachers in writing classes. Obviously the knowledge you acquire in one economics class should help you with whatever writing you do in any other economics class. And just as obviously, your growing familiarity with the language of the field will be helpful. But you're still going to have to develop some sense of each particular teacher as a reader of your papers: what audience he expects you to write for, what forms he expects you to use, how formal he expects you to be, if you can use personal experience, and so forth. It will still also be useful for you to ask the new teacher to look at drafts and show you sample papers.

This variety is all part of helping you grow as a writer. Some teachers may seem to you quite arbitrary and unreasonable in their demands for your writing. But such an audience exists outside school walls as well as inside them. Some teachers may give you almost no guidelines at all and leave you feeling lost, groping in darkness. But that sort of audience exists outside too. All writing (except personal writing for yourself) involves some balance between your intentions and style as a writer and the needs and expectations of your intended audience. Learning to achieve that balance is what writing in school is all about. It doesn't make writing easier; it will make it better.

Writing in the "Real World"

Just as students may get the impression that writing is relevant only in English courses (and it's especially easy to get that impression when teachers of other subjects do not give out many writing assignments!), students may also believe that writing assignments end as soon as they graduate. Not so. Writing is very much a part of the working world outside school.

Although the types of writing assigned in the "real world" may differ from the writing assignments you get in college, the components of effective writing that are discussed in this book apply in both cases. The ability to communicate well in writing is just as highly prized in the increasingly competitive job market as it is in school, if not more so. Many of our students who have graduated and entered the working world tell us that writing turned out to be a more important component of their job than they had expected.

Sometimes it is obvious that the field you've chosen or job you've targeted will require a lot of writing. An ad such as the following from a Sunday edition of *The New York Times* clearly illustrates this point:

> College grad: must have at least 1-2 years of experience in sci-tech/professional publishing as a writer. Responsible for writing sound, effective advertising and promotion copy. Individual will be responsible for writing copy for direct mail brochures, card decks, catalogs, posters, educational mailings, etc. Meticulous eye for detail.

More often, however, the role that writing plays in a job, or even an entire career, is not immediately apparent. Take for example the following *New York Times* ad for a high-level position in a bank:

> Manager, bank. Produce accurate financial analyses of U.S. financial markets and opportunities for clients in Far East, upon which clients will rely to make high-value financial decisions. Initiate & supervise gathering of data & information pertaining to or affecting U.S. financial instruments such as T-bonds and notes and equity securities. Provide consultation to bank's clients and employees. Ascertain client objectives; define issues, gather and analyze data as they apply to clients' objectives utilizing theory & principles of financial management; make recommendations based upon analysis. Use bank in-house computers and computer programs to reduce data to information. Prepare written and oral

reports to clients & bank employees. MS or MBA finance & accounting.

The employer who placed this ad is looking for someone with financial and computer expertise. But he is also looking for a competent researcher and writer. Although it is obvious that the employee will be handling quantitative data, many of the final products will be written reports. We venture to guess that at least one-half of the employee's time will be spent at a computer, not computing, but writing. In fairness to the potential candidates for the job, the employer might have added the caveat: "If you don't like to write, this job isn't for you."

The writing you do for your English and other courses does not differ *in essence* from the writing you may have to do on the job. For example, many of the strategies for "beginning to write" and "finishing" that were mentioned earlier in this chapter could apply in other situations as well. Replace the word "teacher" with "boss," and replace "paper" with "report" or "proposal," and you'll notice that although the products may change, the writing *processes* can remain essentially the same. However, there do seem to be some very real differences between writing for school and writing for work especially in terms of the ways in which the writing and the writer are judged. In order to get a clearer understanding of these differences, we interviewed some professionals whose work includes writing and asked them to describe the role that written communication plays in their professions.

I.

Stephen F. is a partner in a law firm where he specializes in corporate law (e.g., mergers, acquisitions, and public and private offerings).

> Before I became a corporate lawyer, I was a litigator. I was an associate in a law firm, and I learned to write from one of the partners in my firm. He would give me an assignment to draft something. (In a law firm, even if a lawyer gives you an assignment and says, "don't worry about it, it's just a first draft," you'll still stay up all night and rewrite it 48 times because you know he's judging you!). I would hand him the document I wrote. Now, there are two ways to respond to a document an associate writes. The first is to write a big "NO!" on it. The other way is to change the writing to make it right. Fortunately, this lawyer would go over my work very carefully. He would give me models. Seeing the way he wrote next to the way I wrote, you didn't have to be Albert Einstein to notice that his way was so much better than mine.

As a litigator I would be in court and I realized that generally people were fighting over ambiguities in contracts. So I became very sensitive to ambiguities in language. The fact that I was a litigator before becoming a corporate lawyer was good because now when I review what associates write I can say "uh-oh, that could be a problem." Associates aren't well prepared. They need more experience in writing. What drives me crazy is a sentence that could refer to one of four different things. In terms of legal consequences, when you're describing a certain situation, you have to cover all the bases.

Now that I am a corporate lawyer, some of the documents I draft are prospectuses that are filed with the Securities and Exchange Commission (SEC) that investors read, and liability accrues to somebody if I don't state or I omit something. There are very real consequences in terms of omissions of ideas. One of the sections in most documents investors see is called "risk factors." If an investor puts money in a particular venture, what are the risks? When you write, you have to ask yourself, what would a reasonable person investing money in a venture want to know before putting money in it?

When I have to prepare a prospectus for a private offering, before I do writing I "do diligence." That means I try to find out everything I can about the company. I sit with the president of the company for several days. He comes to my office and later on I go to his plant to learn as much about the business as I can. I ask what are they selling? How do they manufacture it? What are their sources of supplies? Who are the customers? What is the distribution? When I visit the plant I ask to talk to other people there such as the plant manager. I have to write for an SEC examiner, who is generally a lawyer, and he reads to see if an investor can understand it. The object of an SEC review is disclosure. The theory is that you can sell anything to the public as long as you tell them what it is and what the risks are. And you have to tell them in a fashion they'll understand.

In order to function in the mass of paper I have to deal with and time requirements, my personal writing style is to get my thoughts down on paper right away. My first draft is usually horrible, except that I generally have all the basic ideas down. Then I can shift ideas around, move paragraphs. Especially if I've just come from two days of doing diligence, I've got to get it all down. If I wait for a week to go by, I'll forget. Some of my first drafts consist of dictation into a tape recorder, because I can speak faster than I write.

Steve tells us that he learned to write much the same way that students in writing workshops learn to write: by writing and receiving feedback from one or more readers. In Steve's case, the reader was his boss, so the feedback contained some element of judgment. But his boss also took time out to *show* Steve alternative—and better— ways of expressing his ideas. Learning took place not because the partner rewrote Steve's prose, but because Steve paid attention to the rewrite by comparing it with his own work. He sensitized himself further by listening carefully in court to the nuances of the language used in contracts. In time and with practice, such conscious, critical attention to language becomes internalized, and it can be called upon at will whenever it is time to evaluate one's own or someone else's writing.

As a corporate lawyer, Steve's main activities are researching and writing. Since he has so much paperwork and so little time, he has had to develop a strategy to get his words down on paper fast. He expects to revise, so he doesn't worry if his first draft is rough. As he writes and rewrites, Steve is conscious of his purpose and the needs of his readers. If in the documents he writes Steve fails to "disclose" properly on behalf of his clients, they can be held liable. This points to perhaps the greatest difference between school-related writing and work-related writing. In the "real world" writing has the potential to effect very real and possibly serious consequences. A lot more is at stake than a grade. As Steve suggests, problems with writing can lead to lawsuits.

II.

Diane M., M.D., is a physician who holds an academic position in a medical school where she has teaching, research, and clinical responsibilities.

> On a daily basis, I have to write notes about patients, and it's critical that other people can understand my notes, otherwise all the data and knowledge I have about my patients will be of no use to my colleagues who may also be seeing the patient. For example, I may see a patient with what I think is a neurological problem and take an extensive history and physical. If I don't write it down in a clear and coherent way and then I refer the patient to neurology, the entire work-up I did for an hour is entirely useless. If the neurologist can't gain information about the work-up, she'll have to repeat it. This kind of thing happens often.
>
> I also send very detailed consultation letters to the primary physicians of patients, and these are 3 to 4-page, single-spaced, typed letters. Also in academic medicine we have to write lectures and grant proposals. No matter how good your ideas are, if you don't communicate them well in a grant proposal you won't get funded. And a career in academic medicine depends a lot on being published. Medical literature is notorious for poor writing. Editors have become much more conscious of this, and papers are being rejected on the basis of poor writing. If you can't communicate your good data and good conclusions, why publish?

Medical students struggle like crazy to get their ideas down on paper. They've often done nothing but science courses in college where they weren't expected to write. In medical school, they've done nothing but rote memorization. In terms of sophistication in writing, it's like high school. Medical school is devoid of writing, and this is completely inappropriate. Even though 75% of medical school graduates end up in private practice, they will be writing on a regular basis. They have to send consultation letters to colleagues. If they're ever involved in any administrative function, any institutional function, they'll be writing memos, hopefully conveying their thoughts in a convincing, concise way to others. In medicine, it's a very powerful tool to be able to communicate effectively without a huge amount of struggle.

In the first paragraph of her transcript, Diane, like Steve, describes how poor-quality writing can lead to serious consequences, in this case unnecessary and costly duplication of work already done. In her field of academic medicine, it seems as if a whole career can be made or broken on the basis of writing-related tasks. Not only does one have to be a competent clinician, one also has to be an effective writer. In academic medicine, one's employment often depends on getting research grants, and promotions are contingent on how often one is published—not on seniority or because the chairman of your department likes you. "Publish or perish" is the name of the game in this arena. So if, as Diane points out, editors of medical journals are rejecting papers because they are poorly written, the writers of these papers have more to lose than just their self-esteem.

III.

Peter C. is a property manager for a real estate company. Before switching to a career in business, he taught writing and worked as a freelance writer, so he was able to add a double perspective to our series of interviews with professionals.

Writing is critical in my job. In real estate, contracts are made in writing. The whole business revolves around agreements and understandings that are memorialized not only in legal papers but in letters, memoranda, and other documents. Therefore, everything you say in writing can become a tool that works either in your favor or against you. The *way* you write things can make all the difference.

For example, we have a tenant who stopped paying rent, pleaded poverty, and said he was in real financial distress. I wrote a letter to the owner of the business saying we were prepared to do x,y, and z to help the situation out. But the problem was that when

I wrote the letter I didn't say that there was a limit to my offer, that they had to respond to our offer within ten days or it would be null and void. The way I wrote the letter suggested, in effect, that my offer was open indefinitely, and that wasn't my intention at all. So that letter is something the tenant can point to and say, "But look, you offered this to us." Then it's too late. The document is binding and I can't go back and say, "Oh, but I didn't mean that!"

In business when people anticipate possible problems, conflicts, or legal disputes in the future, a strategy they use is to write letters "to the files." They describe in writing what is going on. That is to say they write letters that may contain redundant and obvious information, but the point of this activity is to put the information on paper and in the files. Then if a dispute ensues, they are able to produce evidence and say, "I told you I was going to do such and such six months ago. It's here in the files; here's the letter. Then two months later I wrote you this," and so on. What you're doing is building a case for possible use in court.

In early stages of negotiations in any kind of business transaction, whether you're holding them orally or in writing, you kind of position yourself: You can be aggressive, you can be conciliatory . . . Handling negotiations or any business deal has to do with the posture you take, how you position yourself. Whether you think you're going to be able to intimidate someone into taking a deal or smooth-talk and persuade them, your correspondence is going to have a lot to do with it. It's very rhetorical. In sticky situations, you can use writing abilities to smooth things over and influence people's feelings. Because my own background isn't in business but more in academic areas, I tend to make communications to tenants a little bit tongue-in-cheek. I'll add some levity to situations, and I'll phrase things a little more decoratively than the average business person would. I think that what this does is it surprises the reader. So that if there is a specific complaint or a gripe or something somebody's angry about, it will sort of surprise them into realizing that on the one hand, there is the physical situation—the problem— and on the other, there are *people* trying to communicate with each other, and that's not an easy thing to do. This technique is not just manipulation either—you're not merely trying to exploit a mode of communication to a certain end. It's a way of feeling you're being honest in situations as well. It's a personal expression. What I'm saying is: this is my work but it's also *me,* too, and I have to combine the two. I'm not just subscribing to the formulaic business communiques. There is something of myself in my messages. The subtext is "I manage this, but I'm going to manage it my way, and I have to put myself into that whole equation." Some of my tenants have complimented me on my memos. They referred to them as "collectibles." They see them as a kind of journal of the building. The memos told the story.

I think that rhetorical strength—the suasive quality of writing— is developed by reading a lot. I've always felt that to be a good writer you have to be a good reader, too, and I think that in general business people are not as well read as they could be. In their writing the MBA's that work with me have a good command of the language, they're grammatically sophisticated, but they lack the subtleties which come from a lot of reading experience.

As in Steve's case, much of the writing Peter does has legal ramifications. The story he tells in the second paragraph of his transcript illustrates once again that keeping one's purpose and target audience in mind when writing is essential.

Peter also brings up another important distinction between school-related writing and writing in the "real world." Much of what students write in school—exams and papers alike—is meant to demonstrate their grasp of a subject to a higher authority, i.e., the teacher. While there may be such a demonstrative purpose to the writing one does in the working world outside school (as in the case of an associate writing a legal brief in part to prove to a partner that he knows the case law), there may be greater opportunities in the 'real world' to influence the behavior of others through effective oral and written communication.

Becoming an effective communicator, however, takes time, practice, and, frequently, help from others. We know of an English professor at a northeast college who also did freelance consulting with local businesses. One of his clients was an aeronautical company that hired him to work with its engineers on their writing. The first day he met these engineers he asked them what percentage of their time they spent writing. Their answer? Sixty to seventy percent! The problem was that they had to write reports for a very diversified audience. They had to write for their superiors who were engineers; they had to write for executives in their company who were most interested in the bottom line; and they had to write for congressional committees that were responsible for appropriations to the company for its work on space-exploration projects. The engineers were having a hard time adjusting and readjusting their writing to the various audiences, and the English professor taught them how to solve this problem in his writing workshop. The engineers were lucky that their company invested in such continuing education—most industries leave employees to fend for themselves.

The interviews presented here are not meant to be an indepth survey of the writing done in the "real world" of work, outside the academic community. We hope, however, that the stories our informants told, including the one about the engineers, convince you of at least three things: 1) There *is* writing after school; 2) It is an important component of many careers; and 3) It's worth working on writing now, while you're still in school (in English and all other classes—even when the teacher doesn't give out writing assignments!), because chances are you'll be doing a lot of it later on.

Appendix: Using This Book

In this appendix, we're going to show you how two students used this book as they moved from the first draft of a paper to the final draft. Obviously, which sections of the book you use will depend on the particular paper you've written. You'll never use the whole book when working on revising a paper. All we can do, then, with these examples is show you how two students used this book and its advice for specific writing projects.

Both students whose work follows had read through this whole book as part of their assigned work for their writing classes. Thus, they were familiar with the general outline and sequencing: the movement from global revision to smaller and smaller elements. At the global revision stage, both students received feedback from their teachers and classmates and revised and restructured their papers fairly extensively. Before beginning the process of editing both students were satisfied with the scope of their papers.

You and your classmates might find it useful to decide what advice you would give each of these students as they move from level to level in this process. And we think you'll notice at many spots how recursive revision is; that is, revision in one spot tends to require some revision in other spots. This is hardly surprising because any piece of effective writing is a unified whole; changing one part thus often leads to changing another part in order to maintain the unity.

Adam

Adam's teacher had brought several newspaper editorials into the classroom for students to read, analyze, and judge. The class talked about what made arguments effective. The teacher then asked them to spend some time reading newspapers to find some subject about which they felt strongly and then write a paper whose purpose would be to persuade others that they were right.

Following is the first draft of Adam's paper.

> There is a significant difference between natural death and induced death. One who is taken life away from, is immoral and slanderous. One who dies of natural cause because of some incur-

able disease is traumatic but morally acceptable. Retardism is an incurable disease but not death causing. It can only be treated for the sake of the victim and with those who he shares his life. Treating it is relatively difficult. The severity is proportional to being incurable. Any additional disease that is death-causing or shortens lives is a natural death, which is morally acceptable in this society.

In the case of Baby Jane Doe, there are problems as described above. One of the problems is that Baby Jane has an incurable and fatal disease. It is a birth defect of a spina bifida, an exposed spinal cord with other physical internal defects. These conditions will allow her to have at most, 2 years to live with no operation. Even with an operation, Baby Jane will only live for 18 years, at most. The question is, does 18 years of living seem to be the greatest gift? 18 years living in agony is just not the same as living 18 healthy years. There will be mental retardism and constant suffering. It has been said by doctors and nurses that the child would be profoundly retarded and would never grow to be normal and productive. One nurse said that she would have paralplegia, incontinence, and seizures. It is believed that Baby Jane would become a mere vegetable with no goal in life.

Because of her severity, her life should be allowed to flow naturally which would lead to her final fate. Each of us, as humans, have a final fate. The government can not and should not determine that for us, especially in this case. The government should not consider the violation of civil rights because natural fate has nothing to do with civil rights. We can only accept our fate. The severity of the situation helps determine our fates. If a person is suffering a disease as cancer, nothing medically possible can be done to cure him, but to allow his fate to come naturally. He has no choice and neither does Baby Jane Doe. The other choice is to have a prolonged vegetative life and accept her same fate given to her in the beginning. One important thing to consider is that, if one person decides to prolong his life then, he also decides to cope with the conditions of his handicap. Since, at the present, Baby Jane is in no condition to make her own decision, it is her parents right to help her. Baby Jane might never get a chance to make her own decision. Whether or not in the future Baby Jane can act upon herself, it is her parents' influence that should guide her. If she does, she's more unlikely able to cope with her physical defects and mental disorder, rationally.

The parents' decision to prevent surgery would lessen the emotional and economical suffering. It would take several painstaking sacrifices to support their daughter. According to a nurse, it takes constant watch and several emergency intervening for such handicap children. Taking care of her would make the parents too busy to take care of other important aspects of their lives. How can they devote any more time to the leisure and welfare of themselves and their children, if they choose to have a larger family? The other choice would only require a few years of such heavy responsibility.

It would also be useless to spend so much money on Baby Jane's medicare just to prolong the agony of her and her parents. The opposite choice seems to be more advantageous economically, emotionally, and timely. More importantly, prevented surgery would be more beneficial to Baby Jane than for her parents. She would not have to experience a life of constant suffering nor would she even be irrationally bewildered. She would not have to deal with perpetual confusion about the world and herself. She might never be able to cope with that.

Therefore, the parents decision to let their child live to her coming fate is a natural decision. With difficulty, the parents are accepting their baby's fate. Her fate will be a natural death because of its incurability. This is morally accepted in our society and it should be dealt in the manner that it is at present. Her fate would prevent Baby Jane Doe from suffering and would give her peace.

I. Global Revision

When Adam shared this draft with his peer group, they responded as follows:

> The arguments and facts seem good and convincing, but it's hard to know exactly what point you're trying to make.
>
> I think you ought to say right away, at the beginning, the issue that's being fought over in court. Also, you say some of the same things over and over—for instance, that fate should take its course. Maybe you don't need to say that so often.
>
> The first sentence confused me because you don't explain what "induced death" you're talking about. Because I was confused at the very beginning, it was hard to follow the argument.

Adam's teacher agreed with the students' comments, adding that he had given good reasons for what he thought, but should say more about the arguments on the other side of this issue. She also suggested that he ask others to pinpoint for him specific sentences which were unclear to them.

Adam realized during the discussion which followed that he had never really stated exactly what the issue was; he had just plunged into giving reasons on either side almost as though he was assuming that the reader would know exactly what the issue was just because it had received extensive coverage in newspapers. On the basis of this feedback, Adam rewrote the first paragraph:

> Baby Jane Doe is the name given to a little girl recently born at the Stony Brook Hospital with spina bifida, an exposed spinal cord. Other aspects of her physical and mental makeup are defective also. Consequently, her parents have decided to not have performed the

operation which would ameleriate the spinal misformation. Hospital authorities have sued for the assumption of responsibility for the baby's welfare because they allege her civil rights are being violated. Were they to succeed, the operation would be undertaken. If their court case were not to succeed, the baby would die. Newspapers have excessively detailed opposing attitudes toward this issue.

Having started his paper somewhat differently, Adam went through all the rest of it to see what other changes he might need to make as a result of this new beginning. While doing this, he also tried to cut out some of the repetition. This is what his second draft looked like:

Baby Jane Doe is the name given to a little girl recently born at the Stony Brook Hospital with spina bifida, an exposed spinal cord. Other aspects of her physical and mental makeup are defective also. Resultingly, her parents have decided to not have performed the operation which would ameleriate the spinal misformation. Hospital authorities have sued for the assumption of responsibility for the baby's welfare because they allege her civil rights are being violated. Were they to succeed, the operation would be undertaken. If their court case were not to succeed, the baby would die. Newspapers have excessively detailed opposing attitudes toward this issue.

There is a significant difference between natural death and induced death. One who is taken life away from, is immoral and slanderous. One who dies of natural cuases because of some incurable disease is traumatic but morally acceptable. Retardism is an incurable disease but not death causing. It can only be treated for the sake of the victim and with those who he shares his life. Treating it is relatively difficult. The severity is proportional to being incurable. Any additional disease that is death-causing or shortens lives is a natural death, which is morally acceptable in this society.

In the case of Baby Jane Doe, there are problems relative to the issues described above. One of the problems is that Baby Jane has an incurable and fatal disease, spinal bifida, which means that without an operation she has only 2 years to live. Even with an operation, Baby Jane will only live for 18 years, at most. The question is, does 18 years of living seem to be the greatest gift? 18 years living in agony is just not the same as living 18 healthy years. There will be mental retardism and constant suffering. It has been said by doctors and nurses that the child would be profoundly retarded and would never grow to be normal and productive. One nurse said that she would have paralplegia, incontinence, and seizures. It is believed that Baby Jane would become a mere vegetable with no goal in life.

Because of her severity, her life should be allowed to flow naturally which would lead to her final fate. Each of us, as humans, have a final fate. The government cannot and should not determine that for us, especially in this case. The government should not consider the violation of civil rights because natural fate has nothing to do with civil rights. We can only accept our fate. If a person is suffering a disease as cancer, nothing medically possible can be done to cure him. He has no choice and neither does Baby Jane Doe. The other choice is to have a prolonged vegetative life and accept her same fate given to her in the beginning. One important thing to consider is that, if one person decides to prolong his life then, he also decides to cope with the conditions of his handicap. Since, at the present, Baby Jane is in no condition to make her own decision, it is her parents right to help her. Baby Jane might never get a chance to make her own decision. Whether or not in the future, Baby Jane can act upon herself, it is her parents' influence that should guide her. If she does, she's more unlikely able to cope with her physical defects and mental disorder, rationally.

The parent's decision to prevent surgery would lessen the emotional and economical suffering. It would take several painstaking sacrifices to support their daughter. According to a nurse, it takes constant watch and several emergency intervening for such handicap children. Taking care of her would make the parents too busy to take care of other important aspects of their lives. How can they devote any more time to the leisure and welfare of themselves and their children, if they choose to have a larger family? The other choice would only require a few years of such heavy responsibility. It would also be useless to spend so much money on Baby Jane's medicare just to prolong the agony of her and her parents. The opposite choice seems to be more advantageous economically, emotionally, and timely. More importantly, prevented surgery would be more beneficial to Baby Jane than for her parents. She would not have to experience a life of constant suffered nor would she even be irrationally bewildered. She would not have to deal with perpetual confusion about the world and herself. She might never be able to cope with that.

Others who argue for the hospital's civil rights aver that medicine is there to prolong life and doctors and hospitals must do whatever incumbents upon them to keep anyone alive. Those who argue this contention argue also that it is immoral for any parents not to accept the child they give birth to and help them again as much longevity as conceivable. The fact that it might cost a considerable amount of money is not the point. These arguments can be reversed on themselves because doctors and hospitals and others should expend their time and effort to help those who have some opportunity for a relatively normal life. Baby Jane Doe doesn't; there are defects she has which no one can improve.

The parents' decision to let their child live to her coming fate is a natural decision. With difficulty, the parents are accepting their baby's fate. Her fate will be a natural death because of its incurability. This is morally accepted in our society and it should be dealt in the manner that it is at present. Her fate would prevent Baby Jane Doe from suffering and would give her peace.

II. Paragraphs

Adam next followed our directions for labeling paragraphs with "says" and "does" statements. Here's what that looked like:

Baby Jane Doe is the name given to a little girl recently born at the Stony Brook Hospital with spina bifida, an exposed spinal cord. Other aspects of her physical and mental makeup are defective also. Consequently, her parents have decided to not have performed the operation which would ameleriate the spinal misformation. Hospital authorities have sued for the assumption of responsibility for the baby's welfare because they allege her civil rights are being violated. Were they to succeed, the operation would be undertaken. If their court case were not to succeed, the baby would die. Newspapers have excessively detailed opposing attitudes toward this issue.

Says: what the difference of opinion is

Does: introduces my whole paper and gives the background for understanding the issue.

There is a significant difference between natural death and induced death. One who is taken life away from, is immoral and slanderous. One who dies of natural cuases because of some incurable disease is traumatic but morally acceptable. Retardism is an incurable disease but not death causing. It can only be treated for the sake of the victim and with those who he shares his life. Treating it is relatively difficult. The severity is proportional to being incurable. Any additional disease that is death-causing or shortens lives is a natural death, which is morally acceptable in this society.

Says: how natural death and induced death are different and how that relates to retardism.

Does: Begins to build my argument.

In the case of Baby Jane Doe, there are problems relative to the issues described above. One of the problems is that Baby Jane has an incurable and fatal disease, spinal bifida, which means that without an operation she has only 2 years to live. Even with an operation, Baby Jane will only live for 18 years, at most. The question is, does 18 years of living seem to be the greatest gift? 18 years living in agony is just not the same as living 18 healthy years. There will be mental retardism and constant suffering. It has been said by doctors and nurses that the child would be profoundly retarded and would never grow to be normal and productive. One nurse said that she would have paralplegia, incontinence, and seizures. It is believed that Baby Jane would become a mere vegetable with no goal in life.

Says: What Baby Jane Doe's problems are and what her life would be like if she lived.

Does: Gives specifics of this case and continues to build my argument.

Because of her severity, her life should be allowed to flow naturally which would lead to her final fate. Each of us, as humans, have a final fate. The government cannot and should not determine that for us, especially in this case. The government should not consider the violation of civil rights because natural fate has nothing to do with civil rights. We can only accept our fate. If a person is suffering a disease as cancer, nothing medically possible can be done to cure him. He has no choice and neither does Baby Jane Doe. The other choice is to have a prolonged vegetative life and accept her same fate given to her in the beginning. One important thing to consider is that, if one person decides to prolong his life then, he also decides to cope with the conditions of his handicap. Since, at the present, Baby Jane is in no condition to make her own decision, it is her parents right to help her. Baby Jane might never get a chance to make her own decision. Whether or not in the future, Baby Jane can act upon herself, it is her parents' influence that should guide her. If she does, she's more unlikely able to cope with her physical defects and mental disorder, rationally.

Says: the government should not interfere with the natural course of this baby's life because nothing can really help her. Also, she cannot speak for herself so her parents have to make the decisions.

Does: Gives two reasons for my side of the argument.

The parent's decision to prevent surgery would lessen the emotional and economical suffering. It would take several painstaking sacrifices to support their daughter. According to a nurse, it takes constant watch and several emergency intervening for such handicap children. Taking care of her would make the parents too busy to take care of other important aspects of their lives. How can they devote any more time to the leisure and welfare of themselves and their children, if they choose to have a larger family? The other choice would only require a few years of such heavy responsibility. It would also be useless to spend so much money on Baby Jane's medicare just to prolong the agony of her and her parents. The opposite choice seems to be more advantageous economically, emotionally, and timely. More importantly, prevented surgery would be more beneficial to Baby Jane than for her parents. She would not have to experience a life of constant suffering nor would she even be irrationally bewildered. She would not have to deal with perpetual confusion about the world and herself. She might never be able to cope with that.

Says: How expensive and time-consuming it would be to care for her and not having the operation would keep her from living a suffering life.

Does: Gives more reasons for my opinion.

Others who argue for the hospital's civil rights over that medicine is there to prolong life and doctors and hospitals must do whatever incumbents upon them to keep anyone alive. Those who argue this contention argue also that it is immoral for any parents not to accept the child they give birth to and help them gain as much longevity as conceivable. The fact that it might cost a considerable amount of money is not the point. These arguments can be reversed on themselves because doctors and hospitals and others should expend their time and effort to help those who have some opportunity for a relatively normal life. Baby Jane Doe doesn't; there are defects she has which no one can improve.

Says: That doctors should prolong life but not a life that will just be unacceptable.

Does: Gives the other side of the argument and my counter argument.

The parents' decision to let their child live to her coming fate is a natural decision. With difficulty, the parents are accepting their baby's fate. Her fate will be a natural death because of its incurability. This is morally accepted in our society and it should be dealt in the manner that it is at present. Her fate would prevent Baby Jane Doe from suffering and would give her peace.

Says: That the parents are right because their decision is moral and will save the baby from a life of suffering.

Does: States my conclusion with the most important reasons.

Adam discussed with his teacher these "says" and "does" statements and began to realize that his main point had to do with the difference between interfering with a natural process which would cause additional difficulties and letting nature take its course. The Baby Jane Doe case was simply one instance which had focused people's attention on this point. With this in mind, he decided to reverse the first two paragraphs. Adam discussed with his teacher whether his paper might not be more effective if the arguments against his opinion were presented before the reasons for his conclusion. He also saw from looking at the "says" and "does" statements that the paper spoke of the baby's future suffering in several paragraphs and that the horror of this future might be better emphasized if it had a paragraph of its own. He also decided that his response to the argument about the insignificance of money in a moral debate would be more effective if included in the paragraph where he spoke of the possible financial burden. He tried the paper this way and decided it *was* better.

Here is Adam's third draft:

There is a significant difference between natural death and induced death. One who is taken life away from, is immoral and slanderous. One who dies of natural cuases because of some incurable disease is traumatic but morally acceptable. Retardism is an incurable disease but not death causing. It can only be treated for the sake of the victim and with those who he shares his life. Treating it is relatively difficult. The severity is proportional to being incurable. Any additional disease that is death-causing or shortens lives is a natural death, which is morally acceptable in this society.

This issue has come to the fore in the debate over Baby Jane Doe, the name given to a little girl recently born at the Stony Brook Hospital with spina bifida, an exposed spinal cord. Other aspects of her physical and mental makeup are defective also. Consequently, her parents have decided to not have performed the operation which would ameleriate the spinal misformation. Hospital authorities have sued for the assumption of responsibility for the baby's welfare because they allege her civil rights are being violated. Were they to succeed, the operation would be undertaken. If their court case were not to succeed, the baby would die in less than two years. Newspapers have excessively detailed opposing attitudes toward this issue.

Those who argue for the hospital's civil rights over that medicine is there to prolong life and doctors and hospitals must do whatever incumbents upon them to keep anyone alive. Those who argue this contention argue also that it is immoral for any parents not to accept the child they give birth to and help them gain as much longevity as conceivable. It's frightening to conceive of where this could advance to. How retarded and damaged might a child have to be not to be helped? Also, the case should not be argued on the basis of expense, for one cannot put a monetary value on human life.

In the case of Baby Jane Doe, there are problems relative to the issues described above because her life would be one of mainly suffering. The problem is that Baby Jane has an incurable and fatal disease, spinal bifida, which means that without an operation she has only 2 years to live. Even with an operation, Baby Jane will only live for 18 years, at most. The question is, does 18 years of living seem to be the greatest gift? 18 years living in agony is just not the same as living 18 healthy years. There will be mental retardism and constant suffering. It has been said by doctors and nurses that the child would be profoundly retarded and would never grow to be normal and productive. One nurse said that she would have paralplegia, incontinence, and seizures. It is believed that Baby Jane would become a mere vegetable with no goal in life. An operation would only allow her to experience a life of constant suffering and irrational bewilderment. She would have to deal with perpetual confusion about the world and herself. She might never be able to cope with that.

Because of her severity, her life should be allowed to flow naturally which would lead to her final fate, a natural death. Each of us, as humans, have a final fate. The government cannot and should not determine that for us, especially in this case. The government should not consider the violation of civil rights because natural fate has nothing to do with civil rights. We can only accept our fate. If a person is suffering a disease as cancer, nothing medically possible can be done to cure him. He has no choice and neither does Baby Jane Doe. Since, at the present, Baby Jane is in no condition to make her own decision, it is her parents right to help her. Baby Jane might never get a chance to make her own decision. Whether or not in the future, Baby Jane can act upon herself, it is her parents' influence that should guide her.

The parent's decision to prevent surgery would lessen the emotional and economical suffering. It would take several painstaking sacrifices to support their daughter. According to a nurse, it takes constant watch and several emergency intervening for such handicap children. Taking care of her would make the parents too busy to take care of other important aspects of their lives. How can they devote any more time to the leisure and welfare of themselves and their children, if they choose to have a larger family? The other choice would only require a few years of such heavy responsibility. It would also be useless to spend so much money on Baby Jane's medicare just to prolong the agony of her and her parents. The opposite choice seems to be more advantageous economically, emotionally, and timely. Doctors and hospitals should expend their time and effort to help those who have some opportunity for a relatively normal life. Baby Jane Doe doesn't; there are defects she has which no one can improve. There are many children and people already living who can benefit from the good doctors and hospitals can do.

The parents' decision to let their child live to her coming fate is a natural decision. With difficulty, the parents are accepting their baby's fate. Her fate will be a natural death because of its incurability. This is morally accepted in our society and it should be dealt in the manner that it is at present. Her fate would prevent Baby Jane Doe from suffering and would give her peace.

III. Sentences, Phrases, and Words

Adam was now satisfied with the overall structure and paragraphing of his piece and was ready to move to the next step. His teacher provided time in the classroom for Adam and his classmates to exchange papers in order to get help with sentence structure, punctuation, phrase structure, and spelling. Adam's partner circled and underlined sentences, phrases, words, and punctuation marks that he considered questionable. Following are some of these sentences and some comments about how Adam went about making changes.

1. *One who is taken life away from, is immoral and slanderous.*

After some thought and discussion with his teacher about what he what trying to say, Adam realized he was trying to combine two ideas:

There are two kinds of death.

One kind of death occurs when life is taken away forcibly.

To do this is immoral and slanderous.

He then reconnected these ideas as follows:

> One kind of death, when life is taken away forcibly, is immoral and slanderous.

(In this book, we call this sort of approach "Major Surgery.")

2. *It can only be treated for the sake of the victim and with those who he shares his life.*

Adam approached this sentence in the same way: by concentrating first on what he was trying to say and, only after doing that, breaking the sentence down into its separate ideas:

> It can be treated for the sake of the victim.
> It can also be treated for the sake of those he shares his life with.

His teacher pointed out to him that the repetition of so many words suggests that a sentence with parallel structure might make his ideas clearer. Adam reread the section in this book on parallel structure and after several rewritings came up with the following rewriting:

> It can only be treated for the sake of the victim and for those he shares his life with.

3. *Because of her severity, her life should be allowed to flow naturally which would lead to her final fate, a natural death.*

Adam's editing partner wasn't sure what was wrong with this sentence, but she didn't think it was clear. Adam discussed this sentence with his teacher who first asked him what was severe. Adam recognized that it was the disease, not the baby, which was severe. He then tried rewriting the sentence several ways:

> Because of its severity, her disease should be allowed to flow naturally to her final fate, a natural death.
> Because of its severity, her disease was going to flow naturally to death, her final fate.
> Because she was born severly ill, she would naturally die soon.
> Because she was born severly ill, her final fate (dying young) would come about quite naturally.

Adam thought this last sentence came closest to what he was trying to say.

4. *Her fate will be a natural death because of its incurability.*
Adam tried several different ways of expressing his ideas:

> Her fate is to lead to natural death because she's incurable.
> Her death will be natural because she's incurable.
> Her death will be her natural fate because it's incurable.
> Her fate is natural death at a young age because she's incurable.

At this point, Adam sought help from his teacher who again pointed out to him the importance of looking at pronouns (*its* in this case) and thinking about what they refer to. This helped Adam to produce the following rewriting:

> Her fate is an early death because her disease is incurable.

5. *Those who argue for the hospital's civil rights over that medicine is there to prolong life and doctors and hospitals must do whatever incumbents upon them to keep anyone alive.*
Adam's editing partner misread this sentence at first and suggested to him that he needed a comma. After checking the list on pages 104–105 of this book, Adam understood that he had written a compound sentence and that a comma was necessary before *and.* While discussing this sentence, he asked his teacher about the used of *incumbents;* the teacher suggested he check how it is used in his dictionary. Fortunately, Adam had a dictionary which included sample sentences in definition. All this led to the following rewritten sentence:

> Those who argue for the hospital's civil rights over that medicine is there to prolong life, and doctors and hospitals must do what is incumbent upon them to keep anyone alive.

6. *Consequently, her parents have decided to not have performed the operation which would ameleriate the spinal misformation.*
After discussion and looking through the section in the book on sentences, neither Adam nor his editing partner could figure out why this sentence seemed awkward to them. Their teacher suggested they look through the phrase section of the book. They checked subject— verb agreement and the possibility of a double negative, but found no problems there. However, when they looked for an infinitive in the sentence, they realized that there was one and that it was split in an awkward way. Adam was then able to rewrite as follows:

> Consequently, her parents have decided not to have performed the operation which would ameleriate the spinal misformation.

But Adam still didn't like the sound of the sentence and rewrote it once more:

Consequently, her parents have decided not to have the operation performed which would ameleriate the spinal misformation.

But still Adam was dissatisfied and turned again to his editing partner who suggested using *against*. Here's Adam's final rewriting:

Consequently, her parents have decided against having the operation which would ameleriate the spinal misformation.

7. *Each of us, as humans, have a final fate.*

Adam realized, once his peer editor had circled *have* that it was not the right verb. When Adam checked the book's discussion of *each,* he understood he had to change *have* to *has* because *each* is singular.

Each of us, as humans, has a final fate.

8. *Since, at the present, Baby Jane is in no condition to make her own decision, it is her parents right to help her.*

During the classroom editing session, Adam's teacher looked over the work he and his partner were doing and circled *parents* (which Adam's partner had not circled). Adam realized almost immediately that he should have used an apostrophe here. Since two parents are involved in this decision, the apostrophe must follow the *s*. While rewriting this sentence, Adam decided that *right* wasn't the word he really wanted and changed it to *duty* which he felt made his point much more effectively.

Since, at the present, Baby Jane is in no condition to make her own decision, it is her parents' duty to help her.

Having rewritten this sentence, Adam recognized almost immediately that *parent's* in the first sentence of the following paragraph had to be changed to *parents'*.

9. *According to a nurse, it takes constant watch and several emergency intervening for such handicap children.*

At first, Adam decided the sentence needed parallelism and he changed *watch* to *watching*. His peer editor thought there should be an *s* on *intervening* since there was more than one. But then the teacher suggested they see what the dictionary had to say about this word. After checking in the dictionary, Adam decided to use *interventions* instead. In the process of making these changes, Adam decided that *several* was not really strong enough; it seemed less strong than *constant* and, in a way, even weakened his idea. He decided to use *numerous* instead. During this discussion, his editing partner also pointed out that an *-ed* was lacking at the end of *handicap*. When Adam wrote out *handicaped,* he didn't think it looked right. The dictionary helped here also. Here's Adam's final revision:

> According to a nurse, it takes constant watching and numerous emergency interventions for such handicapped children.

10. *This is morally accepted in our society and it should be dealth in the manner that it is at present.*

Adam's editor did not know what Adam meant by the second half of this sentence. (She also pointed out the typographical error.) After a fairly lengthy discussion about what he meant, Adam rewrote the sentence.

> Such a death is morally acceptable to our society; thus the hospital should accept the parents' decision and let nature take its course.

After rewriting these and other sentences, Adam began to look at the individual words his editor had circled. He also used the spell-checker on his computer to catch some spelling errors. The spell-checker identified the following words as misspelled: *cuases, ameleriate, paralplegia, operatin, dealth, severly,* and supplied the corrected words. The spellchecker could not identify *retardism* and *misformation,* so Adam checked these in a dictionary. He discovered that his words were not accepted ones, and he replaced them with *retardation* and *deformation.*

Here is Adam's final draft. It is not perfect, of course. We think that Adam is too concerned with sounding academic, but this draft is far better than his first draft.

> There is a significant difference between natural death and induced death. One kind of death, when life is taken away forcibly, is immoral and slanderous. The second kind of death, when life ends naturally because of some incurable disease, is traumatic but morally acceptable. Retardation is an incurable disease but not death causing. It can only be treated for the sake of the victim and for those he shares his life with. Treating it is relatively difficult. The severity is proportional to the incurability. Any additional disease that is death-causing or shortens lives is a natural death, which is morally acceptable in this society.
>
> This issue has come to the fore in the debate over Baby Jane Doe, the name given to a little girl recently born at the Stony Brook Hospital with spina bifida, an exposed spinal cord. Other aspects of her physical and mental makeup are defective also. Consequently, her parents have decided against having the operation which would ameliorate the spinal misformation. Hospital authorities have sued for the assumption of responsibility for the baby's welfare because they allege her civil rights are being violated. Were they to succeed,

the operation would be undertaken. If their court case were not to succeed, the baby would die in less than two years. Newspapers have excessively detailed opposing attitudes toward this issue.

Those who argue for the hospital's civil rights over that medicine is there to prolong life, and doctors and hospitals must do whatever is incumbent upon them to keep anyone alive. Those who make this argument also argue that it is immoral for any parent not to accept the child they give birth to and help them gain as much longevity as conceivable. It's frightening to conceive of where this could advance to. How retarded and damaged might a child have to be not to be helped? Also, the case should not be argued on the basis of expense, for one cannot put a monetary value on human life.

In the case of Baby Jane Doe, there are problems relative to the issues described above because her life would be one of mainly suffering. The problem is that Baby Jane has an incurable and fatal disease, spinal bifida, which means that without an operation she has only 2 years to live. Even with an operation, Baby Jane will only live for 18 years, at most. The question is, does 18 years of living seem to be the greatest gift? 18 years living in agony is just not the same as living 18 healthy years. There will be mental retardation and constant suffering. It has been said by doctors and nurses that the child would be profoundly retarded and would never grow to be normal and productive. One nurse said that she would have paraplegia, incontinence, and seizures. It is believed that Baby Jane would become a mere vegetable with no goal in life. An operation would only allow her to experience a life of constant suffering and irrational bewilderment. She would have to deal with perpetual confusion about the world and herself. She might never be able to cope with that.

Because she was born severely ill, her final fate (dying young) would come about quite naturally. Each of us, as humans, has a final fate. The government cannot and should not determine that for us, especially in this case because natural fate has nothing to do with civil rights. We can only accept our fate. If a person is suffering from a disease such as cancer, nothing medically possible can be done to cure him. He has no choice and neither does Baby Jane Doe. Since, at the present, Baby Jane is in no condition to make her own decision, it is her parents' duty to help her. Baby Jane might never get a chance to make her own decision. Whether or not in the future, Baby Jane can act upon herself, it is her parents' influence that should guide her.

The parents' decision to prevent surgery would lessen the emotional and economical suffering. It would take several painstaking sacrifices to support their daughter. According to a nurse, it takes constant watching and numerous emergency interventions for such handicapped children. Taking care of her would make the parents too busy to take care of other important aspects of their lives. How can they devote any more time to the leisure and welfare of themselves and their children, if they choose to have a larger family? The other choice would only require a few years of such heavy responsibility. It would also be useless to spend so much money on Baby Jane's medicare just to prolong the agony of her and her parents. The opposite choice seems to be more advantageous economically and emotionally and would represent a more satisfactory use of time. Doctors and hospitals should expend their time and effort to help those who have some opportunity for a relatively normal life. Baby Jane Doe doesn't; there are defects she has which no one can improve. There are many children and people already living who can benefit from the good doctors and hospitals can do.

The parents' decision to let their child live to her coming fate is a natural decision. With difficulty, the parents are accepting their baby's fate. Her fate is an early death because her disease is incurable. Such a death is morally acceptable in our society; thus the hospital should accept the parents' decision and let nature take its course. Her fate would prevent Baby Jane Doe from suffering and would give her peace.

One final note on this extensive revision. We're sure you noticed, as we did, that one revision often led to others. This is how revision works. As we've stressed over and over in this book, words never occur in isolation and they don't "mean" in isolation either. Too often students make *only* the changes their teachers or classmates suggest and don't check to see if these changes require other changes. You always have to stay aware of how words interact when you change any one of them. You have to make sure you continue to get the interactions you want. This is what makes it possible for readers to come away from your text with a good sense of what you were saying.

David

The second revision process that we describe presents a completely different set of problems. The student who wrote the next essay is from Taiwan—English is not his first language—and he therefore had more grammatical problems than did Adam. And since the essay he wrote is descriptive rather than analytical, he had much fewer problems with organizing his content than Adam did. As you read through our description below, note how the student uses special strategies to help him gain control of English grammar.

David's ESL composition class was reading an anthropology textbook which focused on cultural conflict, and the students' first essay was about the problems they faced while adapting to life in New York City. After a brief class discussion of typical problems that immigrants face in a new country, the students wrote their first drafts at home. David's first draft follows.

How I Adapted the Living in New York

"Where is every body?" In the first day I arrived New York, no one took me in the airport. Being for mistakes in communication, those who I support saw in airport did not show up. So the first experience in the U.S. of me was tried to find a hotel in Manhattan with my broken English. Fortunately, I am familiar with the living in big city. New York, Tokyo, or Taipei does not make many differences except language. After all, I found the bus from New Wark Airport to Pen Station and a hotel in nearby. And there was the second surprise in the U.S.—the cost of hotel in downtown Manhattan.

Maybe those cities that be called as international city are pretty similar in many ways. In New York, I found the domiciliary room, applied telephone line, social security card, bank account and all the others things myself. In fact, it is not until I confided in English then I began to deal with some others Taiwanese and Chinese. I guess the most thing that I confused is when and how much tip should I give. In Taiwan, we do not have this custom. Until now, I still can not hold on all the tip-problems very smoothly and properly.

I remembered in the first several days in New York, I had some difficult in eating. I was not sure of the food and the behaviors in the restaurant. Although I am familiar with the manner in formal restaurants of Taiwan, how to order some meals from a strange manu, and if my behavior is proper in here that were another problems. Especially is the tip, that really is a big problem to me. In the first several months, I only ate in some fast food restaurants. Although there is an official price of tip—15%, how to make well use of tip is another problem. Beside, I always forget to leave some bills in table, I was not used to.

The other way is the politeness of a gentleman, such as open the door for young ladies, yield seat in the subway . . . etc. I think it's naturally to do these for elder citizens, but for young ladies, I never saw before. Science man and woman should have equal position, why ladies have the privileges? Although I am not think it is a bad habit, I do not yield my seat to young ladies even in now. However, I learned a lot from these gentlemen. Their manner taught me the mean of "the higher the bamboo growth, the lower it bow," I learned how to humble and how to respect others.

In Taiwan, I confided in proper and tender behavior. But in the U.S., I can only sure that I am doing right in some formal situations. In most of times, I guess I was too serious. I had to, I am not familiar in the ways of American-style social communication. Beside, keeping distance can protect me from many troubles. I guess that also is one purpose of politeness, no one can understand or hurt other from such a distance.

I have to say that I do not like the dirty of New York. In compare with many cities in the world, I feel that New York is a very dirty one. Everyday walking to school, I can even see the dunghill in the road. Not only the road is unusual dirty, but also the subway, and some houses. I am also surprise at there are so many homeless people. In Taiwan, such a small island, twenty million people crowds in forty thousand square kilo-meter ground. The competition of survival is extremely hard. For example, every who can studies in university should defeat at least sixty thousand classmates in enter-college examination. But there are few homeless persons. To make a living in the U.S. is much easier than in Taiwan, and the social welfare of the U.S. is much better than Taiwan. But in Taiwan, the total number of homeless persons which I have ever seen is less than ten. I guess somebody should think about "why?"

Anyway, to some others Taiwanese students, I do too well in adapting American culture and do not like a Taiwanese any more. Maybe I should spend some time in readapting Taiwan society when I go back to Taiwan. I believe that even I need to spend this time, it will not a long time. After all, my ability in adapting new environment is not too bad.

I. Global Revision

David's response group gave the following comments to his first draft:

In which ways are international cities similar? Should you give some more information about Taiwan?

Can you say more about your process of learning—is it still going on? Are you still adapting to other things?

The paragraph about eating and restaurants confused me. I think the part about tipping should be in a different paragraph.

You wrote, "no one took me in the airport" in your first paragraph. Do you mean that no one was there to meet you? And "I support saw"—do you mean "I was supposed to see"? That's a nice introduction, just a little bit unclear in those two parts.

David's teacher agreed that he should consider adding more background information about Taiwan, so that she and his classmates would have a clearer idea of the kinds of adjustments he had to make to live in New York. She also suggested that he add more examples of the adjustments he had to make in New York.

David had already sensed, as he was reading aloud to his group, that he could include more information about life in Taiwan, and the responses he got convinced him he should make these additions.

Note also, in the second draft below, the additional paragraphs on the subway and the New York City "run-around" (paragraphs 5 and 6).

"Where is every body?" In the first day I arrived New York, no one picked me up in the airport. Being for mistakes in communication, those who I expected saw in airport did not show up. So the first experience in the U.S. of me was tried to find a hotel in Manhattan with my broken English. Fortunately, I familiarize with the living in big city. New York, Tokyo, or Taipei does not make many differences except language. After all, I found the bus from New Wark Airport to Pen Station and a hotel in nearby. There was the second surprise waiting for me—the cost of hotel in downtown Manhattan.

Maybe those cities that be called as international cities are pretty similar in many ways. In New York, I found the domiciliary room, applied telephone line, social security card, bank account and all the others things myself. In fact, it is not until I confided in English then I began to deal with some others Taiwanese and Chinese. I guess the most thing that I confused is when and how much tip should I give. In Taiwan, we do not have this custom. Until now, I still can not hold on all the tip-problems very smoothly and properly.

I remembered in the first several days in New York, I had some difficult in eating. I was not sure of the food and the behaviors in the restaurant. Although I am familiar with the manner in formal restaurants of Taiwan, to order some meals from a strange manu, and to behavior as properly as a gentleman were not so easy to hold on. Especially is the tip, that really is a big problem to me. In the first several months, I only ate in some fast food restaurants. Although there is an official price of tip—15%, how to make well use of tip is another problem. Beside, I always forget to leave some bills in table, I was not used to.

The other thing that strange to me is the politeness of a gentleman, such as open the door for young ladies, yield seat in the subway . . . etc. I think it is naturally to do these for elder citizens, but for young ladies, I never saw before. Since man and woman should have equal position, why ladies have the privileges? Although I am not think it is a bad habit, I do not yield my seat to young ladies even in now. However, I learned a lot from these gentlemen. Their manner taught me the mean of "the higher the bamboo growth, the lower it bow," I learned how to humble and how to respect others.

To live in a new place always take time to adapt. When I first took the subway train in New York, I did not know there are many different lines. I think it is like the subway in Taipei which only has one line. So I walked to 74 street Jackson Height station in Queens, and took the first train that I met in New York. In the trunk, I felt more and more strange. "Where are we going? Why there seems to be many different tracks? . . . " I thought. At least, I had to ask other passengers in the train to show me the way. This unfortunately guy who I met in subway train leaded me the way and gave me a subway map. I want say "Thank you" to this poor man, the manager of fast delivery department of New York Transit Authority.

My new live established little by little with some stories like this. I experienced waiting a long time in social security office, running between several different offices of New York telephone to "donate" some deposit. Although in comparing with residents of some others places, New Yorkers are more cooler than them (maybe that is the city-symptom). I found my way to live.

In Taiwan, I confided in proper and tender behavior. But in the U.S., I can only sure that I am doing right in some formal situations. In most of times, I am too serious. I had to, I am not familiar in the ways of American-style social communication. Beside, keeping distance can protect me from many troubles. I guess that also is one purpose of politeness, no one can understand or hurt other from such a distance.

I have to say that I do not like the dirty of New York. In compare with many cities in the world, I feel that New York is a very dirty one. Everyday walking to school, I can even see the dunghill in the road. Not only the road is unusually dirty, but also the subway, and some houses. I am also surprise at there are so many homeless people. In Taiwan, such a small island, twenty million people crowds in forty thousand square kilo-meter ground. The competition of survival is extremely hard. For example, every one who can studies in university should defeat at least sixty thousand classmates in enter-college examination. But there are few homeless persons. To make a living in the U.S. is much easier than in Taiwan, and the social welfare of the U.S. is much better than Taiwan. But in Taiwan, the total number of homeless persons which I have ever seen is less than ten. I guess somebody should think about "why?"

Anyway, to some others Taiwanese students, I do too well in adapting American culture and do not like a Taiwanese any more. Maybe when I go back to Taiwan I will need spend some time in readapting Taiwan society when I go back to Taiwan. I believe that even I need to spend this time, it will not a long time. After all, my ability in adapting new environment is not too bad. Beside, Taiwan is the place that I born and grow up.

II. Paragraphs

David next labeled paragraphs with "says" and "does" statements.

"Where is every body?" In the first day I arrived New York, no one picked me up in the airport. Being for mistakes in communication, those who I expected saw in airport did not show up. So the first experience in the U.S. of me was tried to find a hotel in Manhattan with my broken English. Fortunately, I familiarize with the living in big city. New York, Tokyo, or Taipei does not make many differences except language. After all, I found the bus from New Wark Airport to Pen Station and a hotel in nearby. There was the second surprise waiting for me—the cost of hotel in downtown Manhattan.

Says: Experiences of first day

Does: Introducing paper

Maybe those cities that be called as international cities are pretty similar in many ways. In New York, I found the domiciliary room, applied telephone line, social security card, bank account and all the others things myself. In fact, it is not until I confided in English then I began to deal with some others Taiwanese and Chinese. I guess the most thing that I confused is when and how much tip should I give. In Taiwan, we do not have this custom. Until now, I still can not hold on all the tip-problems very smoothly and properly.

Says: Big cities are similar, but tipping hardest for me

Does: Introduces an idea about little problems are difficult to hold

I remembered in the first several days in New York, I had some difficult in eating. I was not sure of the food and the behaviors in the restaurant. Although I am familiar with the manner in formal restaurants of Taiwan, to order some meals from a strange manu, and to behavior as properly as a gentleman were not so easy to hold on. Especially is the tip, that really is a big problem to me. In the first several months, I only ate in some fast food restaurants. Although there is an official price of tip—15%, how to make well use of tip is another problem. Beside, I always forget to leave some bills in table, I was not used to.

Says: Restaurants are problems, especially tipping

Does: Continuing to explain about tipping

The other thing that strange to me is the politeness of a gentleman, such as open the door for young ladies, yield seat in the subway . . . etc. I think it is naturally to do these for elder citizens, but for young ladies, I never saw before. Since man and woman should have equal position, why ladies have the privileges? Although I am not think it is a bad habit, I do not yield my seat to young ladies even in now. However, I learned a lot from these gentlemen. Their manner taught me the mean of "the higher the bamboo growth, the lower it bow," I learned how to humble and how to respect others.

Says: Politeness is different here

Does: Another example of difficult adjustment

To live in a new place always take time to adapt. When I first took the subway train in New York, I did not know there are many different lines. I think it is like the subway in Taipei which only has one line. So I walked to 74 street Jackson Height station in Queens, and took the first train that I met in New York. In the trunk, I felt more and more strange. "Where are we going? Why there seems to be many different tracks? . . . " I thought. At least, I had to ask other passengers in the train to show me the way. This unfortunately guy who I met in subway train leaded me the way and gave me a subway map. I want say "Thank your" to this poor man, the manager of fast delivery department of New York Transit Authority.

Says: Problem on NYC subway

Does: Another example

My new live established little by little with some stories like this. I experienced waiting a long time in social security office, running between several different offices of New York telephone to "donate" some deposit. Although in comparing with residents of some others places, New Yorkers are more cooler than them (maybe that is the city-symptom). I found my way to live.

Says: Problem of bureaucracy and "cool" New Yorkers

Does: Another example

In Taiwan, I confided in proper and tender behavior. But in the U.S., I can only sure that I am doing right in some formal situations. In most of times, I am too serious. I had to, I am not familiar in the ways of American-style social communication. Beside, keeping distance can protect me from many troubles. I guess that also is one purpose of politeness, no one can understand or hurt other from such a distance.

Says: About formality of my behavior

Does: Explains about how I adjusted to new culture

I have to say that I do not like the dirty of New York. In compare with many cities in the world, I feel that New York is a very dirty one. Everyday walking to school, I can even see the dunghill in the road. Not only the road is unusually dirty, but also the subway, and some houses. I am also surprise at there are so many homeless people. In Taiwan, such a small island, twenty million people crowds in forty thousand square kilo-meter ground. The competition of survival is extremely hard. For example, every one who can studies in university should defeat at least sixty thousand classmates in enter-college examination. But there are few homeless persons. To make a living in the U.S. is much easier than in Taiwan, and the social welfare of the U.S. is much better than Taiwan. But in Taiwan, the total number of homeless persons which I have ever seen is less than ten. I guess somebody should think about "why?"

Says: I don't like dirty of NY and I don't understand homelessness—it not like this in Taipei

Does: Explains something I'm still adjusting

Anyway, to some others Taiwanese students, I do too well in adapting American culture and do not like a Taiwanese any more. Maybe when I go back to Taiwan I will need spend some time in readapting Taiwan society when I go back to Taiwan. I believe that even I need to spend this time, it will not a long time. After all, my ability in adapting new environment is not too bad. Beside, Taiwan is the place that I born and grow up.

Says: I'm American now, maybe I have problems adjusting again to Taiwan

Does: Ending for paper—summary

David showed his "says" and "does" statements to his tutor, and they discussed changes he could make. The tutor said that long "says" statements might mean a paragraph was trying to do too much, and she suggested David look for long "says" statements and then think about ways to rearrange or redivide those paragraphs. Following this advice, David looked through his paper and decided to divide his next-to-last paragraph into two smaller paragraphs, one about litter and the other about homelessness:

> I have to say that I do not like the dirty of New York. In compare with many cities in the world, I feel that New York is a very dirty one. Everyday walking to school, I can even see the dunghill in the road. Not only the road is unusually dirty, but also the subway, and some houses.
>
> I am also surprise at there are so many homeless people. In Taiwan, such a small island, twenty million people crowds in forty thousand square kilo-meter ground. The competition of survival is extremely hard. For example, every one who can studies in university should defeat at least sixty thousand classmates in enter-college examination. But there are few homeless persons. To make a living in the U.S. is much easier than in Taiwan, and the social welfare of the U.S. is much better than Taiwan. But in Taiwan, the total number of homeless persons which I have ever seen is less than ten. I guess somebody should think about "why?"

David liked his final paragraph, so he didn't revise it, even though its "says" statement was long. But he was reminded of his group member's comment about the section on tipping when he saw "tipping" in two "says" statements, and he decided that he could revise these two paragraphs. Here are the revised paragraphs:

> Maybe those cities that be called as international cities are pretty similar in many ways. In New York, I found the domiciliary room, applied telephone line, social security card, bank account and all the others things myself. In fact, it is not until I confided in English then I began to deal with some others Taiwanese and Chinese.
>
> I remembered in the first several days in New York, I had some difficult in eating. I was not sure of the food and the behaviors in the restaurant. Although I am familiar with the manner in formal restaurants of Taiwan, to order some meals from a strange manu, and to behavior as properly as a gentleman were not so easy to hold on.
>
> I guess the most thing that I confused is when and how much tip should I give. In Taiwan, we do not have this custom. In the first

several months, I only ate in some fast food restaurants. Although there is an official price of tip—15%, how to make well use of tip is another problem. Beside, I always forget to leave some bills in table, I was not used to. Until now, I still can not hold on all the tip-problems very smoothly and properly.

III. Sentences, Phrases, and Words

David now felt satisfied with what he had written, and he was ready to begin editing. He spent some time with his editing partner, a non-Chinese speaking student, carefully going over each paragraph. From his editing journal, he knew that his punctuation was usually good, but that his most important problems were with vocabulary and phrases that didn't "sound" English, and with verb forms. So he asked his partner to point to places where she was confused by what he had written or to places where she thought he had used the wrong word or phrase, and together the two of them came up with a clearer phrasing.

Here are some of the sentences that David and his partner worked on. Note where he makes entries in his editing journal.

1. "So the first experience in the U.S. of me was . . ." became "My first experience in the U.S. was . . ." (in paragraph 1)

2. "familiarize with" became "am familiar with" (paragraph 1; note that David had the correct phrase in his first draft, but changed it in his revision, in order to make his paper sound more "academic.")

3. "I found the domiciliary room, applied telephone line, social security card, bank account . . ." became "I solved the housing problem, applied a new telephone line from New York Telephone for my telecommunication, applied the social security card, opened bank account and some other things myself." (paragraph 2)
Editing journal entry: "domiciliary" is too formal

4. "were not so easy to hold on" became "were not so easy to handle" (paragraph 3)
Editing journal entry: "to hold on" means in the hand; "to handle" means to deal with. Two times in this paper.

5. "in the trunk" became "in the car" (paragraph 6)

6. "I found my way to live" became "Despite all these problems, I found a way to live" (paragraph 7)

7. "I confided in proper and tender behavior" became "I trusted in finding correct behavior" (paragraph 8)
   Editing journal entry: "confide" I need to be careful with this word. Ask my teacher for examples:
   I confided in my friend = I told her my problem
   I'm confident in myself = I know I am capable

8. "do not like a Taiwanese any more" became "do not act like a Taiwanese anymore" (paragraph 11)

Finally, David carefully checked all the verb forms in his paper, making sure that they were all in the correct tense and that they agreed with their subjects. He didn't try to check for any other problems because his teacher wanted him only to focus on clarity and verb forms. As soon as he had better control of these, he would begin checking for other types of errors.

David's final draft, below, still contains errors and unclear passages, but it shows that his effort to look closely and carefully at what he had written, alone and with the help of others, paid off. It's a much stronger and clearer paper than his first draft, and in the process of revising and editing it David gained even more understanding of how English "works."

"Where is every body?" In the first day I arrived New York, no one picked me up in the airport. Being for mistakes in communication, those who I expected saw in airport did not show up. My first experience in the U.S. was tried to find a hotel in Manhattan with my broken English. Fortunately, I am familiar with the living in big city. New York, Tokyo, or Taipei does not make many differences except language. After all, I found the bus from New Wark Airport to Pen Station and a hotel in nearby. There was the second surprise waiting for me—the cost of hotel in downtown Manhattan.

Maybe those cities that be called as international cities are pretty similar in life style and the outlook. In New York, I solved the housing problem, applied a new telephone line from New York Telephone for my telecommunication, applied the social security card, opened bank account and some other things myself. In fact, it was not until I confided in English then I began to deal with some others Taiwanese and Chinese.

I remembered in the first several days in New York, I had some difficult in eating. I was not sure of the food and the behaviors in the restaurant. Although I am familiar with the manner in formal restaurants of Taiwan, to order some meals from a strange manu, and to behave as properly as a gentleman were not so easy to handle.

I guess the most thing that I confused was when and how much tip should I give. In Taiwan, we do not have this custom. In the first several months, I only ate in some fast food restaurants. Although there was an official price of tip—15%, how to make well use of tip was another problem. Beside, I always forgot to leave some bills in table, I was not used to. Until now, I still can not handle all the tip-problems very smoothly and properly.

The other thing that strange to me was the politeness of a gentleman, such as open the door for young ladies, yield seat in the subway and some other "strange" manner. I think it is naturally to do these for elder citizens, but for young ladies, I never saw before. Since man and woman should have equal position, why ladies have the privileges? Although I am not think it is a bad habit, I do not yield my seat to young ladies even in now. However, I learned a lot from these gentlemen. Their manner taught me the mean of "the higher the bamboo grows, the lower it bows," I learned how to humble and how to respect others.

To live in a new place always take time to adapt. When I first took the subway train in New York, I did not know there are many different lines. I think it is like the subway in Taipei which only has one line. So I walked to 74 street Jackson Height station in Queens, and took the first train that I met in New York. In the car, I felt more and more strange. "Where are we going? Why there seems to be many different tracks? . . . " I thought. At least, I had to ask other passengers in the train to show me the way. This unfortunately guy who I met in subway train leaded me the way and gave me a subway map. I want say "Thank your" to this poor man, the manager of fast delivery department of New York Transit Authority.

My new live established little by little with some stories like this. I experienced waiting a long time in social security office, running between several different offices of New York telephone to "donate" some deposit. Although in comparing with residents of some others places, New Yorkers are more cooler than them (maybe that is the city-symptom). Despite all these problems, I found my way to live.

In Taiwan, I trusted in finding correct behavior. But in the U.S., I can only sure that I am doing right in some formal situations. In most of times, I am too serious. But I have to, I am not familiar in the ways of American-style social communication. Beside, keeping distance can protect me from many troubles. I guess that also is one purpose of politeness, no one can understand or hurt other from such a distance.

I have to say that I do not like the dirty of New York. In compare with many cities in the world, I feel that New York is a very dirty one. Everyday walking to school, I can even see the dunghill in the road. Not only the road is unusually dirty, but also the subway, and some houses.

I am also surprise at there are so many homeless people. In Taiwan, such a small island, twenty million people crowds in forty thousand square kilo-meter ground. The competition of survival is extremely hard. For example, every one who can study in university should defeat at least sixty thousand classmates in enter-college examination. But there are few homeless persons. To make a living in the U.S. is much easier than in Taiwan, and the social welfare of the U.S. is much better than Taiwan. But in Taiwan, the total number of homeless persons which I have ever seen is less than ten. I guess somebody should think about "why?"

Anyway, to some others Taiwanese students, I do too well in adapting American culture and do not act like a Taiwanese any more. Maybe when I go back to Taiwan I will need spend some time in readapting Taiwan society when I go back to Taiwan. I believe that even I need to spend this time, it will not be a long time. After all, my ability in adapting new environment is not too bad. Beside, Taiwan is the place that I born and grew up.

Index